# THE HISTORY OF THE

## BRITISH LIONS

MAINSTREAM · SPORT

# THE HISTORY OF THE BRITISH LIONS

## CLEM THOMAS

MAINSTREAM
PUBLISHING

EDINBURGH AND LONDON

First published in Great Britain in 1996 by
MAINSTREAM PUBLISHING COMPANY (EDINBURGH) LTD
7 Albany Street
Edinburgh EH1 3UG

ISBN 1 84018 498 1

Reprinted 1996, 1997, 1998
This edition 2001

A catalogue record for this book is available from the British Library

Typeset in Palatino
Printed and bound in Great Britain by
Cox and Wyman Ltd

# Contents

I dedicate this book to my wife Joyce, who is my rock, and to our children Christopher, Caroline, Gregory, Mark, Linda and Nic, who give me so much pleasure.

*Sadly, Clem Thomas died suddenly on 5 September 1996, a month before this book was first published. His family are proud to dedicate it to his memory.*

# Acknowledgements

I am grateful for the references and help I have received from the following publications:

Beaumont, Bill, Andy Dalton, Terry McLean and Ian Robertson, *Lions v. All Blacks 1983*; Bennett, Phil, *Everywhere for Wales*; Chester, R.H. and N.A.C. McMillan, *Men in Black: 75 Years of New Zealand Rugby, Centenary: 100 Years of All Black Rugby*; Clayton, K. (ed.), *The Legends of Springbok Rugby, 1889–1989*; Craven, Danie, *Springbok Annals, 1891–1958*; Dobson, Paul, *Rugby in South Africa: A History 1861–1988*; Edwards, Gareth, *An Autobiography*; Frost, David, *Lions' 83*; Gallaher, D. and W.J. Stead, *The Complete Rugby Footballer* (1906); Godwin, Terry, *The Complete Who's Who of International Rugby*; Greyvenstein, Chris, *Springbok Saga: 100 Years of Springbok Rugby*; Griffiths, John, *British Lions*; Harding, Rowe, *Rugby Reminiscences and Opinions*; Hastings, Gavin and Clem Thomas, *High Balls and Happy Hours*; Hopkins, John, *British Lions 1980, Life with the Lions*; James, Carwyn and Colin Welland, *Tommy David*; James, Carwyn and John Reason, *The World of Rugby*; Jenkins, Vivian, *Lions Rampant*; Marshall, Rev. F., *Football: The Rugby Union Game* (1892); McLean, Terry, *The Lion Tamers, The Best of McLean*; O'Connor, Terry, *How the Lions Won*; Parker, A.C., *The Springboks 1891–1970*; Raeburn, Wallace, *The Lions*; Rea, Chris, *Rugby*; Reason, John, *The 1968 Lions, The Victorious Lions, The Unbeaten Lions, Backs to the Wall*; *Rothmans Rugby Union Yearbooks*; *The Rugby Almanack of New Zealand, 1951*; Starmer-Smith, Nigel, *The Barbarians, Rugby: A Way of Life*; Thomas, J.B.G., *Lions on Trek, The Lions on Trek Again, The Roaring Lions, Trial of Strength, Wounded Lions*; Williams, Bleddyn, *Rugger: My Life*.

I must also thank many people for their unstinting assistance, support and encouragement, including John Griffiths, Terry Godwin, Alan Watkins, Geoff Cooke, Ian McGeechan, Gavin Hastings, Hermas Evans, Clive Rowlands, Harry Bowcott and the countless British Lions who told me so much. My thanks also to Tommy David for permission to republish the hilarious story involving him and Bobby Windsor in the Kruger Park Game Reserve.

A very special thank-you goes to John Lawrence and Bob Weighill for their invaluable information and generosity of spirit, which helped me understand what goes on behind the scenes of a Lions tour, without which the Lions would simply not exist.

If I have made any errors of fact, memory or omission, or damned with faint praise, it was through no lack of effort or intention on my part. They will be irrelevant to the intention of the book, which is to chronicle and celebrate the concept of the British and Irish Lions, at a time when they are being seriously threatened by events which may or may not be beneficial to the future of the game.

I am indebted to my wife Joyce for her total support and for watching over my punctuation and manuscript with the keenest of eyes. I must thank my son Christopher for reading the proofs and making many useful suggestions, and also Mike Burrows for proof-reading. I also received assistance from another son, Greg, who is the media and public relations manager for the Australian Rugby Union.

My thanks also go to Cathy Mineards, my editor at Mainstream, for all her patience and hard work.

Finally, my gratitude to Willie John McBride, the greatest Lion of them all, for his encouragement and for consenting to write the introduction.

# Introduction

BY WILLIE JOHN MCBRIDE

I won my first cap for Ireland in 1962 and it was a momentous occasion, but to obtain the ultimate prize of selection for the Lions tour to South Africa in the same year, at the age of 21, was completely overwhelming. Little did I think that it was the beginning of a Lions playing career which spanned five tours and a total of over 18 months of Lions rugby, and which continued until 1974.

I can well recall setting off for South Africa, not knowing what to expect. It quickly became obvious to me that South African rugby was superior to ours in many ways. They were more committed, they were fitter, they were better organised and they had a far greater pride and will to win than any team in these islands.

I wanted to make the Test team, and my chance came in the third and fourth Tests. We lost the third in the dying minutes with a missed tackle on Keith Oxlee, but I survived for the fourth Test, when we were routed at Bloemfontein. On reflection, I do not know how we survived in those years, with no replacements for injury, and little medical or physiotherapy support. The Lions who made an impression on me during that tour were Dickie Jeeps, Bill Mulcahy, Syd Millar, Alan Pask, Dewi Bebb and Bryn Meredith. We were very much runners-up in the series, which is not surprising as management in those days was reward for services to the game, and all the preparation and the direction of the tour was left to the captain and the players.

The tour in 1966 was a similar experience and, although we walked through the first eight games in Australia, we reached the real world when we hit New Zealand and lost our first game. The tour developed many difficulties and it was not a happy one. All the games were tough and uncompromising, but I enjoyed the challenge, and the hospitality was great. We were thrashed in the first Test and I got my big break and partnered Delme Thomas for the second, and played for the rest of the series. We lost all four Tests.

There were signals coming through loud and clear to me. I can remember Colin Meads telling me, 'You guys from the British Isles believe in fairy tales. There is no way, with your haphazard approach and attitude, that you will ever beat us.' Those words rang clearly in my ears for the years to come and I knew he was right.

We seemed to have good players, but we were not organised and, as far as winning was concerned, it was all dreams. There was no doubt that we were second string, both in South Africa and New Zealand. Many players came home from New Zealand disillusioned in 1966, but there were also many who came back better players and determined that our game would improve.

I returned to South Africa in 1968, when there was still no such thing as a Lions coach, but we regarded the assistant manager, Ronnie Dawson, as such. Again we did not succeed, but we drew the second Test and there were signs that change was in the air. People at home reflected that this tour was a jaunt by a bunch of men intent on enjoying themselves. Perhaps we did overdo the jolliness at times, but it was a happy tour and, more importantly, much was achieved in the development of Lions rugby. Tom Kiernan was a good captain, Ronnie Dawson a clear thinker and, if more players had reacted and believed in themselves, the tour could have achieved much more. David Brooks was different as a manager, but he was closer to the players than any manager on previous tours.

Before the 1971 tour, there had been an upsurge of coaching in these islands. Wales led the way and it was not surprising that the 1971 touring side was largely Welsh. It also had a Welsh captain in John Dawes and a Welsh coach in Carwyn James. I had a premonition that we had at last got it right. We had a great manager, the greatest of my years with the Lions, in Doug Smith. Both he and Carwyn were convinced from the beginning that we could do it, and they made us believe it was possible. History shows us the rest. What a privilege it was to play in that team, and I just love repeating the names of those backs – Edwards, John, Duckham, Bevan, Gibson, Dawes, and J.P.R. Williams. When will we see their like again?

I will never forget that Canterbury game, the loss of Sandy Carmichael and Ray McLoughlin, and the lead-up to the first Test in Dunedin. I remember saying to John Dawes, 'Look, I want the forwards for a few minutes', and saying to them, 'We have spent weeks believing that we can beat the All Blacks and we are not going to let it slip now. Reality tells me that, when we get out there, we are not going to have the ball and they are going to run at us. We are going to knock them down until they are sick. Mentally, we are going to be as tough and, when the break comes, it will be in our favour. Look at our back line! Whose side would you prefer to be on?'

We took the field and, unfortunately, it was very tough, but our line did not yield and we won the day by sheer determination and mental strength. It was that day in Dunedin in 1971 that the Lions stopped believing in fairy tales, and the myth that we could not beat the All Blacks was blown away.

Everyone has a pinnacle in life and, for me, it must be the 1974 Lions tour of South Africa. My selection as captain probably presented me with the greatest challenge of my life, and it was a bonus to have Syd Millar as coach. The dedication to training was immense and Syd found his philosophy of how we should play well accepted. Winning became a habit. The 1974 team developed a superb balance in touring; they knew when to work and when to enjoy themselves, which is the secret of a good life.

I will never forget the tension before the third and vital Test. We were doing our last scrummaging session on the Wednesday before, Test pack against the rest, and a few of the rest had a point to prove. At the first scrum, they pushed us off the ball and it would be an understatement to say I was upset. I recall taking the Test pack aside and giving them a piece of my mind because we had broken concentration. We got down again and they collapsed in a heap under our feet, and Chris Ralston was left lying there, screaming, with a twisted leg. Ken Kennedy, the hooker, who is a doctor, went to his aid and, as he straightened the knee, Chris yelled out, 'The pain is excruciating!' only for Bobby Windsor to remark unsympathetically, 'He cannot be too bad if he can think of a word like that.' Chris was soon down in the next scrum, but that was the calibre of the side: strong of mind and of body.

The comparison between 1971 and 1974 is difficult; they were two different tours in two different countries. In 1974, we entirely dominated up front and we had a superb back line, with two fine playmakers in Gareth Edwards and Phil Bennett. We never dominated up front in 1971. In 1974 we were almost perfect. What a privilege it was to captain such a team! The bonds created then between us will never weaken.

I managed the 1983 tour to New Zealand, but it was never a substitute for playing. I learned a lot and I wish I could do it again, having gained from the experience.

To tour with the Lions is the supreme prize. To be one of the best 30 players in the four countries and, hopefully, to be one of the best 15 and playing in the Test team, is still the ultimate challenge. Our game is currently at a crossroads, with utter confusion everywhere and seemingly nobody in control. Has anyone pondered and asked what we are trying to achieve? Most important of all, where is this great game we have enjoyed so hugely for over a century going to be even in ten years from now? All I can say is, 'Please, do not let the Lions die. If we do then we will be damned.'

Finally, I am delighted to be asked to contribute this introductory piece and I congratulate Clem Thomas, himself a former Lion of the famous 1955 vintage, in chronicling the history of the British Lions since their beginnings in 1888 to the present day. Here's hoping that Lions rugby continues into the centuries ahead, and that many young men will benefit from the experience.

# Genesis

The origins of the British Isles Rugby Union team belong to those who, just as Britons created the Empire through the flag-following trade, chose to bring other enduring British customs, such as their sport, to the colonies they had created. This, in its turn, brought the concept of competition with the mother country. Nevertheless, the first exchange of tours was not arranged by the establishment (the respective Unions) but by private promoters. Little could they have imagined what they were starting, or that the new fledgling pupils in the vibrant young colonies would soon become their equals and masters at both rugby and cricket.

The first recorded rugby tour undertaken to those virile southern hemisphere countries came at the end of the 1880s in the time of Queen Victoria, when the British Empire was all-powerful. It was also the year when sport's biggest sponsors launched themselves on to an unsuspecting world. In Atlanta, Georgia, a soda fountain bar created a fizzy drink sold as the French wine of cocoa – 'An ideal nerve tonic and stimulant' – called Coca-Cola. In the same year, Tchaikovsky completed his first symphony; Robert Louis Stevenson arrived in Samoa to make his home there when Germany, the USA and the United Kingdom guaranteed Samoan independence and neutrality; and in the UK, the Local Government Act established elected county councils.

During the winter of 1888, 65 years after William Webb Ellis had invented the game which took the name of his school, Messrs Alfred Shaw and Arthur Shrewsbury (who as cricket entrepreneurs were the managers of an England touring team in Australia) together with A.E. Stoddart conceived the idea of an English rugby team to play in the southern colonies. Shrewsbury was W.G. Grace's predecessor as England's cricket captain, while Stoddart succeeded Grace.

When they asked the Rugby Football Union to patronise the tour they were refused, which was typical of the conservatism of that august body, with attitudes which prevailed for the next century. The RFU refused their patronage on the grounds that it was a team which was organised for the benefit of individual promoters, who were not under the umbrella of any recognised sporting body. They saw no reason, however, to interfere with the project, as long as the promoters and the players did not infringe the principle that it was an amateur game.

The fact that it was not under the auspices of the Rugby Football Union considerably weakened the strength of the side, as fewer international players took part than would otherwise have done so. Nevertheless, Shaw and Shrewsbury secured the services of 20 players, including many county players, all but one of whom hailed from the north of England and the Scottish borders. G. Bran, A.E. Stoddart and C. Aubrey Smith (later to become a well-known Hollywood film star), all of whom were already in Australia with the cricket team, were also available.

The team left England on 8 March 1888 and arrived home on 11 November of the same year, having played 53 games in all with only 22 players, making a mockery of complaints by the modern player of too many matches. There was nothing amateur about this number of games.

The team was sufficiently powerful to give a good account of itself and the players not only gave Australia and New Zealand an indication of the strength of English rugby, but upheld their country's honour by winning 27 of the 35 matches played in New Zealand and Australia under Rugby Union laws, with six draws and two defeats.

The extraordinary feature of the tour was that 18 further games were played under Victorian or Australian Rules. Inevitably, the results here were not as good, with 11 defeats, one draw and only six wins. These matches were undertaken as a means of making money for the promoters, who were underwriting the costs. As there was little or no rugby in areas like Victoria, it was sold on the basis of seeing the Englishmen in exhibition games. Had the tour been under the auspices of the RFU, then no such matches under alien rules would have been permitted.

Indeed, it was remarkable that the tourists, who were totally ignorant of the Victorian rules, let alone the finer points and combinations, picked up the game so quickly. A.E. Stoddart, in particular, was remarkable in the speed at which he mastered the game. He became extremely popular with the colonials because of his remarkable skill in both codes, and he was the undoubted hero of the tour.

The tour began disastrously and memorably with the disqualification of J.P. Clowes of Halifax who, on the eve of departure, was declared a professional by the Rugby Union. The account of these remarkable events is chronicled in the Rev. F. Marshall's book, *Football: The Rugby Union Game*, published in 1892, which is the great and definitive reference book from the formation of the Rugby Union in 1871 to that time.

I had been searching for a copy of this rare book for many years until, in 1980, during the Lions tour to South Africa, I was travelling with Carwyn James, my old friend from the days when we played for the Welsh Secondary Schools together in 1947, and arguably the greatest Lions coach of all time. One day, with great glee, he presented me with a copy of this spendid work, which he had found in a second-hand bookshop in Johannesburg, beautifully inscribed in his own hand, 'Clem, Pob dymuniadde, De Gyfall, Carwyn', which means 'All best wishes to my friend, Clem'. Needless to say, it is one of my most cherished possessions.

According to the Rev. Marshall:

The Yorkshire Cup competition is answerable for this exposure of professionalism, as it has also been for many others. The match Dewsbury v Halifax at Dewsbury on March 3rd, 1888, was the occasion leading to the arraignment of Clowes. Mr Turner, the agent in England of Messrs Shaw and Shrewsbury, had approached Lockwood, Stuart and Stadden, of the Dewsbury Club. Lockwood and Stuart had signed agreements to go, and a similar agreement had been sent to Stadden. Lockwood afterwards withdrew from his agreement, and Stadden placed the agreement forwarded to him in the hands of the Dewsbury officials, who were now in a position to lay a trap for the Halifax Club. They had not forgotten the Jones incident in 1883, when Halifax had successfully appealed and caused the match to be replayed; and the opportunity of returning a Roland for an Oliver was not allowed to pass by. Dewsbury left Stuart out of their team, and entered the contest in the delightful position of standing upon velvet. They might win but they could not lose. Fortunately for the interests of the Rugby game, Dewsbury lost the match; they then disclosed the negotiations that had passed between Mssrs Turner and Stadden. Stuart, like Stadden, was a Welshman, and had received £15 from Mr Turner for his outfit and preliminary expenses. This he had told to Stadden, and so the Dewsbury club charged Clowes with having received the same sum for the same purposes. Clowes acknowledged in an open manly manner that such was the case, and he admitted having spent the money in providing himself with clothes and other articles necessary for the trip. The Yorkshire Committee found: 1. That J P Clowes of the Halifax Club, having received £15 from Mr Turner of Nottingham for an outfit in connection with a football tour of Australia, has thereby received money consideration for playing football, and, in the opinion of this committee, is a professional football player according to the Union rules as to professionalism adopted in October 1886. 2. That the Halifax Club have played Clowes in ignorance of his receipt of this money, and the committee therefore order that the match be replayed, on Wednesday, on the Bradford ground. It may be interesting to remark that Halifax won the match, and were eventually the winners of the Yorkshire Cup for that season.

The Yorkshire Committee then communicated with the committee of the Rugby Football Union, and a special meeting of the latter was held at Leeds on March 7th, when the following resolution was adopted: 'The Rugby Football Union has decided, on the evidence before them, that J P Clowes is a professional within the meaning of their laws. On the same evidence they have formed a very strong opinion that others composing the Australian team have also infringed those laws, and they will require from them such explanation as they think fit on their return to England.' On the return of the team, each player was required to make an affidavit that he had received no pecuniary benefit from the tour, and there the matter ended.

In spite of this Clowes toured with the party, but he never played a game, because the organisers feared that the Unions in the colonies, who were affiliated to the RFU, might refuse to play them if he did. In addition, Clowes playing might professionalise and disqualify the rest of the party on their return to England. Thus, the power and influence of the Rugby Union was never more strongly exemplified than in this matter, which entrenched the authority of the relatively new governing body of the game in England, and which was, in its time, a huge *cause célèbre*.

The tour finally went ahead, but it was not the first of its kind, as New South Wales had blazed the first trail overseas when they visited New Zealand in 1882 with a representative team. They revisited New Zealand in 1886 and New Zealand, in between, had reciprocated with a visit to Australia in 1884 by 19 players, who wore blue jerseys with a gold fernleaf emblem. To them goes the accolade of being the first national rugby team of any country to tour abroad.

Touring abroad was a new concept for rugby, but cricket tours had been going on between Australia and England since 1868. It was thought at the time that Australia would be the greatest rugby rival for the mother country, just as it became in cricket; and so Australia dominated the early rugby tours to the antipodes and, in 1899, had a British tour to itself.

It was to emerge that the young neighbour, New Zealand, was the paramount force and, from 1908 onwards, the emphasis on these tours moved to New Zealand. That was the year when Australia became the only other country in the world wholeheartedly to embrace professional Rugby League, a game which is still confined, in the main, to two counties in the north of England and two states, New South Wales and Queensland, in Australia. Nowadays, there are other pockets in Papua New Guinea, France, Fiji, New Zealand and Western Samoa.

Canada was brought into the Lions equation in 1959, but it is true to say that until very recently, when Australia became a major force by winning the World Cup, it was only tours to South Africa and New Zealand which really mattered. It has been these two protagonists who have been slugging it out over the years for the title of world champions, and it is South Africa who have always held the edge, for the All Blacks had never managed to win a full series in the Republic until 1996.

The anomaly is that the British Lions have been far more successful in South Africa and, apart from 1971, their record in New Zealand has been abysmal ever since they lost the first Test match against the All Blacks in 1904. In contrast, the British sides won their first series in South Africa with a whitewash in 1891, and also won their second series in 1896, drew in 1955 and won in 1974.

## R.L. SEDDON'S 1888 BRITISH TEAM

These were the trailblazers and pathfinders, who were to set the tradition of overseas tours by British Isles rugby teams. They played 16 matches in Australia, of which they won 14, lost none and drew two. In New Zealand they played 19, won 13, lost two and drew four. In addition to these games under Rugby Union laws, according to rugby historian Marshall, they played 18 exhibition games in the state of Victoria, winning six, drawing one and losing 11. These matches were played under Australian Rules, which enraged the Rugby Union. It is interesting to gauge the thinking of the time, views which have only recently been changed, when Marshall refers to the exhibition games by saying, 'The only objectionable feature of the tour was the arrangement of matches under Australian rules.'

Although no Test matches were played, nowadays the mind boggles at such an itinerary with so few players, and at the achievement of Harry Eagles, a forward who played in every tour match between 28 April and 3 October, setting a record which never has been and probably never will be surpassed.

It was a tour and a year touched by tragedies for rugby men, when the popular captain, Bob Seddon, was drowned in the early part of the tour. While sculling on the Hunter river, he capsized and his feet apparently became entwined in the foot strappings. The same year, the captain of the New Zealand national team, Joe Warbrick, was killed when he was engulfed in a lava flow from a volcanic eruption on his return to New Zealand.

Much later, Andrew Stoddart, the star of the tour who replaced Seddon as captain, was also to die tragically when, as a member of the Stock Exchange, he committed suicide in April 1915. John Nolan, another outstanding back on the tour, was killed at work in 1907.

Although not truly representative, the 1888 side had players from all four Home Unions. W.H. Thomas was the first Welshman to tour Australia and New Zealand. Angus Stuart of Dewsbury played for Cardiff in the early 1880s, but he was of Scottish extraction. He was to stay in New Zealand and tour Australia as the senior member of the New Zealand team in 1893, before returning to England, where he became the trainer of Dewsbury Rugby League team. A.P. Penketh was the only Isle of Man player to tour with a British team; J.T. Haslam was credited with being the first man to introduce the dummy pass to New Zealand; Harry Speakman of Cheshire stayed in Australia and later captained Queensland. Arthur Paul of Lancashire, the only Irish-born member of the side, was the principal goal-kicker of the team and a distinguished cricketer, who partnered Archie MacLaren against Somerset at Taunton, when he established the English batting record of 424 runs in a first-class innings. He was later to play goalkeeper for Blackburn Rovers.

## Rugby Union results of the 1888 British team in Australia and New Zealand

P 35  W 27  D 6  L 2  F 300  A 101

| | | | |
|---|---|---|---|
| Otago | W | 8 | 3 |
| Otago | W | 4 | 3 |
| Canterbury | W | 14 | 6 |
| Canterbury | W | 4 | 0 |
| Wellington | D | 3 | 3 |
| H. Roberts XV | W | 4 | 1 |

| | | | |
|---|---|---|---|
| Taranaki Clubs | L | 0 | 1 |
| Auckland | W | 6 | 3 |
| Auckland | L | 0 | 4 |
| | | | |
| New South Wales | W | 18 | 2 |
| Bathurst | W | 13 | 6 |
| New South Wales | W | 18 | 6 |
| Sydney Juniors | W | 11 | 0 |
| King's School Sydney | D | 10 | 10 |
| Sydney Grammar Past and Present | D | 3 | 3 |
| Bathurst | W | 20 | 10 |
| New South Wales | W | 16 | 2 |
| University of Sydney | W | 8 | 4 |
| Newcastle | W | 15 | 7 |
| Queensland | W | 13 | 6 |
| Queensland Juniors | W | 11 | 3 |
| Queensland | W | 7 | 0 |
| Ipswich | W | 12 | 1 |
| Melbourne | W | 15 | 5 |
| Adelaide XV | W | 28 | 3 |
| | | | |
| Auckland | W | 3 | 0 |
| Auckland | D | 1 | 1 |
| Hawke's Bay | W | 3 | 2 |
| Wairarapa | W | 5 | 1 |
| Canterbury | W | 8 | 0 |
| Otago | D | 0 | 0 |
| South Island | W | 5 | 3 |
| South Island | W | 6 | 0 |
| Taranaki Clubs | W | 7 | 1 |
| Wanganui | D | 1 | 1 |

## R.L. Seddon's 1888 British team

**Full-backs**

| | |
|---|---|
| J.T. Haslam | Yorkshire and Batley |
| A. Paul | Lancashire and Swinton |

**Three-quarters**

| | |
|---|---|
| J. Anderton | Lancashire and Salford |
| H. Brooks | Durham and Edinburgh University |
| H.C. Speakman | Cheshire and Runcorn |

**Half-backs**

| | |
|---|---|
| W. Bumby | Lancashire and Swinton |
| W. Burnett | Roxburgh County and Hawick |
| J. Nolan | Rochdale Hornets |

**Forwards**

| | |
|---|---|
| T. Banks | Lancashire and Swinton |
| P. Burnett | Roxburgh County and Hawick |
| J.P. Clowes | Yorkshire and Halifax |
| H. Eagles | Lancashire and Swinton |
| T. Kent | Lancashire and Salford |
| C. Mathers | Yorkshire and Bramley |
| A.P. Penketh | Douglas, Isle of Man |
| R.L. Seddon (capt.) | Lancashire and Swinton |
| D.J. Smith | Corinthians and Edinburgh University |
| A.J. Stuart | Yorkshire and Dewsbury |
| W.H. Thomas | Cambridge University and Wales |
| S. Williams | Lancashire and Salford |

Managers: A. Shaw and A. Shrewsbury

The 1888 team was away for nine months, three months of which were spent in arduous and, indeed, perilous travel. Wallace Raeburn relates in his book, *The Lions*, something of the conditions which prevailed at the time in his home country of New Zealand, with quotes from various newspapers:

'There was considerable interest in town last evening on the departure of the members of the club from Katikati. Five started on horseback and six in a drag, and the remainder will proceed today by steamer, when the goalposts and flags will also be forwarded.'

'It was miraculous how players escaped injury, there being stumps and roots all over the paddock.'

'Budge played well, only missed securing a force down for Wellington when the ball caught in the telephone wires which ran across the field.'

'A Nelson man, who was thrown headfirst into a may hedge adjoining the touchline, seemed not at all disconcerted and picked the thorns out of his head as the opportunity offered.'

'Our footballers started yesterday for Kawakawa and if they ever get there, which is doubtful, they are going to play a match.'

The reports of the matches all had a common denominator, which was that the most impressive aspect of the visitors was their back play, which was to become the characteristic, indeed, the hallmark, of Lions teams for the next century. It was the first time that New Zealand had seen organised back moves which delighted them, and they were quick to start adopting the same tactics.

O.L. Owen wrote in his *History of Rugby Union Football*, 'The New Zealanders, though highly critical, realised that the Englishmen had a much better conception than themselves of the passing game and, furthermore, knew how to exploit what in those days was called the practice of heeling from the scrummage, without which passing in the open could not hope to develop.'

T.R. Ellison, who was to captain the 1893 New Zealand side and who was the author of *The Art of Rugby*, was highly critical of the tour and said, 'Beyond learning the minor, though petty and effective, trick of feign passing from Mr Haslam, and learning to disregard the strict laws of offside play as regards forwards in the scrum, I challenge anyone to tell me what else the 1888 side taught us.' He had a point, because it took 83 years after the first tour of New Zealand for the British Lions to win a Test series in that country.

In their book *The Complete Rugby Footballer*, published in 1906, Dave Gallaher (who captained the 1905 All Blacks) and his collaborator, W.J. Stead, refuted this and clearly stated:

It was left to Stoddart's British team to show Maoriland the fine points of the game and the vast possibilities of combination. The exhibitions of passing which they gave were most fascinating and impressive to the New Zealander, who was not slow to realise the advantages of these methods. One may safely say that, from that season, dates the era of high-class rugby in the colony.

Consequently, the splendid tradition of exciting back play by touring British teams was established from the very beginning. Despite the fact that the team in 1888 played no Test matches and was essentially an English, not a British, side, it nevertheless pioneered the concept of overseas tours by a British team.

## W.E. MACLAGEN'S 1891 BRITISH TEAM

1891 was the year that the zip fastener was invented, and that *The Picture of Dorian Gray*, *The Adventures of Sherlock Holmes* and *Tess of the D'Urbervilles* were first published. A Boston architect, Louis Sullivan, made buildings ten storeys high that 'scrape the sky', by using a new type of special steel girders, and the periscope was invented in France.

The team that toured South Africa in 1891 was the first to formalise the concept of international rugby competition by playing three Test matches. As hosting the tour was a step into the unknown by the newly formed South African Rugby Board, the tour was organised by Western Province Union. Once more it was cricket which had set the example, and it was the visit of Major Wharton's cricket team to the Cape which led to the idea of a British rugby team visiting the Province. Mr Harold, the honorary secretary of the Western Province Rugby Football Union, was the initiator of the project. The tour was underwritten by Cecil Rhodes, the Prime Minister of the Cape, who eased the rugby authorities' minds when he said, 'Let them come. I shall stand firm for any shortfall.' President Kruger of the Transvaal Republic also promised support and gave his blessing.

Rugby has always despised racial and religious intolerance, and it faced one of its greatest crises when Prime Minister Verwoerd introduced apartheid into South Africa in the '50s; now happily resolved, largely because of a sporting boycott. The game has always crossed boundaries and has been a great unifying force, whatever a player's religion or political persuasion. The co-operation between Rhodes and Kruger in those early days was another such example.

This time, the Rugby Union approved of the tour and gave it their full support. However, in their time-honoured tradition, they were extremely cautious in making their arrangements, as they wanted to be sure that there would be no repeat of the events of the tour to Australia three years earlier when, in their view, the amateur ethic was abused. They were determined this time to exercise strict control of the affair and to ensure that the team leaving England, and those sides encountered in Africa, should be composed of amateurs. Their reservations concerning the possibility of a financial loss on the tour were satisfied by Cecil Rhodes himself accepting responsibility.

The length of the tour was fixed at 30 days, and all the players were recruited from England and Scotland. Most of the uncapped players were Cambridge Blues, which was in contrast with the more working-class composition of the 1888 team. They made sure, too, that the tour was managed by an establishment man. This was Mr Edward Ash, a member of Richmond and a former secretary of the RFU, whom the players called 'Daddy', and whose credentials were impeccable.

They sailed from Southampton on board the *Dunottar Castle* on 20 September 1891, with the captain, W.E. Maclagen, entrusted with a beautiful silver cup donated by Sir Donald Currie of the Union Castle Shipping Line, to be given to the colonial club who did best against his team. It was won by Griqualand West. The cup was to be held by that club until the next season and then to be competed for by the clubs of South Africa. It is now the trophy, indeed the holy grail, for the South African Provincial Championship, which did so much to keep up their playing standards during the years of the sporting boycott caused by apartheid.

When the team arrived in Kimberley to play Griqualand West, they were horrified to find themselves playing on a sun-baked ground which was as hard as concrete and without a blade of grass. (It had not changed when I toured with the Lions in 1955, and we could hear our studs drumming on the rock-hard ground.) One of the players described it as 'like playing on a pavement', and the field was covered with a red dust, which saw 30 pairs of boots creating miniature sandstorms. The home side, being hardened to the conditions, gave the visitors, who had never seen a pitch like it in their own green and pleasant land, such a hard time that they won by only 3–0 from a try by Bill Maclagen and a penalty by A. Rotherham. Consequently, at the end of the tour, Griqualand were handed Donald Currie's cup.

The second Test was played in Kimberley, which at the time was a town of some note and prosperity, due to the diamonds mined from the biggest man-made hole in the world. For this, the first time a Test had been played in the town, the entrance fee was four shillings for the main stand, three for the temporary stand and two for standing. The team stayed in the Central Hotel for ten shillings per head.

They became the most successful side to tour South Africa in history in terms of results, for they won every match and amazingly conceded only one point, which was a solitary try in the first game against Cape Town Clubs. They whitewashed the South Africans in the Test matches, winning 4–0, 3–0 and 4–0. The scores in the first and third Tests were two tries and a conversion to nil, and in the second it was a drop goal from a mark.

In fact, though, the achievement of the 1974 Lions was by far the greater, for it must be remembered that in 1891 South Africa were the duffers on the international rugby scene and, because rugby was still in its infancy in the colony, they had scant knowledge of the game at that time. Consequently, they found that the dribbling skills of the visiting forwards and the passing movements of the backs were too sophisticated for mere beginners.

One must appreciate that the accent in those days was on kicks. A try, which at the time was called a touchdown, had no value apart from earning a try at goal which, if successful, counted as only one point. A penalty was worth two points, a drop goal three points and a conversion goal two points. A touchdown, therefore, would create cries from the crowd of 'A try!', which later would have a totally different meaning as the name for a touchdown, which over the years became the principal objective and increased in value.

The first Test match took place in Port Elizabeth on 30 July, and was the first ever played by a representative South African team. It was very much a social occasion, being played on a Thursday, and according to *The Cape Times*, 'the pavilion was crowded with ladies, all intent on the game.' Apparently, the crowd of 6,000 were not disappointed with the football. Maclagen, the British captain, had to claim several penalties, which was the custom in those days, all of which were granted. Many marks were made and many drop goals attempted, all of which were missed. There were no stands, so the crowd were kept on their toes by countless dribbling rushes, which sometimes covered the length of the field. The British won by two tries and a conversion scored before half-time.

Quaintly, it was reported that 'during the interval, the two teams received instructions from well-known backers of either side and enjoyed lemons and sundry'. Although the South African forwards were on top for long periods of the second half, there was no more scoring.

It is difficult to ascertain why South Africa were such slow starters, but some clue may be found in the fact that, when the British team was still at sea before arriving at Cape Town after a 16-day voyage (which was a record at the time), the locals, Western Province, organised a trial match to test their own strength before their arrival. It was a disaster, as many invited players failed to turn up because, as reported in *The Cape Times*, 'the doubtful aspect of the weather and the arrival of the mail mitigated against a strong muster'.

The dominant rugby personality of the tour was the Blackheath and Cambridge University centre R.L. Aston who, at 6ft 3in and 15 stone, used his remarkable size for a back in those days to score 30 tries, the most ever scored by any British player on one tour to the southern hemisphere. In spite of the tiresome travelling, three players – MacMillan, Hammond and Mitchell – played in every game, while the captain, W.E. Maclagen, with 26 caps for Scotland, missed only one match.

On their return, they reported on the very hard grounds, the thin atmosphere on the high veldt, and the long journeys between some major centres by horse-drawn vehicles. Furthermore, the train journey from Cape Town to Kimberley took two days and nights and, even though they met Barney Barnato, the mining entrepreneur, on the train, it was a tedious experience. They also told of the good times, of the dry and sunny winter climate, the shooting parties and the hectic party round, numerous receptions and the principal amusement of the day, the smoking concert. Most of these have never changed, apart from aircraft replacing the train and the horse.

The team arrived back in England aboard the *Garth Castle* on 28 September, and it was said by the Rev. Marshall that 'the team of footballers to the Cape have initiated the colonists of South Africa into the fine points and science of the Rugby game'.

In the official book produced by the South African Rugby Board to celebrate its 75th anniversary, entitled *Rugby in South Africa*, there is no mention of the pioneer tours of 1891 and 1896, when they were trounced in both Test series. Perhaps they thought that the British had taken an unfair advantage and, therefore, they did not count. Happily, other historical books such as *Springbok Annals*, written in 1960 by South Africa's greatest rugby personality Dr Danie Craven, and later books by those eminent South African writers, Paul Dobson and Chris Greyvenstein, rectified such omissions and gave a fair account of the events.

## Results of the 1891 British team in South Africa

I discovered that most reference books state that there were only 19 games, but Dr Danie Craven's *Springbok Annals* reveals that there were 20 matches, and although many sources believe that the last match against Stellenbosch was unofficial, I include it.

P 20   W 20   F 226   A 1

| | | | |
|---|---|---|---|
| Cape Town Club | W | 15 | 1 |
| Western Provinces | W | 6 | 0 |
| Cape Colony | W | 14 | 0 |
| Kimberley | W | 7 | 0 |
| Griqualand West | W | 3 | 0 |
| Port Elizabeth | W | 22 | 0 |
| Eastern Province | W | 21 | 0 |
| South Africa (Port Elizabeth) | W | 4 | 0 |
| Grahamstown District | W | 9 | 0 |
| King Williams Town | W | 18 | 0 |
| King Williamstown District | W | 16 | 0 |

| | | | |
|---|---|---|---|
| Pietermaritzburg | W | 25 | 0 |
| Transvaal | W | 22 | 0 |
| Johannesburg | W | 15 | 0 |
| Johannesburg–Pretoria | W | 9 | 0 |
| Cape Colony | W | 4 | 0 |
| South Africa (Kimberley) | W | 3 | 0 |
| Cape Colony | W | 7 | 0 |
| South Africa (Cape Town) | W | 4 | 0 |
| Stellenbosch | W | 2 | 0 |

## W.E. Maclagen's 1891 British team

**Full-backs**

| | | |
|---|---|---|
| E. Bromet | Cambridge University | |
| W.G. Mitchell | Richmond | England |

**Three-quarters**

| | | |
|---|---|---|
| R.L. Aston | Blackheath | England |
| P.R. Clauss | Birkenhead Park | Scotland |
| W.E. Maclagen (capt.) | Edinburgh Academicals | Scotland |

**Half-backs**

| | | |
|---|---|---|
| H. Marshall | Cambridge University | |
| B.G. Roscoe | Manchester | |
| A. Rotherham | Cambridge University | England |
| W. Wotherspoon | Cambridge University | Scotland |

**Forwards**

| | | |
|---|---|---|
| W.E. Bromet | Richmond | England |
| J.H. Gould | Old Leysians | |
| W. Jackson | Cambridge University | |
| J. Hammond | Cambridge University | |
| P.F. Hancock | Blackheath | England |
| R.G. MacMillan | London Scottish | Scotland |
| W.E. Mayfield | Cambridge University | |
| C.P. Simpson | Cambridge University | |
| A.A. Surtees | Harlequins | |
| R. Thompson | Cambridge University | |
| W.H. Thomson | Cambridge University | |
| T. Whittaker | Lancashire | |

Manager: E. Ash

In Pietermaritzburg, they encountered among their opponents a man who was to become a famous military leader: W.E. Tanner, who commanded the South African forces in Flanders in World War I. A week later, in Johannesburg, they played against Christiaan Beyers, who became a general in President Kruger's forces in the Boer War less than nine years later.

The tour which, in a sense, had a strong missionary element, gave South African rugby a huge fillip and, at the farewell dance before they departed for home on the *Garth Castle* on 9 September 1891, both Bill Maclagen and his vice-captain, Johnny Hammond, predicted a great future for the game in the colony. How right they were!

## J. HAMMOND'S 1896 BRITISH TEAM

The year 1896, which brought Queen Victoria's Jubilee and saw Cecil Rhodes make peace with the Matabele after their uprising in Rhodesia, was probably the zenith of the British Empire. Marconi made his first communication by wireless telegraph. Ethiopia routed the Italian army, and a new newspaper, *The Daily Mail*, was established. It was also the year when rinderpest ravaged the bovine herds of southern Africa. This did not prevent British rugby celebrating with a second consecutive visit to South Africa, which was more accessible to them than the antipodes.

The 1896 British team to visit South Africa were to find that the lessons of the early tours had been absorbed and the opposition was stiffer, and although they again put South Africa to the sword, it was to be for the last time until 1974.

An itinerary was worked out by the South African Rugby Board, for which the costs were estimated at £3,300. The figure was made up as follows: passage £1,000, expenses on board £100, railway fares £200, board for 70 days £1,750 and miscellaneous expenses £250. Each Province or Union was allotted matches and levied accordingly; Western Provinces five games and £900; Transvaal five and £1,000; Griqualand West four and £550; Eastern Province four and £550; Border three and £250; Natal £100 and Orange Free State £75. The tour itinerary was laid out a year in advance, and the wealth of each centre had a bearing on the disposition of matches.

As it turned out, the Board was very happy with the tour, which ended with a profit of £600 12s 2d, but regretted that no matches were played in Natal or the Orange Free State. They then began to consider a tour of their own to the UK, but the fixture list was full so they had to wait another decade.

It was to be a colourful tour by virtue of the fact that, for the first time, there was a large Irish contingent, mostly in the pack. British teams soon discovered the value of Irishmen, who are born tourists and who have the knack of introducing a delicious sense of humour into any party which might be in danger of taking itself too seriously.

Discovering that South Africa were beginning to harness their great power in forward play, the British developed the art of wheeling the scrum and created the snap shove on their opponents' put-in, to counter their strength. Consequently, they remained unbeaten until the final Test match in Cape Town when, to scenes of huge delight, South Africa began their march, which was to take them to world supremacy, with a historic victory. The British team complained that the referee, Alf Richards, a former South African outside-half, had repeatedly penalised them in the scrummages for wheeling the scrum, claiming that they fell offside during the wheel. This was also the tour when it was decided that neutral referees would be used and not drawn from players in the games.

Thus began an ongoing battle between the two hemispheres, concerning different interpretations of the always too complex laws of Rugby Football. Being so far apart and with little contact apart from infrequent tours, it was inevitable that differences in the interpretation and styles of play would develop. This persisted until the modern day when, belatedly, the IRB introduced exchange referees, and the holding of a World Cup every four years began to provide far more uniformity of thought.

Johnny Hammond captained the side, and he and P.F. Hancock were the only survivors from the 1891 team. From then on, British teams were often identified and recognised by the name of their captain. Thus they became known as Karl Mullen's or Robin Thompson's Lions, but only until the coach became the dominant personage. Nowadays, as the captain's role diminishes, we are more likely to remember them as Carwyn James's, Syd Millar's or Ian McGeechan's Lions.

The British team arrived in Cape Town on board the *Tartar* too late at night to disembark, so the South African officials and enthusiasts, impatient to greet the players, chartered the tug *Enterprise* and sailed out to board the liner. They spent the night talking to the team and had breakfast with them, before they landed and streamed off to the Royal Hotel, where the team was again quartered.

The team was variously described at the time either as the Anglo-Irish team, the English team or the British team, as it was made up only of English and Irish players. England were undergoing a period of recovery after the breakaway of the northern clubs of Lancashire and Yorkshire over the issue of refusal to pay compensation for broken time. It was the start of Rugby League. Ireland had won the championship that year for the first time, beating England and Wales and drawing with Scotland. Fittingly, it was that great character of the tour, Tommy Crean of Dublin Wanderers, who had scored the winning try against Wales, which clinched the championship.

Strangely, their captain, Johnny Hammond, despite having taken part in two tours, never played for England. Having played in every match on the 1891 tour as vice-captain, he played in only seven out of 21 on this tour. It was always said that the real captain of the tour was the incredible Irish character, Tommy Crean, who became a doctor at the age of 22. Standing 6ft 2ins and over 17 stone, he was a huge man for the time, handsome and with great energy. He was a typical fighting Irishman, witty and devil-may-care; probably the Tom Reid and Moss Keane of his day, all rolled into one.

He was to win a Victoria Cross, extraordinarily, as was Robert Johnston. No other representative team in history could boast such valour in their ranks. Another of the team who was to receive a high military decoration was the Rev. M. Mullineux, a Blackheath half-back, but he never captained his country, although he was to captain and manage the side to Australia three years later. He won an MC as a gazetted Chaplain-Captain in France in World War I.

The Rev. Walter Carey, one of the tourists, who was to coin the Barbarians' motto, 'Rugby football is a game for a gentleman of all classes, but never for a bad sportsman of any class', and who later became the Bishop of Bloemfontein, said of Tommy Crean, 'He was the most Irish, the most inconsequent, the most gallant, the most lovable personality one could ever imagine and he made the centre of the whole tour.'

Tommy won the VC at Elandslaagte during the Boer War. The story goes that, when with the First Imperial Light Horse Brigade attacking the Boer forces, he was hit and bowled over. Dazed, he shouted, 'By Christ, I'm kilt entoirely.' Happily, he got up and found that, although not dead, he was badly wounded so, with his Irish dander up, he let out some wild yells and led a bayonet charge to take a vital Boer stronghold, for which he received the supreme award for gallantry.

He and another of the VC winners, Robert Johnston, were to plough similar furrows; not only did both of them play for Dublin Wanderers, Ireland and the 1896 Lions, but both settled in South Africa and turned out for Transvaal. In the Boer War, they were both captains in the Imperial Light Horse.

There is a nice little story concerning the only other blight on the team's record apart from the Test defeat, which was the drawn game against Western Province early in the tour. Apparently, they took lunch with the Prime Minister, Sir Gordon Sprigg, who had succeeded Cecil Rhodes after the Jameson raid in 1895, and despite Tommy Crean telling his players that they could only have four tumblers of champagne, apparently that was only starters. Needless to say, the game they were lucky to get away with was a pointless draw, but when they returned to play Western Province in the penultimate match of the tour, sans alcohol, they won 32–0.

The first Test victory by South Africa is worth recording for its historical value. The tourists had won the first three and, with the series already won, were looking for the Grand Slam. The South African captain was Barrie Heatlie, amusingly known as 'Fairy', before its modern connotation. He was probably the first of the many great personalities of South African rugby, and played against three British teams, those of 1891, 1896 and 1903. He led South Africa in the final Test of 1903, when they won the series for the first time.

Heatlie decided to issue green jerseys to the team from his Old Diocesan club in Cape Town and therefore, coincidentally, South Africa won their first game wearing the colour they were to adopt as their national colour. It was obvious from the beginning that the South African forwards would be a force to be reckoned with, led from the front, as they were, by Heatlie. The forward rushes of the South Africans kept the British on the back foot and the vital score came midway through the first half, when the Brits won the ball from a lineout and got it to the strong-running Byrne in the centre. He was tackled by Freddie Aston, brother of R.L. Aston, star of the 1891 British side, who was living in South Africa. The South African centre 'Biddy' Anderson darted in, snatched the ball from Byrne's hands and bolted upfield, to draw the full-back Meares and to put the South African fly-half, Alf Larard, over for what was to be the winning score. Hepburn converted and South Africa were leading 5–0. Although the posts were peppered by drop and penalty goal attempts in the second half, South Africa held out amidst huge excitement, and the players and spectators were beside themselves with joy on the final whistle, knowing history had been made.

The British team objected violently to the score, on the grounds that the ball was illegally taken from Byrne. The next day, *The Cape Times* agreed that it was illegal, severely criticising Anderson. Their reporter said, 'It was a pity that the match should have been decided on a piece of sharp practice. A player less inclined than Anderson to take every advantage he can get, whether lawfully or unlawfully, would have left Byrne in charge of the ball and allowed a scrum to be formed over the place he was held.'

Apparently the score stood, but even so it was hotly disputed. It was also felt that the try scorer, Alf Larard, should not have been playing, for he had played professional rugby in the north of England during the broken-time dispute, but was accepted to play in the amateur ranks when he emigrated to South Africa. Nevertheless, it was generally considered that South Africa had earned and deserved their first of many Test triumphs.

Walter Carey described the tour as being 'a very happy one, as the play of our opponents was scrupulously fair. I hope and pray that South African teams will always play like gentlemen. Rugby football is a game for gentlemen: it is so easy to cheat at it and so destructive for this wonderful game. If a man wants to do dirty tricks, let him do it at ninepins in his own back yard, but let him keep clear of rugby football.' In the new professional era, rugby needs to preserve this kind of ethic.

It is of note that it was in that year of 1896 that the South African Coloured Board was formed.

## Results of the 1896 British team in South Africa

P 21   W 19   D 1   L 1   F 320   A 45

| | | | |
|---|---|---|---|
| Cape Town Clubs | W | 14 | 9 |
| Suburban Clubs | W | 8 | 0 |
| Western Province | D | 0 | 0 |
| Griqualand West | W | 11 | 9 |
| Griqualand West | W | 16 | 0 |
| Port Elizabeth | W | 26 | 3 |
| Eastern Province | W | 18 | 0 |
| South Africa (Port Elizabeth) | W | 8 | 0 |
| Grahamstown | W | 20 | 0 |
| King Williams Town | W | 25 | 0 |
| East London | W | 27 | 0 |
| Queenstown | W | 25 | 0 |
| Johannesburg–Country | W | 7 | 0 |
| Transvaal | W | 16 | 3 |
| Johannesburg–Town | W | 18 | 0 |
| Transvaal | W | 16 | 5 |
| South Africa (Johannesburg) | W | 17 | 8 |
| Cape Colony | W | 7 | 0 |
| South Africa (Kimberley) | W | 9 | 3 |
| Western Province | W | 32 | 0 |
| South Africa (Cape Town) | L | 0 | 5 |

# J. Hammond's 1896 British team

**Full-back**

| | | |
|---|---|---|
| J.F. Byrne | Moseley | England |

**Three-quarters**

| | | |
|---|---|---|
| C.A. Boyd | Dublin University | |
| L.Q. Bulger | Dublin University | Ireland |
| O.G. Mackie | Cambridge University and Wakefield Trinity | |
| J.T. Magee | Bective Rangers | Ireland |
| C.O. Robinson | Northumberland | |

**Half-backs**

| | | |
|---|---|---|
| S.P. Bell | Cambridge University | |
| L.M. Magee | Bective Rangers | Ireland |
| M.M. Mullineux | Blackheath | |

**Forwards**

| | | |
|---|---|---|
| W.J. Carey | Oxford University | |
| A.D. Clinch | Dublin University | Ireland |
| T.J. Crean | Dublin Wanderers | Ireland |
| J. Hammond (capt.) | Cambridge University and Blackheath | |
| P.F. Hancock | Blackheath and Somerset | England |
| R. Johnston | Dublin Wanderers | Ireland |
| G.W. Lee* | Northumberland | |
| A.W.D. Meares | Dublin University | |
| W. Mortimer | Cambridge University and Marlborough Nomads | |
| R.C. Mullins | Oxford University | |
| J. Sealey | Dublin University | Ireland |
| A.F. Todd | Blackheath | |

Manager: R. Walker

* Replacement

## REV. M.M. MULLINEUX'S 1899 BRITISH TEAM

The 1899 tour of Australia was unique in that it was the only time, apart from 1989, that they had a British tour to themselves. Usually both the Lions and the Springboks set aside only a small part of their visit to the antipodes for Australia who, increasingly, were being seen as taking more interest in their own Australian Rules game, a form of Gaelic football brought in by many immigrants of Irish ancestry. Also, to the fury of the Rugby Union establishment, they were even more inclined to throw in their lot with professional Rugby League. The mind boggles at what they might have achieved had they concentrated on Rugby Union instead of their more insular games, which never allowed their young footballers to perform on the world stage.

It was the year when the Boer War broke out, when the *Uitlanders* (foreigners) were refused voting rights, and so war ensued between the British, based in Natal and Cape Province, and the Boers from Transvaal and the Orange Free State. It started at the end of the Australian tour, when the Boers, after delivering an ultimatum regarding the withdrawal of British troops from the colony, finally invaded. It was the year of Kimberley, Mafeking and Ladysmith. In the rest of the world, Elgar's Enigma Variations were performed for the first time; the Samoan Islands were split up between the USA and Germany; and a 16-year-old anarchist attempted to assassinate the Prince of Wales in Brussels.

The British tour was both captained and managed by the Rev. Matthew Mullineux of Blackheath, a veteran of the 1896 tour to South Africa, who was aware of the growing problems in that country but was oblivious to the imminence of these events. Mullineux was the only captain of a British side who never played in a Four Home Unions international; nor did he play in an England trial and, while at Cambridge, did not get a Blue. A Blackheath player, he was a curate in south-east London and a teacher at the Royal Naval School at Eltham. He played in the first Test and, after the defeat, wisely stood down for Frank Stout, an experienced English international forward, to captain the side in the remainder of the rubber.

Although the team was far from being fully representative of the best in the British Isles, as the majority of the players had never won a cap, the side still carried more internationals than the first prototype tour to Australia and New Zealand in 1888. The party of 21 included seven caps: two English, two Scottish, two Irish and one Welsh.

In the team was the legendary Gwyn Nicholls of Wales who, they said at the time and for a long time after he finished, was the finest three-quarter ever to play the game. He was always a maker rather than a scorer of tries and, in his time with Cardiff, he averaged no more than seven tries a season. The Welsh always claimed him, as he played all his rugby in Wales, where he became the great exponent of centre play in that first Welsh golden era of the early 1900s, but he was, in fact, an Englishman from Gloucestershire.

Nicholls enchanted the Australians with his innovative back play, but not even his presence could save the touring team from defeat in the first of four Tests; then they won the last three, the third by the narrowest of margins: a solitary point. Coincidentally, they and Finlay Calder's 1989 team were the only teams to tour Australia exclusively, and were also the only British teams to win a series abroad after losing the first Test. Losing, it seems, often concentrates the mind, for the triumphant 1971 Lions to Australia and New Zealand also lost their first match of the tour to Queensland.

The team was described as the English football team by *The Times*, who in those days seemed disdainfully unaware of the contribution of the other components of the United Kingdom and Ireland. They lost two other matches against Queensland and Metropolitan, but they won the series in the end by 3–1.

## Results of the 1899 British team in Australia

P 21   W 18   L 3   F 333   A 90

| Central Southern | W | 11 | 3 |
|---|---|---|---|
| New South Wales | W | 4 | 3 |
| Metropolitan | W | 8 | 5 |
| Australia (Sydney) | L | 3 | 13 |
| Toowoomba | W | 19 | 5 |
| Queensland | L | 3 | 11 |
| Bundaberg | W | 36 | 3 |
| Rockhampton | W | 16 | 3 |
| Mount Morgan | W | 29 | 3 |
| Central Queensland | W | 22 | 3 |
| Maryborough | W | 27 | 8 |
| Australia (Brisbane) | W | 11 | 0 |
| New England | W | 6 | 4 |
| Northern | W | 28 | 0 |
| New South Wales | W | 11 | 5 |
| Metropolitan | L | 5 | 8 |
| Western | W | 19 | 0 |

| Australia (Sydney) | W | 11 | 10 |
|---|---|---|---|
| Schools | W | 21 | 3 |
| Victoria | W | 30 | 0 |
| Australia (Sydney) | W | 13 | 0 |

## Rev. M.M. Mullineux's 1899 British team

**Full-backs**

| E. Martelli | Dublin University |
|---|---|
| C.E.K. Thompson | Lancashire |

**Three-quarters**

| A.M. Bucher | Edinburgh Academicals | Scotland |
|---|---|---|
| G.P. Doran | Landsdowne | Ireland |
| E.G. Nicholls | Cardiff | Wales |
| E.T. Nicholson | Birkenhead Park | |
| A.B. Timms | Edinburgh University | Scotland |

**Half-backs**

| C.Y. Adamson | Durham |
|---|---|
| G. Cookson | Manchester |
| M.M. Mullineux (capt.) | Blackheath |

**Forwards**

| A. Ayre-Smith | Guy's Hospital | |
|---|---|---|
| F.C. Belson | Bath | |
| G.V. Evers | Moseley | |
| J.S. Francombe | Manchester | |
| G.R. Gibson | Northern | England |
| H.G.S. Gray | Scottish Trialist | |
| J.W. Jarman | Bristol | |
| W. Judkins | Coventry | |
| T.M.W. McGown | North of Ireland | Ireland |
| F.M. Stout | Gloucester | England |
| B.I. Swannell | Northampton | |

Manager: Rev. M.M. Mullineux

This was the end of the easy ride for British teams in the antipodes and South Africa, as the colonies quickly absorbed the message of those missionary-style tours. From now on, it was going to be a grim uphill struggle for the Lions, who were forced to soldier, as exhaustingly as the old Crusaders, against these young, virile nations who saw rugby as an extension, or at least an expression, of their manhood.

# Nuts and Bolts

Before I continue with the story of the Lions in chronological order, it is necessary to understand that an overseas tour by a British Isles rugby union team does not just happen. Instead it requires an enormous amount of thought and preparation, which is undertaken by the Tours Sub-Committee of the Committee of the Four Home Unions. This consists of a member from each country, one of whom is the Chairman, and includes an Honorary Secretary and Honorary Treasurer who, at the time of writing, are R.H.G. Weighill and John Lawrence.

By the time of publication of this book, there will be a permanent paid Secretary/Treasurer of the Committee of the Four Home Unions and, for tax purposes, he will be based, like the International Board, in Dublin. He will be responsible not only for the day-to-day running of all matters relating to co-operation between the Unions, which includes tours, but also for the running of the new European Cup competition and all other related matters. The new man is Roger Pickering, who played for England at scrum-half in 1967 and 1968. The current honorary officers, Bob Weighill and John Lawrence, will stay in post until after the Lions tour to South Africa in 1997.

In its amateur past, almost everything in rugby was controlled and run by a vast army of unpaid voluntary helpers who were always in an honorary capacity and were extraordinarily powerful figures. Too often, they were and still are depicted by that lavatorial phrase employed by Will Carling, which further damaged their image. Nevertheless, it must be said that these people, although old-fashioned, were men of considerable integrity who did a terrific job in organisational terms and who were invaluable.

By custom, tradition and experience, they established procedures for matters such as a Lions tour which were almost foolproof, which I can illustrate by giving details of what happened on the most recent of Lions tours in 1993. Principles are already laid down and precedents set which authorise the secretary to begin the initial planning.

The whole process begins with the acceptance of an invitation from Australia, New Zealand or South Africa to host the tour. Each member Union is then invited to submit nominations for the management posts, with the curricula vitae of their nominees. Plans are then made to interview for the posts of honorary manager, honorary assistant manager, coach (still known as the assistant manager) and assistant coach. They are nowadays appointed before the start of the season preceding the tour, in time for the selection of players and the appointment of medical personnel.

Each Union is also asked to nominate their representatives for the Selection Committee. Each candidate should have had experience as a national selector, but not be a current member of a national selection committee. The nominations are then reviewed by the committee and, if there is any imbalance in the composition, further nominations are called for. The Honorary Manager then receives the title of Chairman of the Selection Committee and directs the programme for the coming season.

Next the itinerary, always the subject of considerable discussion and correspondence, is approved and confirmed. In the case of the 1993 tour, it was decided that the team should leave the UK on 14/15 May 1993 and return on 6/7 July 1993. It was agreed with the New Zealand RFU that the acclimatisation period from 15 to 21 May would be spent in Waitangi, prior to the first match in Whangerei.

It was further agreed that for the first time ever the party, 35 in number, would travel club class, using the best available route organised by the Four Home Unions' own travel agent. The Unions would pay the cost, but the NZ RFU would then refund the price of the economy fare. That, of course, is a nonsense; considering the vast amount of money generated by these tours, why should the host country only refund economy fares?

Further agreements were entered into with regard to training and assembly of the team and it was decided that, subject to the wishes of the manager and coach, the party should assemble at the Oatlands Park Hotel, Weybridge, Surrey for a familiarisation and training weekend on 23/24/25 April 1993, and reassemble again at midday on Tuesday, 11 May, for departure from Heathrow on Thursday, 13 May 1993, at 1410 hours.

The Honorary Secretary reported that, as previously agreed, he had invited Umbro to be the main kit providers for the tour. They had duly undertaken to provide all training and playing kit, and some leisure wear, at no cost to the Home Unions.

At the time, there was no copyright in the Lions badge, so it was agreed that the current badge should be used for the tour. This has now been rectified and the new badge of the shield of the Four Home Unions, with a Lion Guardant above it, has been duly registered at a cost of some £20,000, for future commercial advantage. It will be interesting to see whether England, who are demanding the lion's share of the television income from the Five Nations tournament, will in future demand a larger cut of the Lions' merchandising.

There were discussions regarding the possibility of various forms of sponsorship for the 1993 Lions tour. The reaction was that there should be no exploitation of the Lions in New Zealand, but the subject was referred to a later meeting of the Committee of the Four Home Unions, who are regarded by most people these days as being too conservative. In the new world of professionalism, sponsorship could be a major factor for the tour to South Africa in 1997.

The committee also discussed a request by London Weekend Television for approval for a camera team to accompany the party to make a video of the tour from assembly to dispersal. Although it offered commercial advantage, they decided that it would be too disruptive and intrusive for the tour party and so it was not allowed.

Prior to this firming-up of arrangements, there are guides and check lists for planning such tours, based on past experience. The following is the check list currently available.

### General

1. Composition of party
2. Terms of reference – aim of tour
3. Programme of work – dates of meetings
4. Study of previous tour reports
5. Itinerary for tour:
   Check (a) Frequency of games
         (b) Distances to be travelled
         (c) Mode of travel
         (d) Hotels, including provision of team rooms
         (e) Time changes
         (f) Availability of training facilities (floodlights)
         (g) Adequate free time
         (h) Obtain Tour Agreement to check daily allowances rate, provision of match tickets, replacement procedures etc.

6. Availability of players
7. Selection
8. Appointment of captain
9. Notification to tour party of addresses, telephone numbers, next of kin details
10. Training schedule for work-up period
11. Kitting: design of tour tie, badge; issue of blazers, slacks, track suits, bags etc.
12. Outline of duties for officials, players, baggage-master
13. Assembly before departure
14. Final check of medical fitness
15. Dispersal at end of tour
16. Press liaison
17. Talk by appropriate Embassy official
18. Farewell party for the players by the Committee of the Four Home Unions
19. Training facilities prior to departure

## Administration

1. Brochure for the tour
2. Adequate copies of nominal role for a variety of purposes
3. Pen pictures and photographs of players and officials for publicity
4. Documentation: passports, visas etc.
5. Medical, dental and physiotherapy requirements, inoculations
6. Finances: Imprest account, foreign exchange
7. Postal arrangements
8. Emergency contacts
9. Dress
10. Baggage details, weights etc.
11. Insurance
12. Local information
13. Reciprocal entertainment
14. Arrangements for return by sea of excess baggage

## Other items

1. Playing kit (shoes, shirts, stockings, boots with various studs, laces)
2. Medical kit
3. Balls for training
4. Name tags
5. Autograph sheets

6. Tickets for games
7. Badges, crests, ties etc. for giving away
8. Tour stationery
9. Thank-you cards
10. Baggage labels
11. Party photo
12. Touch flags
13. Flag
14. Spare studs, laces and blazer buttons
15. Large numbered discs for marking baggage
16. Training kit

Further pre-tour arrangements are:

1. Confirmation of appointments
2. Manager/Chairman of Selectors must set duties of the selectors, scheduling games and players to be watched
3. Selectors to watch players of other countries apart from their own
4. Secretary of a Union must be informed well in advance that a visiting Lions selector will attend their international games so that accommodation, match and function tickets can be arranged
5. Tour manager to arrange interim meetings of selectors to discuss requirements and personnel necessary to win on tour
6. Selectors' out-of-pocket expenses to be submitted to CHU Honorary Treasurer for reimbursement
7. Letters of availability to be sent to Home Union National Squad panels or final trial teams
8. Date of final selection meeting to be arranged following last Five Nations international

One can, therefore, see the immense amount of meticulous thought and preparation which goes into sending the Lions overseas; something, perhaps, of which the teams and their supporters have no conception.

There was a standard letter sent from the Committee of the Four Home Unions, announcing to the players that they were selected for the 1993 tour of New Zealand. Sent together with this letter from the manager, Geoff Cooke, was an acceptance form and a memorandum of guidance, plus an application for tour allowance and compensation for loss of income caused by participation in the tour.

Prior to this tour, no consideration was given to loss of income, and many players on previous tours survived on meagre pocket-money and savings. I remember that in 1955 we received one pound ten shillings a week pocket-money. Furthermore, a number of players on that and subsequent tours gave up their jobs for the honour, pleasure and privilege of going on tour with the Lions, which they saw as the pinnacle of their rugby careers, and a matter which would give them immense satisfaction for the rest of their lives. After visiting those virile countries of the southern hemisphere on such a tour, you are left battle-hardened and, from there on, you are more confident in everyday life and in managing situations.

In an increasingly competitive world, and with jobs harder to find, it was right and proper that such a state of affairs be ended and, after over a century of touring as amateurs, all those pressures have now forced the administrators to make the game professional. The problem now is what the middle and professional classes will do for a new sport, for surely we will have a different game, a different ethos and a different type of person out there on the pitch? Already they are writing 'professional rugby player' on their application forms for passports.

The crucial document, which covers all eventualities, is the 'Tour Agreement'. This is a standard document, formulated and issued by the International Rugby Board for all major tours under their jurisdiction. It is the bible by which all Lions tours are run and it is legally binding. Its importance must never be underestimated, for it addresses every possible eventuality and the extraordinary number of matters which pertain to these tours.

It is because of this document, and its meticulous nature and legal implications, that a controversy such as the Wade Dooley affair in 1993 arose. Wade had to return home on the sad occasion of the death of his father, and the subsequent events became so misunderstood by the touring party, who felt deeply about the inflexibility of the Tours Committee on such a highly emotive matter, that it became a considerable issue. The whole sorry story is fully explored in Chapter 9, The Last Amateurs, covering the 1993 tour.

From the moment the British Lions assemble to go on tour, everything is organised and provision is made for all circumstances. No deviations are allowed, and no leave is granted except in special circumstances of illness or injury. The cost and responsibilities for replacements are catered for and so are all tour expenses, except for personal matters such as phone calls, cables or faxes, and room service. Meals are restricted to table-d'hôte breakfast, lunch and dinner; à la carte meals are not authorised but, in addition to the menu provided, and with the agreement of the liaison officer, soft drinks, fruit juices, milk, beer or wine may also be provided with luncheon or dinner.

All travel and baggage are free, with a baggage man provided for the whole tour, and everything is insured. Taxis for medical treatment are paid for.

Match replacements are, according to IRB regulations and match officials, for foul play and misconduct, all governed by IRB procedures. A commissioner is appointed by the IRB from a neutral country for foul-play hearings, with full discretion as to the punishment. Sanctions for foul play should not be less than:

| | |
|---|---|
| Punching | 30 days |
| Kicking, raking or unlawful use of the boot | 60 days |
| Head butting | 60 days |
| Offences in the tackle | 60 days |
| Other forms of assault | 60 days |
| Abuse of a match official | 120 days |
| Striking a match official | *sine die* |

It has, however, been seen that officials tend to be more lenient, sometimes absurdly so, when touring teams are involved. Nowadays it has become fashionable for players to be cited from television evidence and this must occur within 24 hours of the offence.

Playing kit, laundry and medical arrangements are all clearly defined, as are allocations of match tickets. Each player is entitled to two complimentary tickets and is able to purchase a limited number of extra tickets at the discretion of the manager and the host Union. Everything is covered, including discipline and the use of drugs.

The agreement is signed by the host and visiting Unions and by each player or official in the touring party.

In place of pocket-money, the players will now receive handsome payment. This will be discussed in more detail in Chapter 10, entitled 'The Future'.

# Tables Turned

The start of the twentieth century brought a rude awakening for British rugby, as their missionary days ended and they were forced to face the stark reality of the vigour of the emerging sportsmen from the new worlds of Africa and Australasia.

Trouble was now brewing elsewhere in the world, as the Bolsheviks split the Russian Socialists and Serbian army officers murdered their King and Queen. Delegates at the Zionist conference clashed over plans to set up a Jewish state in Uganda. Women were coming into their own, as Madame Curie won the Nobel Prize for the discovery of radium, and Emmeline Pankhurst formed the militant Women's Social and Political Union in Manchester. Chekhov's *The Cherry Orchard* and George Bernard Shaw's *Candida* had their premières, and the first western movie, *Kit Carson*, was filmed.

In 1904, the Automobile Association was founded and Charles Rolls and Henry Royce began to build the best motor cars in the world. The New York underground opened and *Peter Pan* was produced on stage. The psychologist Alfred Brint invented intelligence tests, and Jules Verne died. Norway declared independence from Sweden and the Russians surrendered to the Japanese at Port Arthur.

The guns in South Africa became silent as the Boer War ended on 31 May 1902, and the Commandos returned to their farms. The British, who thought they had won (although in retrospect they had not), lost no time in sending a rugby team back to what they already knew to be an extremely pleasant country to tour. In 1903 they sent a team to the colony, and in the following year another side went to Australasia. The rude awakening came when Morrison's team lost the first ever Test series to South Africa and then, following an unbeaten run through Australia, Bedell-Sivright's team lost the Test against New Zealand.

## MARK MORRISON'S 1903 BRITISH TEAM

1903 was the watershed, which saw the emergence of South Africa as the most powerful force in world rugby. After being whitewashed in 1891 and winning only one Test in 1896, they shocked the rugby world by winning the three-Test series by one match to nil, with two matches drawn. No one expected it, least of all the British team, who were not to know that South Africa would not lose another Test series for over half a century, until their 1956 series in New Zealand.

Taken by surprise, Morrison's team were beaten in a really tight series. Even though the 1903 Lions fought hard to stop South Africa embarking on what was to be a period of unparalleled success, and although the result of the series was in doubt right up to the last minutes of the final Test, they were unable to prevent a dramatic second-half victory by South Africa in the ultimate match.

Their tour record of 11 wins in 22 matches, which included defeats in the first three matches of the tour, also brought them close to the ignominy of being the first British team to have lost more matches than they won. The first actually to do so was the 1924 Lions side to South Africa.

I have been careful not to refer to the South African team as 'the Springboks', as they were not called that until they adopted the emblem in 1906. It is equally wrong to call New Zealand 'the All Blacks' before 1905, and, strictly speaking, to refer to 'the Lions' before 1924. However, I have called the British teams before that time 'Lions', largely because I believe they were Lions in all but name, and also for ease of reference.

Wales and Scotland were the strongest teams of the first decade of the twentieth century and produced the leading players of the 1903 and 1904 tours. The 1903 side in South Africa was weak at three-quarter, with the one exception of Reg Skrimshire, the Newport and Wales centre. He was miles better than his other backs but he could not do it all on his own, even though he was played in every match. Bill Scott, a fine forward from the West of Scotland, was another who did not miss a game.

Reg, who scored ten tries and 59 points on the tour, was the undoubted British star and was much liked and respected by the South African public. Another in the line of fine Welsh centres, he was on his own against South African backs who were to become household names for generations to come, such as fly-half Paddy Carolin and three-quarters Japie Krige and Bob Loubser. For all that, Skrimshire was ignored by the Welsh selectors and never got another cap after the tour.

There was no problem with the forwards, with players of the calibre of Tedford of Ireland, who was regarded as one of the best Irish forwards of his or any other time. He was the sort of Irishman who, over the generations, became a template for players like Fergus Slattery and many others who have created such mayhem in the home countries championship. He was supported by other international-class forwards like his captain Morrison, 'Darky' Bedell-Sivright (a future Lions captain), W.P. ('Bummer') Scott, and Frank Stout.

Neither was there any problem at half-back, and many experts at the time reckoned the series could have been saved had some of them been employed in the threes. There was also a grave weakness at full-back and, in the last two Tests, the Lions were forced to play Neill, one of the halves, at full-back.

Mark Morrison, who was capped as a teenager (which was and still is extremely rare for a forward), was a hugely popular leader. In the first Test he captained the side against his opposite number Alex Frew, who was captain of South Africa, but he had also played under him in the Triple-Crown-winning Scottish side of 1901. The referee was another Scottish international, with whom Morrison had played in the 1896 Four Nations championship; perhaps it was no surprise, then, that the match was a draw.

In South Africa, the combination of Loubser and Krige became legendary and Danie Craven, in his book, *Springboks Down the Years*, was to call the latter 'the finest centre the game has ever produced'. With Loubser as his wing, he enchanted not only South Africa, but also the British public when he toured Britain with the Springboks of 1906–1907. Under the captaincy of Paul Roos, the team adopted the Springbok as their emblem on the jersey, which led to them and all future generations of South African sportsmen and women becoming known as Springboks. Loubser was also part of that renowned Stellenbosch three-quarter line, which included Krige, de Villiers and Stegmann.

With such a poor overall record, Morrison's team did well to draw the first two Tests. In the first half of the first game in Johannesburg, they even led 10–0 at half-time, but blew up in the second half due to setting too high a pace early on at the high altitude. Skrimshire scored a tremendous try from half-way after feinting to drop at goal and Cave, in the forwards, also scored a try, with Gillespie converting both. After surviving the early attacks in the second half, South Africa took charge and scored tries through Fred Dobbin and Jimmy Sinclair, the famous cricketer with a penchant for hitting sixes, and Heatlie added the points for a draw.

The second Test was, as they say, a match of two halves, this time with South Africa being on top in the first and the British coming back to dominate the second period. There was no score at the end, but the British had the satisfaction that the man of the match was P.S. Hancock, the young Richmond half-back.

The third and final historic Test was to give South Africa their first ever Test rubber. In the odd manner of South African team selection in those days, there was no national selection committee, and it was the Union staging the match which was also responsible for selection. Nepotism was, therefore, fairly rife and, with 11 Western Province players and only four Transvaalers in the side, there are no prizes for guessing which province staged the match.

Heatlie, who was once again captain of South Africa, once more brought out the Old Diocesan green jerseys, which had proved so lucky in the 1896 match against the British. They deservedly won by 8–0 to clinch the series, and as a result South Africa decided that, in future, they would always wear green.

It poured with rain on the morning of the match (a common occurrence in temperate Cape Town), and the British were delighted, for they thought that the wet and the mud would be entirely in their favour, considering that their strength lay in the forwards.

It was not to be, however, as 6,000 spectators braved the weather in what became known as 'the umbrella Test' to see South Africa attempting to attack with their superior backs, even though the ground was a mud bath. Although Loubser, van Renen and Krige were magnificent in the conditions, and Skrimshire got over for the British just before the whistle, it was adjudged a forward pass and there was still no score at half-time. The second half saw South Africa overcoming their opponents' forward skill at dribbling the ball, and they scored when they moved the ball to the left wing, Barry, who plunged through the water for an unconverted try in the corner. Amid huge excitement, South Africa kept up the pressure, and pressed home their superiority when Hobson made the crucial break before handing on to Reid, a forward who remarkably eluded three defenders. According to the British, the defenders stood still, because they believed that Hobson's pass was well forward. Few close games are without controversy, but the consensus was that South Africa deserved their win and their first Test series.

# Results of the 1903 British team in South Africa

P 22   W 11   D 3   L 8   F 229   A 138

| | | | |
|---|---|---|---|
| Western Province (Country) | L | 7 | 13 |
| Western Province (Town) | L | 3 | 12 |
| Western Province | L | 4 | 8 |
| Port Elizabeth | W | 13 | 0 |
| Eastern Province | W | 12 | 0 |
| Grahamstown | W | 28 | 7 |
| King Williams Town | W | 37 | 3 |
| East London | W | 7 | 5 |
| Griqualand West | L | 0 | 11 |
| Griqualand West | L | 6 | 8 |
| Transvaal | L | 3 | 12 |
| Pretoria | W | 15 | 3 |
| Pietermaritzburg | W | 15 | 0 |
| Durban | W | 22 | 0 |
| Witwatersrand | W | 12 | 0 |
| Transvaal | L | 4 | 14 |
| South Africa (Johannesburg) | D | 10 | 10 |
| Orange River Colony | W | 17 | 16 |
| Griqualand West | W | 11 | 5 |
| South Africa (Kimberley) | D | 0 | 0 |
| Western Province | D | 3 | 3 |
| South Africa (Cape Town) | L | 0 | 8 |

## Mark Morrison's 1903 British team

**Full-back**

| | | |
|---|---|---|
| E.M. Harrison | Guy's Hospital | |

**Three-quarters**

| | | |
|---|---|---|
| G.F. Collett | Gloucestershire | |
| I.G. Davidson | North of Ireland | Ireland |
| A.E. Hind | Cambridge University | |
| R.T. Skrimshire | Newport | Wales |
| E.F. Walker | Lennox | |

**Half-backs**

| | | |
|---|---|---|
| J.I. Gillespie | Edinburgh Academicals | Scotland |
| L.L. Greig | United Services | |
| P.S. Hancock | Richmond | |
| R.M. Neill | Edinburgh Academicals | Scotland |

**Forwards**

| | | |
|---|---|---|
| D.R. Bedell-Sivright | Cambridge University | Scotland |
| W.T. Cave | Cambridge University | |
| T.A. Gibson | Cambridge University | |
| J.C. Hosack | Edinburgh Wanderers | |
| M.C. Morrison (capt.) | Royal High School FP | Scotland |
| W.P. Scott | West of Scotland | Scotland |
| R.S. Smyth | Dublin University | Ireland |
| F.M. Stout | Richmond | |
| A. Tedford | Malone | Ireland |
| James Wallace | Wanderers | |
| Joseph Wallace | Wanderers | Ireland |

Manager: J. Hammond

The next British tour to South Africa was not until 1910, by which time the name 'Springboks' had become firmly established and was to gain respect wherever the game was played. Although there are other versions, the authenticity of a letter by J.C. Carden, the tour manager of the 1906 tour, is undeniable. He states in the letter to Ivor Difford, 'The fact is that the Springbok, as a badge, existed when my team left South Africa, and here is proof positive. We landed at Southampton on the evening of 20 September 1906 and, from *The Daily Mail* of 20 September, I culled this paragraph: "The team's colours will be myrtle green jerseys with gold collar. They will wear dark blue shorts and dark stockings and the jerseys will have embroidered, in mouse silk on the left breast, a Springbok, a small African antelope, which is as typical of Africa as the kangaroo is of Australia."'

Carden continues: 'As to the adoption of the name. No uniforms or blazers had been provided and we were a motley turn-out at practice in Richmond. That evening I talked with Paul Roos, the captain, and Carolin, and pointed out that the witty London Press would invent some funny name for us if we did not invent one ourselves. We thereupon agreed to call ourselves the Springboks and to tell pressmen that we desired to be so named. I remember this distinctly, for Paul [Roos] reminded us that Springbokken was the correct plural.

However, *The Daily Mail*, after our first practice, called us the Springboks and the name stuck. I at once ordered the dark green, gold-edged blazers and still have the first Springbok badge that was made.'

## D.R. BEDELL-SIVRIGHT'S 1904 BRITISH TEAM

The captain, D.R. Bedell-Sivright, was the only player to tour in both 1903 and 1904. Apparently he was a man after my own heart, being a rough handful as a player. He was one of the first in a long line of Scottish forwards to master the art of wing-forward play, and had the reputation of breaking up opposing teams with his marauding spoiling. He was the Douglas Elliot or the John Jeffrey of his day. He played in four Varsity matches for Cambridge and 22 internationals for Scotland between 1901 and 1908, and was one of the best forwards produced by the British Isles in the first decade of the twentieth century.

He had only three other capped forwards in his side: D.D. Dobson of England, R.W. Edwards, who had one cap for Ireland, and the redoubtable A.F. ('Boxer') Harding of Wales; all nine of his remaining forwards were merely of club standard. In the backs, however, he had a galaxy of talent, including five Welshmen who are still household names: Tommy Vile, Percy Bush, Rhys Gabe, Teddy Morgan and Willie Llewellyn. Had Gwyn Nicholls been available, then Wales would have supplied all the backs except the full-back for the Test team. These were the players who carried Wales through their first golden era, when they won the international championship five times in seven seasons.

I knew four of these old players – Rhys Gabe, Tommy Vile, Teddy Morgan and little Willie Llewellyn – and often enjoyed long discussions with them concerning this tour and, of course, the most controversial try of all time, which All Black Bob Deans claimed that he scored in 1905 at Cardiff Arms Park. Willie Llewellyn told me that it was not a try, as he wriggled over after the tackle, and Rhys Gabe claimed, 'He was struggling to go forward, so I pulled him back, as I knew he had not got to the line'; but Teddy Morgan, who put in the original tackle after covering from the other wing, was always of the belief that he had scored. Remarkably, David Gallaher, the All Blacks captain, made no reference to it in his book published in 1906, but then real gentlemen never complain over spilt milk.

Many was the time that I discussed the early tours with these first tourists of the early 1900s who were now legends, comparing them with my own tour with the Lions of 1955. I was always surprised at how little we differed in our views of our particular eras for, apart from the differences resulting from technological progress in areas such as travel, accommodation and facilities, our personal experiences of the marvellous hospitality we received, and the adventure of it all, tallied exactly.

In Australia, Bedell-Sivright's team became the first side to win all its Australian games, playing and winning 14 matches and scoring 265 points against 51, and they rattled up 50 points to three in the three Tests. In their three games against New South Wales, always seen as close to Test standard, they scored 61 points against six. In these games, their brilliant Welsh backs swept all before them, beginning a long tradition of such talent on Lions tours.

The orchestrator of the superb back play was Percy Bush. He was greatly admired by the Australians, who adored his magical, almost ethereal play, which has its modern parallel in that of Barry John during the 1970s.

It was the most successful British side to visit Australia, being the only one to win all of its matches on a major visit and, following the New Zealand leg of the tour, this was to change vastly British conceptions concerning the antipodean colonies.

In New Zealand it was a very different story, particularly after Bedell-Sivright unhappily broke his leg in the opening game at Canterbury and did not play again on tour. Teddy Morgan, later to be immortalised for scoring the Welsh try in that unforgettable Welsh victory over New Zealand in 1905, took over as captain.

New Zealand rugby was reaching its first peak and events took a rapid turn for the worse after the heady success in Australia. The British won the first game at Canterbury by a mere conversion, and won the next against Otago in another tight game, before losing to New Zealand in Wellington, drawing at Taranaki and finally losing heavily to Auckland.

It was the beginning of that now familiar tale of annihilating New Zealand forward play wiping out the brilliance of British back play. The British were completely thrown by the New Zealand forward formation, which was to pack 2–3–2, and by a forward known as a 'Rover', who never packed down and made a huge nuisance of himself in defence. This was to be abandoned after the acrimony of the 1930 Lions tour to New Zealand, when the law was changed to force them to put three men in the front row. The All Blacks also differed, as they do to this day, with having two five-eighths, a first and a second, as opposed to a fly-half and two centres. The theory was to get the ball to the wings by going through the same sequence of hands, and to work out moves to combat the loose forwards, whereas the old British system of a left and a right centre meant a change of position alongside the fly-half or once removed from him, dependent on whether you are going left or right. There is no difference, however, between a second five-eighth and a player picked as an inside centre.

It was the time when the vernacular of rugby was about invincibles and immortals, and certainly many famous names were beginning to emerge as rugby stars. Billy ('Carbine') Wallace was one of the first, and I was again privileged to have met and talked to him. He scored a career record of 379 points for New Zealand, which stood for 50 years, until bettered by Don Clarke.

Another was the mighty Dave Gallaher, a tremendous thinker concerning the game, who was to captain the 1905 team to Britain and so displease the crowds with his role as a destructive 'Rover'. There was also Charlie ('Bronco') Seeling, who was famous for his flying tackles, and regarded as one of the finest of all New Zealand forwards to visit the UK.

The coach of the New Zealand team which beat Bedell-Sivright's team was another fine strategist, Jimmy Duncan, who was also to coach the 1905 All Blacks team which came to Britain and lost only one game, against Wales. Like Markotter of South Africa and Adrian Stoop of England, he was among the great rugby innovators of the time, and it was he who devised the New Zealand five-eighth system.

Two of the 1904 tourists were, in fact, New Zealanders. Pat McEvedy and Arthur O'Brien were medical students at Guy's Hospital when they were selected to tour, and both ultimately practised medicine in New Zealand, where McEvedy became President of the NZ RFU. Blair Swannell, who toured South Africa with Mullineux, emigrated to Australia in 1905 and played for Australia that year against New Zealand. Swannell, a hard forward, was to die heroically, leading a charge at Gallipoli on Anzac day 1915, while his captain, Bedell-Sivright, was to die a few months later in the same theatre of war.

There was terrific interest in the Test match, which drew 20,000, a huge crowd in those days, to Athletic Park. The game was attended by the Governor, the Prime Minister and most of the Ministers of the Crown, and New Zealand kicked off in perfect conditions. Wallace drew first blood with a penalty after half an hour, but Harding replied with one for the British to make it 3–3 at half-time. In the second period, the New Zealand forwards got well on top and Duncan McGregor scored two fine tries, to make the final score 9–3. He was carried off shoulder high by the crowd who, amid scenes of intense excitement, had invaded the pitch.

Bedell-Sivright admitted that his team had been beaten by a better side, but thought that they were tired and out of sorts after all their travelling. He also suggested that the lavish New Zealand hospitality could have damaged their cause.

Just as many Welsh team members in New Zealand in 1969 returned to gain revenge with the 1971 Lions, so the Welsh players returned to Wales to plot the downfall of Gallaher's 1905 All Blacks, who would have been invincible had they only beaten Wales. Five of the Welsh side had played in Wellington and so they were experienced in the New Zealand tactic of seven forwards and a 'Rover'. Consequently, they too detached a forward and played Cliff Pritchard as an extra roving back. He subdued the All Blacks' five-eighths, Hunter and Mynott, who had been instrumental in their team's success throughout the tour, thus allowing Wales to win by the narrow margin of 3–0.

## Results of the 1904 British team in Australia and New Zealand

P 19   W 16   D 1   L 2   F 287   A 84

| | | | |
|---|---|---|---|
| New South Wales | W | 27 | 0 |
| Combined Western Districts | W | 21 | 6 |
| New South Wales | W | 29 | 6 |
| Metropolitan Union | W | 19 | 6 |
| Australia (Sydney) | W | 17 | 0 |
| Northern Districts | W | 17 | 3 |
| Queensland | W | 24 | 5 |
| Metropolitan Union | W | 17 | 3 |
| Queensland | W | 18 | 7 |
| Toowoomba | W | 12 | 3 |
| Australia (Brisbane) | W | 17 | 3 |
| New England | W | 26 | 9 |
| Australia (Sydney) | W | 16 | 0 |
| New South Wales | W | 5 | 0 |
| | | | |
| South Canterbury, Canterbury & West Coast | W | 5 | 3 |
| Otago–Southland | W | 14 | 8 |
| New Zealand (Wellington) | L | 3 | 9 |
| Taranaki, Ranganui & Manawatu | D | 0 | 0 |
| Auckland | L | 0 | 13 |

## D.R. Bedell-Sivright's 1904 British team

**Full-back**

| | | |
|---|---|---|
| C.F. Stanger-Leathes | Northern | |

**Three-quarters**

| | | |
|---|---|---|
| J.L. Fisher | Yorkshire | |
| R.T. Gabe | Cardiff | Wales |
| W.F. Jowett | Swansea | Wales |
| W.M. Llewellyn | Cardiff | Wales |
| P.F. McEvedy | Guy's Hospital | |
| E.T. Morgan | Guy's Hospital | Wales |
| A.B. O'Brien | Guy's Hospital | |

**Half-backs**

| | | |
|---|---|---|
| P.F. Bush | Cardiff | |
| F.C. Hulme | Birkenhead Park | England |
| T.H. Vile | Newport | |

**Forwards**

| | | |
|---|---|---|
| D.R. Bedell-Sivright (capt.) | Cambridge University | Scotland |
| T.S. Bevan | Swansea | |
| S.N. Crowther | Lennox | |
| D.D. Dobson | Oxford University | England |
| R.W. Edwards | Malone | Ireland |
| A.F. Harding | London Welsh | Wales |
| B.F. Massey | Yorkshire | |
| C.D. Patterson | Malone | |
| R.J. Rogers | Bath | |
| S.M. Saunders | Guy's Hospital | |
| J.T. Sharland | Streatham | |
| B.I. Swannell | Northampton | |
| D.H. Trail | Guy's Hospital | |

Manager: A.B. O'Brien

## A.F. Harding's 1908 Anglo-Welsh team

In 1908, Asquith became Prime Minister, and men and women over 70 in Britain began to draw the first old age pensions. In America, Jack Johnson KO'd Tommy Burns to become the first black heavyweight champion of the world. An international conference in Switzerland banned night work for children under 14 years old. Picasso held a banquet for Henri Rousseau in Paris, and anti-British articles in *The Daily Telegraph* by the Kaiser caused consternation. The Model-T Ford was built in Detroit, bringing transport to the masses.

Similarly, sporting teams were becoming more mobile. The 1908 team was in no sense a fully representative British side and, at first, I was reluctant to include it in a book about the Lions. However, some of those early 'pioneer' teams were also hardly representative and, after all, A.F. Harding's players did play two Tests against the All Blacks, which was sufficient for them to qualify. It was the first and last Anglo-Welsh team to go on tour.

These tourists failed to gel as a team, and they managed to sustain two of the worst defeats in Lions history, losing the first and third Tests in New Zealand by 32–5 and 29–0 respectively. The experiment was never repeated, but the basic problem was the selection of so many players without international experience. Only 11 of the 28 tourists had played for their country, although several were to be capped later.

They played in red jerseys with broad white hoops, a combination of English and Welsh colours. For the first time, the New Zealand part of the tour became larger and more significant than the Australian section. They played only nine games in Australia with no Test match, and 17 in New Zealand with three Test matches.

This was strange, because rugby was popular in Sydney in 1907, with crowds of over 45,000 going to see the touring All Blacks. Somehow, this tour heralded the beginning of the decline of Australia as a rugby world force over the next 70 years. Not until the 1980s did the Aussies finally stop the decline and reorganise themselves into a side capable of making the Grand Slam against the four home nations in 1984, of winning the World Cup in 1991, and consistently capable of beating the All Blacks.

In contrast with the 1904 team, there was no star-studded back division, with no backs of the stature of Rhys Gabe, Percy Bush, Willie Llewellyn or Tommy Vile. Only E.J. Jackett, the Cornish England full-back, A.F. Harding, the captain, and R. Dibble, who was capped 19 times by England, made any sort of a name for themselves.

They narrowly won a three-game rubber 2–1 against New South Wales, and then managed to win only nine of their 17 games in New Zealand. They drew the second Test, played in shocking conditions in Wellington, but got hammered in the other two, in Dunedin and Auckland, to concede the series.

At the first Test in Dunedin, they met an All Blacks team which was in its heyday and which contained no fewer than eight players who had been outstanding in that magnificent tour to Britain in 1905, losing only the one game. The crowd were incensed at the excessive price of the ground tickets, which had gone up to two shillings, so they tore down the corrugated fence and hundreds poured through the gap onto the terraces, with the police powerless to stop them. A crowd of 23,000 saw the game, which was played in brilliant sunshine. The All Blacks were vastly superior in every phase of play and ran out easy winners by 32–5, which was a gigantic score in those days.

The British had to contend with Jimmy Hunter at fly-half, who was famous for his sniping runs and his speciality of walking in tries once he had broken the defence. In 1905, he scored an all-time record of 44 tries on a single tour. The All Blacks also had the great Bob Deans at centre, who scored the hotly disputed try against Wales which is still argued about whenever Welshmen and New Zealanders meet. At scrum-half they had Freddy Roberts, again one of the best scrum-halves New Zealand has ever had and, of course, Charlie Seeling, the great exponent of the feared dive tackle. Harding had no such ammunition in his locker.

The second Test, three weeks later at Wellington, was played in such wretched conditions that only 10,000 spectators braved the cold and wet to see what they believed was going to be a one-sided affair. In the event, the British played some excellent wet-weather rugby and surprised their opponents by the strength of their scrummaging, to draw the match. There was no score at half-time, but in the second half Francis put New Zealand ahead with a penalty goal for offside, before 'Ponty' Jones scored a try under the posts from a forward rush which, calamitously, Harding failed to convert. The All Blacks were lucky to escape with a draw and the series was again very much alive.

An interesting feature of the match against Wellington came when Jackett left the field for an extended period of time with an injury. The Wellington captain, Freddy Roberts, offered a substitute, a practice often used following a typically pragmatic decision made in the southern hemisphere, but one which made the British-dominated International Board furious. The gesture was declined on the grounds that it transgressed the laws of the game, which typifies some of the conservative attitudes of the game's administrators which lasted for far too long. Because of the physical nature of rugby in the southern hemisphere, the Lions often suffered grievously with injuries; therefore, those who refused to change the laws on substitution can be seen to have contributed to a number of their defeats.

However, in the third Test played at Potter's Park, Auckland, New Zealand showed that the second Test was an aberration, and punished the British side for their final week of much festivity at places like Rotorua after they had lost to Auckland. Apparently that last week at Rotorua was a lot of fun, with sightseeing every day and dancing every night. They even played an unofficial game against a Maori team on the Tuesday.

They left for Auckland in poor shape on the Thursday, and it was no surprise when it became a one-sided game, particularly after they lost their captain, Harding, in the opening minutes. New Zealand led 12–0 at half-time, with two tries by Mitchinson and one each from Hunter and Glasgow. In the second half, Gillett, Hayward, Mitchinson, Deans and Francis all scored further tries, but the goal kicking was appalling and only one try out of the nine was converted by Colman. The Brits were lucky, then, to get away with losing only 29–0.

Another interesting fact was that there were five Old Boys from the Welsh public school Christ's College, Brecon, on the tour, which is probably a record for any school.

## Results of the 1908 Anglo-Welsh team in Australia and New Zealand

P 26   W 16   D 1   L 9   F 323   A 201

| New South Wales | W | 3 | 0 |
| New South Wales | W | 8 | 0 |
| Western | L | 10 | 15 |
| Metropolitan | W | 16 | 13 |
| Newcastle | W | 42 | 0 |
| New South Wales | L | 3 | 6 |
| Queensland | W | 20 | 3 |
| Queensland | W | 11 | 8 |
| Brisbane | W | 26 | 3 |
| Wairarapa–Bush | W | 17 | 3 |
| Wellington | L | 13 | 19 |
| Otago | L | 6 | 9 |
| Southland | W | 14 | 8 |
| New Zealand (Dunedin) | L | 5 | 32 |
| South Canterbury | W | 12 | 6 |
| Canterbury | L | 8 | 13 |
| West Coast–Buller | W | 22 | 3 |
| Marlborough–Nelson | W | 12 | 0 |
| New Zealand (Wellington) | D | 3 | 3 |

| | | | |
|---|---|---|---|
| Hawke's Bay | W | 25 | 3 |
| Poverty Bay | W | 26 | 0 |
| Manawatu–Horowhenua | W | 12 | 3 |
| Wanganui | W | 9 | 6 |
| Taranaki | L | 0 | 5 |
| Auckland | L | 0 | 11 |
| New Zealand (Auckland) | L | 0 | 29 |

## A.F. Harding's 1908 Anglo-Welsh team

**Full-backs**

| | | |
|---|---|---|
| J.C.M. Dyke | Coventry | Wales |
| E.J. Jackett | Falmouth | England |

**Three-quarters**

| | | |
|---|---|---|
| F.E. Chapman | Hartlepool Rovers | |
| R.A. Gibbs | Cardiff | Wales |
| R.B. Griffiths | Newport | |
| J.P. 'Ponty' Jones | Pontypool | Wales |
| J.P. 'Tuan' Jones | Guy's Hospital | |
| P.F. McEvedy | Guy's Hospital | |
| H.H. Vassall | Oxford University | England |
| J.L. Williams | Cardiff | Wales |

**Half-backs**

| | | |
|---|---|---|
| J. Davey | Redruth | England |
| H. Laxon | Cambridge University | |
| W.L. Morgan | London Welsh | |
| G.L. Williams | Liverpool | |

**Forwards**

| | | |
|---|---|---|
| H.A. Archer | Guy's Hospital | |
| R. Dibble | Bridgewater Albion | England |
| P.J. Down | Bristol | |
| R.K. Green | Neath | |
| A.F. Harding (capt.) | London Welsh | Wales |
| G.R. Hind | Guy's Hospital | |
| F.S. Jackson | Leicester | |
| G.V. Kyrke | Marlborough Nomads | |
| E. Morgan | Swansea | |
| W.L. Oldham | Coventry | England |
| J.A.S. Ritson | Northern | |

| T.W. Smith | Leicester | |
| L.S. Thomson | Penarth | |
| J.F. Williams | London Welsh | Wales |

Manager: G.H. Harnett

The teams were now growing in size, as the resistance grew and the tours became harder.

When the storm clouds gathered over Europe, Australia and New Zealand were soon to become Britain's firm allies in World War I, when so many young men of both countries of the antipodes would make the ultimate sacrifice on Britain's behalf, particularly at Gallipoli. The 1908 side was the last team to visit Australasia for another 22 years.

## DR TOM SMYTHE'S 1910 BRITISH TEAM

There was only to be one more tour before Europe went up in flames in 1914, and the flower of Britain's youth were to undertake a far more dangerous and deadly contest. Their visit to South Africa coincided with George V succeeding to the throne, and the Union of South Africa becoming a Dominion of the British Empire. Also in that year, Tolstoy died as a hermit. Dr Crippen was hanged, Florence Nightingale died aged 90, the suffragettes went on hunger strike in prison and Captain Scott set out for the South Pole.

No longer was it a question of missionary work and the spreading of the message that rugby was the best character-building game of all, with its huge demand on physical and mental bravery. These, together with its more intellectually stimulating requirements, were all qualities which saw the colonials, tempered in hard and tough environments, taking to the game like ducks to water. It has often occurred to me that rugby always seems to find its spiritual home where life is at its toughest and most unsophisticated, as in those southern hemisphere places, which even in relatively modern times are new frontiers, and in the south-west of France and the mining valleys of Wales.

Instead, the 1910 tour was all about survival and the British took out 26 players, only four short of what has become the normal full complement of 30 players for a Lions tour. This was further evidence of the increasing strength of rugby in places like South Africa and New Zealand, and the growing realisation that the former pupils were becoming the masters.

It was the first time that Wales was fully represented in a British Isles touring team to South Africa, when no less than eight Welshmen were included and seven of them were from Newport, a record for a club's representation on a Lions tour.

One of the team was Watsonian L.M. Speirs, who had played for Scotland when they beat Paul Roos's team during the Springboks' tour of Britain in 1906. The Springboks had lost only to the Scots, drawing with England and beating Wales and Ireland; and so South Africa held no fears for at least one member of the touring party.

The old Springboks system of selection by the Province in which the Test was played had been amended slightly. For the three Tests, however, there were still three different panels, with the centre where the Test took place providing two selectors, and the other Test centres one each. Griqualand, having lost their Test match, were still allowed to have a selector on the panel.

One of the two matches against Border was considered unofficial by the British team, as they thought the tour was getting too strenuous by its inclusion. They therefore played in their club, not their tour, jerseys.

This was to be known as C.H. ('Cherry') Pillman's tour. Seldom has a tour been so completely dominated by one man, as this one was by this Blackheath and England loose forward. The Springboks captain, Billy Millar, considered him to be the greatest wing forward of all time, and said that Pillman revolutionised the South African concept of forward play. By now, the new strategies of forward play with an emphasis on the loose head were coming into use and this, together with Pillman's skill, was to establish a pattern of forward technique which remained for 70 years, until they began to curb the wing forward, who had become far too destructive.

In South Africa, it was Pillman who made the template for future generations of superb Springboks loose forwards, such as Hennie Muller, Doug Hopwood, Jan Ellis and many others who became cult figures in the game. Billy Millar also stated categorically that it was Pillman who single-handedly inspired the British to their unexpected victory in the second Test when, astonishingly, he operated at fly-half.

Pillman also operated as a place kicker of remarkable accuracy and easily headed the points-scorers for the tour with 65 points, even though he was an unrecognised kicker when he went on tour. It is easy to see, therefore, why the South Africans were in awe of this remarkable young man, who was only 22 years old, stood 6ft 3ins tall and weighed 173lbs. A leading critic of the day wrote that 'he played as though he had invented the game himself'.

The original tour party included 14 internationals of the time, and three were capped later. Three of the four replacements were also internationals. The British team's overall record was similar to that of Morrison's side, as they, too, lost eight matches and drew three, but they played two more fixtures and had 13 wins against 11. Their Test record was worse, as they lost two matches and won one whereas the 1903 side lost only one and drew the other two. They were also to sport their new colours of a dark blue jersey, instead of the red and white stripes. The shorts were white and the stockings red.

Apart from the new concept of a winging forward, Tommy Smythe's team was also credited with having been the first side in South Africa to introduce half-backs in the fixed positions of scrum-half and fly-half; previously they had played on a left and right, or even a first-up, basis. The South African Provinces quickly adopted this system with the exception of Western Province, who waited another four years.

The first Test was played at the Wanderers ground and, in line with the terrible injury problems which plagued the whole tour, their star player, Pillman, was unable to play in what was a most exciting affair. The British had by far the better of the first half, but at half-time the scores were level with a try apiece from A.R. Foster and de Villiers. South Africa then seemed to have the game comfortably won, when a try by Duggie Morkel, and another by Richard Luyt, converted by Morkel, made it 11–3. Then a drop goal by 'Ponty' Jones (who was on his second tour to South Africa) and a try by J.A. Spoors made it a thriller and anybody's game at 11–10.

It was the splendid Morkel who won the game for South Africa, after they had been put on the rack of repeated British attacks, when he put in an intelligent kick to the left flank for Hahn to gather in his stride and score. South Africa won a most thrilling game by 14–10. The Morkel family from Somerset West became a legend in South Africa, as ten members won Springboks colours in the period from 1903 to 1928 – a feat unlikely ever to be repeated.

The second Test at the Crusader ground in Port Elizabeth saw South Africa as hot favourites to win, but they had not counted on the return of the dreaded Pillman, who was an inspired choice to play at fly-half. Even more astonishingly, South Africa dropped Duggie Morkel. The game was largely won by the performance of the forwards, who played out of their skins (in particular, H. Jarman and P.D. Waller), and by the scrum-half, George Isherwood, who had the game of his life.

Playing with the wind, the Springboks were 3–0 up at half-time following a try by Mills. In the second half, Pillman took over so completely that Bill Millar, the South African captain that day, wrote years later: 'My memories of this game are all dwarfed by Pillman's brilliance. I confidently assert that, if ever a man can be said to have won an international match through his own unorthodox and lone-handed efforts, it can be said of the inspired, black-haired Pillman I played against on the Crusader ground on 27 August 1910.'

Pillman started both his team's second-half match-winning tries, first with a kick over Allport's head for Spoors to score. Two minutes later he was at it again, when he initiated a try for the winger, M.E. Neale, which he also converted, and the game was won 8–3.

The third Test to decide the rubber, poised at one win each, was played at Newlands in Cape Town. Unfortunately, and again in keeping with the tour's unlucky chapter of injuries, the British lost their full-back in the opening ten minutes and played with 14 men for the rest of the game. They stood little chance after that and were well beaten 21–5. The only first-half score was a try by Gideon Roos, converted by Duggie Morkel. In the second half, Luyt scored a try which was again converted by Morkel, who also kicked a penalty. Although Spoors scored a try (as he had done in the previous two Tests), which was converted by Pillman, a further try by Reynecke, converted by Morkel, saw the British team well beaten. This match also marked the introduction of 'Boy' Morkel who, at the time and for a long time after, was regarded as the best all-round forward in the world.

In that third Test, a member of the pack was Clive van Ryneveld, father of the double Oxford Blue of the same name, who played rugby for England at centre in 1949, and captained South Africa at cricket against Peter May's side in 1960–61.

Harry Jarman, who was a British stalwart in the pack, was to die tragically and courageously. His illustrious football career ended when he threw himself into the path of a runaway tram at a South Wales colliery, as it headed for a bunch of youngsters playing in its path. His heroic action saved the children's lives, as he managed to derail the wagon, but he was mortally wounded.

This was the end of another era and, as the lights went out finally all over Europe during World War I there was to be no further rugby contact between teams from the British Isles and those from the southern hemisphere for 14 years. Many South Africans fought gallantly for Britain in those hostilities.

## Results of the 1910 British team in South Africa

P 24   W 13   D 3   L 8   F 290   A 236

| | | | |
|---|---|---|---|
| South Western Districts | W | 14 | 4 |
| Western Province (Country) | W | 9 | 3 |
| Western Province (Colleges) | W | 11 | 3 |
| Western Province (Town) | D | 11 | 11 |
| Western Province | W | 5 | 3 |
| Griqualand West | L | 0 | 8 |
| Transvaal | L | 8 | 27 |
| Pretoria | W | 17 | 0 |
| Transvaal (Country) | W | 45 | 4 |
| Transvaal | L | 6 | 13 |
| Natal | W | 18 | 16 |
| Natal | W | 19 | 13 |
| Orange River Colony | W | 12 | 9 |
| Griqualand West | L | 3 | 9 |
| Cape Colony | L | 0 | 19 |
| Rhodesia | W | 24 | 11 |
| South Africa (Kimberley) | L | 10 | 14 |
| North Eastern Districts | D | 8 | 8 |
| Border | W | 30 | 10 |
| Border | D | 13 | 13 |
| Eastern Province | W | 14 | 6 |
| South Africa (Port Elizabeth) | W | 8 | 3 |
| South Africa (Cape Town) | L | 5 | 21 |
| Western Province | L | 0 | 8 |

## Dr Tom Smythe's 1910 British team

**Full-back**
| | | |
|---|---|---|
| S.H. Williams | Newport | |

**Three-quarters**
| | | |
|---|---|---|
| A.M. Baker | Newport | Wales |
| A.R. Foster | Derry | Ireland |
| J.P. Jones | Newport | Wales |
| A. Melville | Newport | |
| M.E. Neale | Bristol | |
| R.C.S. Plummer | Newport | |
| J.A. Spoors | Bristol | |

| C.G. Timms | Edinburgh University | |
| K.B. Wood | Leicester | |

**Half-backs**

| N.F. Humphries | Tynedale | |
| G.A.M. Isherwood | Sale | |
| A.N. McClinton | North of Ireland | Ireland |
| E. Milroy* | Watsonians | Scotland |

**Forwards**

| W.J. Ashby | Queen's College Cork | |
| E. O'D. Crean | Liverpool | |
| F.G. Handford* | Manchester | England |
| H. Jarman | Newport | Wales |
| C.H. Pillman | Blackheath | England |
| O.J.S. Piper | Cork Constitution | Ireland |
| J. Reid-Kerr | Greenock Wanderers | Scotland |
| T.J. Richards* | Bristol | |
| W.A. Robertson | Edinburgh University | |
| D.F. Smith | Richmond | England |
| T. Smythe (capt.) | Malone | Ireland |
| L.M. Speirs | Watsonians | Scotland |
| R. Stevenson | St Andrews University | Scotland |
| W. Tyrrell | Queen's University Belfast | Ireland |
| P.D. Waller | Newport | Wales |
| J. Webb* | Abertillery | Wales |

Managers: W. Cail and W.E. Rees

* Replacements

# Between the Wars

In the 21 years between the two great wars, the rate of touring slowed down and only three teams, the 1924 and 1938 to South Africa and the 1930 to New Zealand, left British and Irish shores. This was largely due to the exhaustion and worry which many felt at that time and to the great world-wide economic depressions of the 1920s and 1930s.

These teams were also officially the first fully representative teams to be sent by the Four Home Unions. However, just as before and later in the Lions' history, they were often weakened by the unavailability of players, who were loath to risk giving up good jobs, as were the employers to give them the time off, as money was short. Nowadays, people have no idea how poor the population was at that time; even after World War II, a meal for a rugby player in Wales, and in parts of England and Scotland, was a valuable commodity.

It is not surprising that in January of 1924 Ramsay MacDonald, a weaver's son from Scotland, became the first Labour Prime Minister. In the October, however, the Tories won a huge election victory after the scare of the Zinoviev Letter, which recently was shown to be fake, and the Campbell case. It was also the year when Lenin died. Stalin denounced Trotsky and Mussolini assumed full dictatorial power in Italy. Harold Abrahams and Eric Liddell triumphed in the Paris Olympic Games and Jan Smuts lost his parliament seat in the South African elections.

When the armistice was signed on 11 November 1918 and the guns fell silent, many rugby players of all nationalities failed to return home from the battlefield. Typically, it was South Africa and New Zealand who were to set the first rugby tours rolling again, for the New Zealanders would go anywhere for a game, especially at the drop of a forage cap. Their New Zealand Imperial Services team, which won the

Inter Services tournament in England at the end of the war, jumped at the chance of visiting South Africa on their way home in 1919 and played 14 matches, winning ten and losing three, with one drawn. This further whetted the insatiable appetite for the game in both these mighty rugby countries, which led to one of the greatest rugby rivalries of all, and to the 1921 Springboks tour of New Zealand and Australia, where they lost only two of 24 matches with two draws, and shared the unofficial Test series with the All Blacks.

## DR RONALD COVE-SMITH'S 1924 LIONS

It took Britain some time to reorganise its rugby after the war, but eventually a tour to South Africa was put in place, and Dr Cove-Smith, a fine and delightful man, was chosen to lead the team that was the first to be called the British Lions. The name had a better journalistic ring to it than the official name of British Isles Rugby Union Team, or BIRUT, on the official notepaper and kit-bags.

From the start this tour was to be ill-fated, as rugby in the British Isles was at a low ebb. This was evidenced by the progress of the 1924 All Blacks, who ran through the four home nations undefeated. On the other hand, South Africa was embarking on a golden period of its noble rugby history.

Once again, Cove-Smith's side was not representative of all the talent of the British Isles, for Lions sides have never been at full strength. In contrast, you always knew that the All Blacks and the Springboks would never dream of missing a rugby tour, gladly giving up jobs and studies for an experience of a lifetime, and you could virtually guarantee that you were watching the full cream of their talent. Many key players, including the legendary Wavell Wakefield, who had led England to the Grand Slam in 1924, and those fine Scottish centres, A.L. Gracie and G.P.S. Macpherson, were unavailable.

Not only were many important players left at home, but injuries also played havoc with the team. So desperate was their plight that they had to call on the services of W. Cunningham, an Irish international living in Johannesburg. He played only four matches, but those included the third Test. Another who was injured for most of the tour was A.T. Young, the splendid England scrum-half. W.S. Gainsford was injured in the very first training session and did not play in a single match, while T.E. Holliday was injured in the opening game and never played again. As both were full-backs, this put a huge responsibility on the Scotsman Dan Drysdale who, although he played marvellously throughout as a running full-back, was a duffer as a goal kicker and did not land one kick throughout the tour. Tom Voyce, who took over the place-kicking duties, was no great shakes at it either, and the total tally of the place kicking on tour was five conversions and three penalties. This was desperately paltry, and one of the main reasons for the team's lack of success.

Tom Voyce, the great Gloucester and England forward, proved invaluable as, whenever needed, he played wing and full-back on the tour. He was at one time a centre, but in the England trials he was put down as a forward, so he set to and played himself into the England team. Along with Tom Voyce, 'Jammie' Clinch and Cove-Smith himself, there was another famous forward on the tour: A.F. Blakiston, the Blackheath and England back-row forward, who later inherited his father's baronetcy.

The team also included the remarkable all-rounder Stanley Harris, who declined an invitation to train for the Olympics in 1920 in order to concentrate on rugby. He was a fine wing, who was actually playing for Pirates in Johannesburg when he was chosen for the 1924 Lions tour. He spent most of his life in South Africa, where he won the amateur light-heavyweight championship, and represented South Africa in the Davis Cup. This *Boy's Own* hero was wounded as a gunnery officer in World War I and, while recuperating, took up dancing and reached the finals of the World Ballroom Dancing Championships. He was taken prisoner by the Japanese in World War II and worked on the Death Railway in Siam. Colonel Stanley Harris CBE also won the All England mixed doubles tennis championship and played water polo for England. What a Lion! I am proud to have met him when I was on the 1955 tour.

In the light of all their problems, it was, perhaps, not surprising that Cove-Smith's team wound up with the worst record of any Lions side. Unthinkably, they won only nine matches out of 21. Only the fourth Wallabies side to the British Isles in 1947–48 suffered such indignity. That 1924 team also scored the lowest number of points ever recorded, with a mere 175.

There were two father and son connections in this Lions side. Herbert Waddell, a 1924 Lion, later to become president of that world-famous and unique rugby club the Barbarians and a member of the International Board, was not only to see his son Gordon play for the Lions in New Zealand and South Africa, but also saw him emigrate to South Africa, where he married Mary Oppenheimer of the family dynasty built on the diamond and gold industry. Gordon Waddell also became a member of the South African Parliament. The other connection was the famous Irish forward 'Jammie' Clinch, whose father, A.D. Clinch, had played with Hammond's team in 1896.

It was in this series that South Africa introduced the 3–4–1 scrum formation, devised by Markotter to protect the scrum-half from the quick-breaking loose forwards. It was also to lead to the far quicker channel-one ball. Although the captain, Albertyn, reverted to the 3–2–3 scrum for the fourth Test, Markotter's system was soon universally adopted and gave South Africa a huge advantage in scrummaging and defensive qualities for over 30 years, before the British finally adopted it in the 1950s.

It was also the year when the fabulous Bennie Osler made his debut for the Springboks. He was to become a true legend, as were Hansi Brewis and Naas Botha in later years, but his influence on this series was less marked than that of the captain, Pierre Albertyn, who began his career as a wing, but became a devastating centre three-quarter with a lethal, blindingly fast sidestep.

It was Osler's drop goal which settled the issue of the first Test at Durban. All the South African scoring came in the first half when they were playing with both the wind and the sun: first came the drop goal, followed by a try from P. Aucamp. In the second half, Whitley scored a fine try for the Lions. Although the Lions were now definitely on top, the splendid Springboks defence held and they failed to score again, therefore losing that psychologically crucial first Test.

As the first Test was so tight, there was huge interest for the second game in Johannesburg, and the gates were locked after the ground's full capacity, 15,000 spectators, had paid to go in. Those locked out, however, broke the locks and swarmed in and it was estimated that over 25,000 saw the game in the end. Again it was an exciting affair in the first half, when the only score was an Osler penalty. In the second half, the Springboks struck form and they scored what was at the time their most convincing win ever in international rugby, when they piled on tries by Starke, Mostert, van Druyten and Albertyn, with Bosman converting the second.

In the third Test, the Lions recovered some of their self-esteem by forcing a draw, but they should have done much better, for once again Drysdale missed an easy conversion of their only try scored by Cunningham at half-back, who had blazed his way over from a five-yard scrum. Drysdale also missed a sitter of a penalty. South Africa scored when van Druyten steamrollered his way over from a lineout on the half-time whistle. Although the Springboks were on the defensive for most of the second half, there was no more scoring and the Lions were in the now familiar territory of losing another series to the Springboks.

However, the final Test at Newlands in Cape Town was an absolute cracker of a game, and many South African critics of the time thought it the perfect game of rugby football. Again South Africa won, but the

Lions matched them all the way with some marvellously inventive and flowing football. Bester scored the first Springboks try and Starke kicked a huge 50-yard drop goal but, a minute later, Tom Voyce actually kicked a penalty to put the Lions back in the game, and South Africa led by 7–3 at the interval. In a sensational second half, tries were scored by Starke for the Springboks and by Harris for the Lions, making it 10–6. Starke, producing an inspired performance, then scored another try for the Springboks, before Voyce charged through for a try to make it 13–9 and, with the game in the balance right up to the death, the Springboks clinched victory with a marvellous unconverted try by Slater on the final whistle. They said at the time that no better Test had ever been played in South Africa.

Cove-Smith's tour may have been a statistical disaster, but it was nevertheless a terrific Test series, which increased the appetite and enthusiasm of South Africans for the game. The goal-kicking lesson should have been learnt by the British selectors, but it never was, and time and again they failed to ensure that there were enough good goal kickers in the party.

The last word on the tour must come from Dr Cove-Smith himself, who wrote in Difford's *History of South African Rugby*:

> Looking back, one cannot help but laugh at the subterfuges to which we were forced to resort in order to place 15 fit men on the field, and I have marvelled many times in retrospect that the fellows were able to put up such a good show in spite of all the handicaps. A tour such as this, where everything is new and fresh, lives long in the memory. The veritable kaleidoscope of ever-changing impressions would be liable to produce mental indigestion, even as the high standard of South African hospitality strains the most robust of gastric organs, were it not for the fact that some of the incidents stand out strongly to dwarf the others.
>
> Perhaps the most noticeable of these was the quietly efficient captaincy of P.K. Albertyn in the Test matches. He always seemed to have his players well in hand and be able to produce the requisite thrust at the right moment.

Writing in 1932, he said about Benny Osler:

> In those days (1924), Benny Osler was just making a name for himself, but even then kicked more than was warranted. I was astounded to see to what extent these kicking propensities had stultified South African three-quarter play, for in 1931 in England we rarely saw a Springboks back-line in action.

Then, as now, the main glory of the team lay in the pack, led by Kruger and ably backed up by Mellish and van Druyten – this last an ubiquitous fellow, who frequently functioned as an auxiliary back, so quick was he in falling back and covering up. His anticipatory play marked him head and shoulders above the others as far as brain power went, while his pace and powerful kicking were rarely at fault.

Against these formidable forwards, we had such stalwarts as Marsden-Jones, J. Clinch, T. Voyce, A.F. Blakiston, Neil Macpherson, J. McVicker and D.S. Davies, but outside the scrum and in the centre we had no one who could deal with the wily Albertyn.

Rowe Harding, who was one of the few British successes behind the scrum and who later became a judge, was to comment in his book published in 1929 and called *Rugby Reminiscences and Opinions* about this ill-fated tour:

Many unkind things were said about our wining and dining, but that was not the explanation of our failures. The long train journeys (often of 48 hours duration), the hard grounds, and a heavy casualty list had taken a heavy toll of players unaccustomed to such conditions. When we played the country districts of the Orange Free State, we had to play eight backs because, of 16 forwards, only seven were fit to play.

Drysdale played wonderfully well at full-back, and Cove-Smith, Macpherson, D.S. Davies, Howie and Blakiston were our best forwards. The British pack was a very fine one and was hardly ever 'worsted', but behind the scrums we seldom rose above mediocrity.

It is not difficult to analyse the reasons for our failure. Dissipation had nothing to do with it. I will not deny there was occasionally what was termed a 'blind'. We were thoughtless and careless of what other people said or thought of us and that contributed to our unpopularity.

The real reason for our failure was that we were not good enough to go abroad as the representatives of the playing strength of these islands. It is not sufficient to send abroad some players of international standard and others who are only second class. Every member of the team must be absolutely first class, or disaster is bound to overtake it.

Later in this book, Rowe Harding made reference to the fact that the governing bodies should take such tours far more seriously and rid themselves of the theory that rugby was only a game when it was played at the representative level. Poor performances damage the respect you receive from the country you are visiting; therefore, only fully representative teams should be sent abroad. Tours have obligations as well as privileges, entailed when visiting a foreign country. Tellingly, Harding relates, 'There has always been too much condescension by the British Rugby authorities about our attitudes, both to our continental neighbours and to the colonies', and even as long ago as 1929 Rowe Harding was questioning the unyielding amateur ethics of the Four Home Unions.

While rugby in South Africa and New Zealand was now embarking on a euphoric period up to World War II, rugby in the British Isles was poorly directed and got nowhere in global terms.

## Results of the 1924 Lions in South Africa

P 21   W 9   D 3   L 9   F 175   A 155

| | | | |
|---|---|---|---|
| Western Province (Town & Country) | L | 6 | 7 |
| Western Province (Universities) | W | 9 | 8 |
| Griqualand West | W | 26 | 0 |
| Rhodesia | W | 16 | 3 |
| Western Transvaal | W | 8 | 7 |
| Transvaal | D | 12 | 12 |
| Orange Free State (Country) | L | 0 | 6 |
| Orange Free State | L | 3 | 6 |
| Natal | D | 3 | 3 |
| South Africa (Durban) | L | 3 | 7 |
| Witwatersrand | L | 6 | 10 |
| South Africa (Johannesburg) | L | 0 | 17 |
| Pretoria | L | 0 | 6 |
| Cape Colony | W | 13 | 3 |
| North Eastern Districts | W | 20 | 12 |
| Border | W | 12 | 3 |
| Eastern Province | L | 6 | 14 |
| South Africa (Port Elizabeth) | D | 3 | 3 |
| South Western Districts | W | 12 | 6 |
| South Africa (Cape Town) | L | 9 | 16 |
| Western Province | W | 8 | 6 |

## Dr Ronald Cove-Smith's 1924 Lions team

**Full-backs**

| | | |
|---|---|---|
| D. Drysdale | Heriot's FP | Scotland |
| W.S. Gainsford | Bart's Hospital | |
| T.E. Holliday | Aspatria | England |

**Three-quarters**

| | | |
|---|---|---|
| J.H. Bordass | Cambridge University | |
| W. Rowe Harding | Swansea | Wales |
| S.W. Harris | Blackheath | England |
| R.M. Kinnear | Heriot's FP | |
| R.B. Maxwell | Birkenhead Park | |
| I.S. Smith | Oxford University | Scotland |
| W. Wallace | Percy Park | |

**Half-backs**

| | | |
|---|---|---|
| W. Cunningham* | Lansdowne | Ireland |
| H.J. Davies* | Newport | Wales |
| V.M. Griffiths | Newport | Wales |
| H. Waddell | Glasgow Academicals | Scotland |
| H. Whitley | Northern | |
| A.T. Young | Cambridge University | England |

**Forwards**

| | | |
|---|---|---|
| A.F. Blakiston | Blackheath | England |
| M.J. Bradley | Dolphin | Ireland |
| T.N. Brand | North of Ireland | |
| J.D. Clinch | Dublin University | Ireland |
| R. Cove-Smith (capt.) | OMTs | England |
| D.S. Davies | Hawick | Scotland |
| R.G. Henderson | Durham University | Scotland |
| K.G.P. Hendrie | Edinburgh University | Scotland |
| R.A. Howie | Edinburgh University | Scotland |
| N. Macpherson | Newport | Scotland |
| J. McVicker | Belfast College | Ireland |
| D. Marsden-Jones | London Welsh | Wales |
| W.J. Roche | Newport | Ireland |
| A. Ross | Kilmarnock | Scotland |
| A.T. Voyce | Gloucester | England |

Manager: H. Packer    * Replacements

## F.D. Prentice's 1930 Lions

The 1930 tour of New Zealand came almost exactly midway between the two great European wars. Times were fitfully peaceful, with Germany not yet aware of resurgent nationalism and the imminent appearance of Adolf Hitler. King George V was on the English throne. It was a time of growing economic depression and uncertainty for the working man but, as ever, the British upper and middle classes were reasonably cushioned from its effects.

In that year, Donald Bradman scored a record 452 not out, and the planet Pluto was discovered. D.H. Lawrence died, white women were given the vote in South Africa, and Haile Selassi was crowned Emperor of Ethiopia. There was uproar in the Reichstag, Berlin, when Nazi deputies arrived in uniforms which were banned. Winston Churchill resigned over a policy of conciliation with Indian nationalism and Mahatma Gandhi was released from prison. Two million people died from famine in China. The BBC formed its own orchestra, and George Gershwin composed *I Got Rhythm*. Marlene Dietrich starred in the film *The Blue Angel*. The Rev. Dr William Spooner (of spoonerism fame) died, and Wallace Carrothers discovered a new synthetic material called nylon.

It must be remembered that, at the time, rugby union was almost entirely in the hands of the middle class in England, Scotland and Ireland. It was not the same in Wales and therefore, at this time, more working-class Welshmen like Dai Parker of Swansea were included in the team. Dai was a character who possessed a marvellous native wit and a physique which overcame and eliminated any pretensions by the varsity and posher elements to be superior; elements which were present in all Lions teams before the war. These men from different social backgrounds had begun to emerge; they had used life as their university and they were no less skilled in the arts of rugby or in debates on important issues than their well-educated counterparts. They may have had something to learn about social graces, as many of them, before touring, had lived extremely confined lives. Some of them had barely moved out of the valleys or the towns they lived in. As ever, they were quick to learn. These were the men that the Rev. Carey was talking about when he made his statement concerning 'gentlemen of all classes'.

Some indication of the middle-class nature of the Lions was the fact that at that time it was necessary, indeed, *de rigueur* to have a dinner jacket, together with a required sum of £80 spending money, before they could embark on such a tour. The dinner jacket was largely for the five- to six-week return boat journey when, every night, they were required to dress for dinner on board. Consequently, the poorer members of the party, especially the Welshmen, were sponsored by their clubs, who gladly passed the hat round to ensure that their players would not be disadvantaged for what became recognised as a trip of a lifetime, and one which brought great honour to the club which they represented.

I am fortunate and privileged to know Harry Bowcott who, I believe, is the only survivor of the 1930 tour, and who, at 89 years of age, has a remarkable memory for all the events of that time. Talking to him added enormously to the authenticity of events concerning that tour, because he was able to give the earliest eye-witness account of the events on a Lions tour.

Harry Bowcott is a lovely man who, as a Welsh player, captain of Wales and Wales selector and administrator, has always carried himself with enormous dignity and decency, which ensured the respect of everyone who met him.

He admitted that the earlier Lions tours were élitist because of the very nature of overseas travel and the meeting of different people and cultures. He told me what an extraordinary adventure it was for young men who otherwise could never afford such luxurious travel, and explained the astonishing experience of seeing far-flung corners of the world, all achieved through rugby union football because of the accident of being talented in the sport.

According to Harry, the dominating side of the late 1920s was Scotland, yet they had only one player in the side. He added that the young men of the time had forgotten the war and were optimistic about the future, despite growing unemployment and the fact that jobs were hard to find. The idea of such a tour was hugely exciting for the young men of the period, as, indeed, it still is today.

They travelled by passenger boat via the Panama Canal and it was a delightful five weeks, with the outward journey providing tremendous fun for the 29 young players and their manager. There was nobody else: no coach, no doctor, no physiotherapist and, said Harry with a smile, 'Thank goodness, no pressmen, which was a wonderful thing, for we could do as we liked without looking over our shoulders. When we got to New Zealand, we picked up a masseur, whose only qualification was experience.

'We were no better and no worse than the young men of today in our behaviour. We drank a bit and enjoyed female company, but we tended to carouse only after matches. Standards of behaviour were left to the individual. I will not say that the manager, Jim Baxter, could not care less, for he was a typical RFU man. It so happened they were all nice people.

'The teams were selected by the senior people in the side, including one from each country, and I was the Welsh representative. Scotland, for a number of reasons, had only one man on the tour, Bill Welsh from Hawick, and even after seven months we could not understand what he was saying! So Scotland were not represented in selection. There were seven players from Wales, five from Ireland and 16 from England.'

According to Harry, they were delightful times; the players had never heard of a coach apart from those they rode in and, in the way of the times, the idea would have been frowned upon by the governing bodies. Any coaching of the Lions, as it was for the next four decades, was left to the captain, F.D. Prentice, who later became the secretary of the Rugby Football Union. At 30, Prentice was, according to Harry, beyond his sell-by date and this was reflected in the fact that he played only in the second of the four Tests against New Zealand and in the single Australia Test.

The Lions' standards and style of play were largely based on the football of the two universities, Oxford and Cambridge, which in those days were immensely powerful. Their adage was 'Let the ball do the work'. Previously, rugby had been more élitist, and Harry explained that more ordinary working-class people went on the 1930 tour.

The manager looked after the £80 belonging to each player and, when a pound or two was required (which had in those days considerable purchasing power), the players went to him as their banker. It must also have had the effect of keeping breakages down to the bare minimum.

The players also received a tour allowance of three shillings a day subsistence but, in the nonsensical ambivalence concerning amateurism at the time, it was received not in money, but in chits from the manager for, let us say, one shilling or sixpence to be spent in the hotel. Money in hard cash form could not be allowed to tarnish the amateur game!

This, however, was virtually only pocket-money, for everything was paid for and, in the manner of nearly all Lions tours that one has been on, it was hard to spend a penny in the face of the overwhelming hospitality of New Zealand or South African rugby people.

New Zealand in the 1930s was not a sophisticated place, particularly outside the main centres such as Auckland, Wellington, Christchurch and Dunedin, and many of the players and the spectators arrived on horseback for the matches. The Lions travelled largely by train and they would stop and, in the leisurely manner of the time, take lunch on the platform as the train waited. The shorter distances were undertaken by coach.

It was a tour marred by off-the-field controversy, almost as fierce as the Australian complaints concerning the body-line bowling of Harold

Larwood. The tour manager, James Baxter, went to war with the New Zealand authorities over their seven-man scrum formation of 2–3–2 and a 'Rover' who put the ball into the scrum.

A British team had not toured New Zealand for 22 years, so inevitably this 1930 tour created huge excitement among rugby supporters throughout New Zealand. However, once again too many leading players were left at home, including none other than Wavell Wakefield, who was expected to be the tour captain. Also left behind were those fine Scottish three-quarters, Ian Smith and Phil Macpherson, and the Irish trio Mark Sugden, Ernie Crawford and captain Harry Stephenson, all unable to spare the time.

The game in the colony had changed considerably from the accepted practices in the UK where, at the time, the laws of the game were made. The Brits were astonished, for instance, when, in the first game of the tour against Wanganui, their opponents trooped off at half-time for a cup of tea and a ten-minute breather.

This, of course, was like a red rag to a bull for that typical establishment man from headquarters at Twickers, the formidable James Baxter. He berated the New Zealand administrators throughout the tour for their flagrant beaches of the laws as laid out by the International Rugby Board. Harry Bowcott told me, 'He slaughtered them in one of his speeches after dinner and one sensed that they became afraid of him.'

He pointed out that they were in violation of the laws of the game, which stated that no player may leave the field of play unless granted in special circumstances. Furthermore, they were allowing the mark when both feet were off the ground. They were also allowing players to appear in advertisements, which gave the British authorities apoplexy – as it continued to do until very recently.

Baxter, being a member of the Rugby Football Union committee and a prominent member of the International Board, pointed out that New Zealand were in defiance of the Tour Agreement, which clearly stated that they were to play to the IRB laws.

He was incensed by the seven-man scrum and the 'Rover', who was the New Zealand captain, C.G. Porter. The latter put the ball into the scrum and then stayed on his feet to harass the opponents if they won the ball, or to support his own backs, while the scrum-half was at the base of the scrum to collect the incredibly quick heel, which was produced by the formation of a front row of two hookers, a second row of a lock binding them together with a flanker on either side and two back-row forwards. Baxter called Porter a cheat, but was powerless to do anything about his harassment of the brilliant England fly-half, Roger Spong.

The ball would squirt out of their 2–3–2 scrum like a pip out of a lemon as the two hookers swung the outside foot and hurtled the ball back through the lock's legs, and so it was essential that the 'Rover' put it in and the scrum-half received it. Such a heel had the huge merit of giving the New Zealand backs so much room that it was to develop those world-class inside backs of the time, Mark Taylor and Bert Cooke.

New Zealand pointed out that the laws never stipulated how many players constituted a set scrum and they did not see why they should discard a method of scrummaging which was not only legal, but which was the one they had adopted ever since the game began organising itself into formations in the 1880s.

The problem was exacerbated as New Zealand had their own rule of not allowing any player to advance beyond the middle of the scrum until the ball was out. As there was no such International Board law, this meant that Porter was able to get at the British halves ridiculously early, to the fury of Baxter who, on his return to England, quickly had the scrummaging laws changed, so that New Zealand had no option but to put three men into the front row.

This meant that, in future, the ball would come back much more slowly to the half-backs, who were also to become easy prey to fast breakaway flankers and so, pragmatically, they changed their style to attritional forward play, supported by kicking half-backs and a strong full-back who, preferably, was their goal kicker. We all know how successful they have been in developing their all-embracing forward game which has become synonymous with winning rugby but which, in the aesthetic sense, set rugby back 50 years. English supporters of their winning team of the last five years will know what I mean.

In the meantime, as the battle raged during after-dinner speeches and in the press, the players continued to enjoy themselves on tour and made themselves very popular with the crowds. They won their first four matches before falling to those two formidable New Zealand provincial teams, Wellington and Canterbury, by the narrow margins of four and six points respectively. Two more wins against West Coast–Buller and Otago finished their preparation for the first Test at Dunedin where, marvellously, they became the first British team to have beaten New Zealand. It was also to be the last until the 1959 Lions achieved what was, and still is, considered a pretty impressive feat.

In that first Test, the All Blacks played in white because of the lack of contrast between black jerseys and the blue of the Lions, which was eventually to influence a change from the blue to the red jersey, with its colourful motif of the Four Home Unions on the left breast.

The All Blacks were soon three points down, when Roger Spong kicked diagonally into the arms of Reeve, who beat Hart and scored in the corner. The score stood at half-time, when the All Blacks were denied their cup of tea in the dressing-room by the wrath of James Baxter, and merely withdrew to the touchline. New Zealand, however, quickly scored after the restart, when Hart went over in the corner from a sweeping three-quarter movement, and George Nepia hit the upright with the conversion. With only seconds to go, Ivor Jones, the great Welsh wing forward, picked up a loose ball in his own 25, broke the defence and brilliantly drew the great Nepia, who had a reputation of mesmerising attackers; Jones committed Nepia to the tackle and gave to Morley, who scored the winning try right on the final whistle. The British had won but, as many a side has found to its cost, the All Blacks regrouped and made sure it would not happen again in that series.

New Zealand made four changes for the second Test and the Lions two, with the captain, Doug Prentice, coming in for Hodgson and Tony Novis replacing the injured Reeve. There was a crowd of 30,000 at Lancaster Park, Christchurch, for a match played on a soft ground in clearing weather. It was typical of all those hard matches which are the hallmark of the province of Canterbury: solid without any brilliance.

Mark Nicholls opened the scoring for the All Blacks with a goal from a mark, but Carl Aarvold struck back with a try after Jack Morley beat Oliver, and Prentice converted to take the lead. Lucas and Porter then made a try for Hart which Nicholls converted for New Zealand to regain the lead, which they kept until half-time. Unfortunately, the Lions lost their scrum-half, Paul Murray, after 30 minutes with a dislocated shoulder, and for the rest of the game Ivor Jones showed his remarkable versatility by taking over at scrum-half.

In the second half Nicholls, the man of the match, made a break and passed to Oliver, who scored in the corner, and Nicholls converted most handsomely from the touchline. The Lions had the last word with a try made by a tremendous break by Ivor Jones; Aarvold was up, changed direction and scored a magnificent try with a 40-yard run. This try, rated as one of the finest seen on this historic ground, was converted by Prentice, but New Zealand grimly held on to their 13–10 lead to win the match. The British believed that, had they not lost a man, they would have won.

New Zealand again changed their back division for the third Test, and the Lions brought the uncapped Howard Poole in at scrum-half for the injured Murray. Hodgson replaced Prentice and Reeve was restored to the wing.

As the series was so close, a record New Zealand crowd packed into Eden Park, Auckland, as the Lions won the toss and opted for the sun at their backs in the first half. They opened the scoring with a try after 13 minutes, when Harry Bowcott made a brilliant break to score under the posts, for the ubiquitous Ivor Jones to convert. New Zealand responded with a well-executed try by Lucas, who gathered a clever kick by Nicholls and went in under the posts, for Strang to convert and level the scores at 5–5 at half-time.

Although the Lions forwards were on top in the tight, they were being outplayed in the loose, where Batty and the newcomer, Hugh McLean, were outstanding. A Nicholls interception made the next try for McLean and the All Blacks went further ahead with a drop goal by Nicholls. McLean scored a second try from a forward drive and New Zealand, at 15–5, seemed to have matters in hand as the rain began falling. The Lions, however, continued to move the ball and Aarvold, showing a fine turn of speed, scored under the posts and Black converted. In spite of this, the All Blacks kept a firm grip on the remaining few minutes, but at least the Lions had the satisfaction of seeing their splendid fly-half, Roger Spong, adjudged the best back on the field, with his speed and elusive swerving which seemed to take him through impossible openings.

Two weeks later, the final Test pulled another record crowd to Athletic Park, Wellington, where New Zealand made only one change, Lilburne replacing the unavailable Nicholls. They scored a decisive victory, running in six tries through Porter (2), Strang, Cooke (2) and Batty, to only one by the Lions, scored by Novis and converted by Black. Dai Parker also kicked a penalty. Batty converted two tries for New Zealand, to make it a comfortable win by 22–8, although with only half an hour to play, there was only one point in it. The Lions had made two changes, Welsh for Hodgson and Novis for Morley.

The New Zealanders had finished their great era of the 1920s in some style, but they were still disgruntled by the actions of Jim Baxter who, they said, had great influence in the halls of power, and who, whilst in New Zealand, plotted to outlaw their roving wing forward and their scrum formation. This soon came about with changes to the scrummage offside and hooking laws in 1932, which, at the time, was seen as being a disadvantage for New Zealand.

# Results of the 1930 Lions in New Zealand and Australia

P 28   W 20   L 8   D 0   F 624   A 318

| | | | |
|---|---|---|---|
| Wanganui | W | 19 | 3 |
| Taranaki | W | 23 | 7 |
| Manawhenua | W | 34 | 8 |
| Wairarapa–Bush | W | 19 | 6 |
| Wellington | L | 8 | 12 |
| Canterbury | L | 8 | 14 |
| West Coast–Buller | W | 34 | 11 |
| Otago | W | 33 | 9 |
| New Zealand (Dunedin) | W | 6 | 3 |
| Southland | W | 9 | 3 |
| Ashburton, South Canterbury & North Otago | W | 16 | 9 |
| New Zealand (Christchurch) | L | 10 | 13 |
| Maoris | W | 19 | 13 |
| Hawke's Bay | W | 14 | 3 |
| East Coast, Poverty Bay & Bay of Plenty | W | 25 | 11 |
| Auckland | L | 6 | 19 |
| New Zealand (Auckland) | L | 10 | 15 |
| North Auckland | W | 38 | 5 |
| Waikato, Thames Valley & King County | W | 40 | 16 |
| New Zealand (Wellington) | L | 8 | 22 |
| Marlborough, Nelson & Golden Bay | W | 41 | 3 |
| | | | |
| New South Wales | W | 29 | 10 |
| Australia (Sydney) | L | 5 | 6 |
| Queensland | W | 26 | 16 |
| Australian XV | W | 29 | 14 |
| New South Wales | L | 3 | 28 |
| Victoria | W | 41 | 36 |
| Western Australia (unofficial) | W | 71 | 3 |

## F.D. Prentice's 1930 Lions team

**Full-backs**

| | | |
|---|---|---|
| J.A. Bassett | Penarth | Wales |
| G. Bonner | Bradford | |

**Three-quarters**

| | | |
|---|---|---|
| C.D. Aarvold | Cambridge University | England |
| H.M. Bowcott | Cambridge University | Wales |
| R. Jennings | Redruth | |
| T. Jones-Davies | London Welsh | Wales |
| J.C. Morley | Newport | Wales |
| P.F. Murray | Wanderers | Ireland |
| A.L. Novis | Blackheath | England |
| J.S.R. Reeve | Harlequins | England |

**Half-backs**

| | | |
|---|---|---|
| T.C. Knowles | Birkenhead Park | |
| H. Poole | Cardiff | |
| W. Sobey | Old Millhillians | England |
| R.S. Spong | Old Millhillians | England |

**Forwards**

| | | |
|---|---|---|
| G.R. Beamish | Leicester | Ireland |
| B.H. Black | Oxford University | England |
| M.J. Dunne | Lansdowne | Ireland |
| J.L. Farrell | Bective Rangers | Ireland |
| J.McD. Hodgson | Northern | |
| H.C.S. Jones | Manchester | |
| I.E. Jones | Llanelli | Wales |
| D.A. Kendrew | Leicester | England |
| S.A. Martindale | Kendal | England |
| H.O'H. O'Neill | Queen's University Belfast | Ireland |
| D. Parker | Swansea | Wales |
| F.D. Prentice (capt.) | Leicester | England |
| H. Rew | Blackheath | England |
| W.B. Welsh | Hawick | Scotland |
| H. Wilkinson | Halifax | England |

Manager: James Baxter

This side was the first team to tour New Zealand and Australia and the British and Irish Lions were the first to carry a supply of gold-plated Lions brooches to give to friends and children.

It was a team popular with the opposite sex, because there were a number of very good-looking men in the party, such as Carl Aarvold. They were a typical Lions team in New Zealand, very creative and fast in the backs, but not strong enough in the front five of the forwards to carry the tour.

## SAMMY WALKER'S 1938 LIONS

As the war clouds began to billow again over a divided Europe, the Four Home Unions squeezed in one more tour to South Africa in 1938. It was the year when Neville Chamberlain promised 'Peace in our Time' as Hitler was welcomed into Austria, and Sigmund Freud fled the Gestapo and came to London. General Franco's troops pushed the Spanish Government forces back to Catalonia, the Moscow show trials ended in the execution of 18 commissars, and the Japanese bombed Canton. In America, Disney released the first full-length feature cartoon, *Snow White and the Seven Dwarfs*. The Anglo-Italian agreement was signed, and the Marquis of Bute sold half the city of Cardiff for £20 million in the biggest property deal in British history. Football pools were condemned as a menace, and Joe Louis KO'd Max Schmelling in a one-round revenge defeat.

Like Joe Louis, South Africa were now the champions of the world, having beaten New Zealand and Australia the previous year. The 1938 Lions had the usual problem with availability of players and, once again, leading players and personalities such as the mercurial Cliff Jones, Willie Davies, Charles Dick and Wilson Shaw, together with the powerful Welsh centre, Wilf Wooller, and fine forwards like George Horseburgh and Fred Huskisson, were all left at home.

The team was led by the Irish international prop forward, Sammy Walker, who had played for Ulster against Benny Osler's Springboks. Five of the team, all forwards, were not internationals, and there were nine Englishmen, eight Irishmen, eight Welshmen and four Scots in the party. There were some considerable personalities in the side who became famous characters in the game, such as Haydn Tanner, who was my first captain when I played for Wales in 1949. I would have no hesitation in putting him forward as one of the very finest scrum-halves of all time. There was Vivian Jenkins, who was to become a notable writer on the game, and Jeff Reynolds, a delightful man and an elegant fly-half who became a hotelier in Cape Town, and whose home I often visited on my many visits to the Cape.

There were Harry McKibbin and Bill Clement, both of whom were destined to be respected administrators of the game in their respective countries, Harry becoming a member of the International Board while Bill became secretary of the Welsh Rugby Union. McKibbin's co-centre, Duncan Macrae, was another classy centre. Because of the usual casualty list sustained on tours of South Africa, the reserve scrum-halves were important, and here Jimmy Giles of England and George Cromey of Ireland were to do well when both played a Test match. Haydn Tanner was out of action for much of the time. The question of taking three scrum-halves was found to be flawed in 1955: because of the durability of Dickie Jeeps and Johnny Williams of England, Trevor Lloyd spent most of the tour kicking his heels. Therefore, once quick replacement by air was possible, they began to take only two.

In the forwards there was the great Irishman Blair Mayne, who was to win the DSO and two bars in the forthcoming war, and another fine Welsh character and hooker, Bunny Travers, who set the example of being one of the world's great hookers for Bryn Meredith to follow on the next Lions tour to South Africa. Laurie Duff of Scotland, Bob Alexander of Ireland and J.A. Waters of Scotland were others who distinguished themselves. The manager was Major B.C. ('Jock') Hartley and the assistant manager was H.A. Haig-Smith of Barbarian fame.

There is always an argument about which was the best Springboks team to represent South Africa. The choice between Benny Osler's 1931 team to Britain, which won all four Tests against the home nations; the 1937 team which won four out of five Tests in Australasia; the 1951 team to Europe, which won all five Tests; or Avril Malan's team, which lost only against the Barbarians at Cardiff. It is, in my view, almost impossible to arrive at a just verdict, because there are too many factors to allow a valid comparison. Suffice to say, these were all teams of the highest quality, whose credentials were impeccable.

Therefore, the 1938 Lions were taking on a Springboks side of immense quality which, in 1937, had been said by the New Zealanders to be the best team ever to leave New Zealand. Those Springboks, on their triumphant tour of Australasia the previous year, had failed by only two matches to become invincible. They lost one match in each country, losing to New South Wales by 17–6, and to New Zealand in the first Test by 13–7. They returned to South Africa as champions of the world, a title they were to hold until 1955, when the Lions drew the series two-all.

Walker's men were taking on not only some of the best South African players of all time, but also some of the best rugby brains they had ever produced. These included the now legendary Danie Craven, who was to captain the team, and Boy Louw, the most-capped Springbok of his time and one of the greatest of all South African forwards, as well as being a huge personality in every sense. He was famous for his malapropisms. Craven tells of Boy looking at a sloppy lineout and saying, 'Why you stand so crooked? Can't you stand in a straight stripe?'

Craven had made a huge name for himself in New Zealand, where he had illustrated his favourite dive pass and had been found to be a most articulate man. This was often the exception and not the rule in Springboks teams, as in those days they were largely men of the soil. He was made captain for what was to be his last year of Test rugby at the age of 27. His vice-captain, Boy Louw, was also at the end of his magnificent Test career, which stretched from 1928.

It was the swansong for Gerry Brand too, who was the Springboks' legendary equivalent of the great Maori full-back George Nepia. Gerry Brand came hotfoot from scoring a record 209 points in Australasia, and the 14 points scored in the first Test of 1938 against the Lions took him to over 300 points for his country. Sadly, injury kept him out of the last two Tests and, because of the war, like so many of his contemporaries he was never to play for South Africa again.

South African rugby was at its finest since its inception and the Lions played only three Test matches, a departure from that strange formula for many Lions tours of playing four Test matches, designed to mirror the number of games that major touring teams played against the teams of the Four Home Unions. Playing an odd number of tests usually guarantees a series winner, therefore a three- or five-match series would have made far more sense. After their success in New Zealand, the South Africans did not play any trial matches and relied on the large nucleus of the 1937 tour and, although Phillip Nel had retired by ceremoniously throwing his boots overboard on the way home from New Zealand and Louis Brabrow had departed to continue his medical studies at Guy's Hospital, all the rest were available and 14 of them were included for the first Test at Ellis Park, Johannesburg.

It was, like so many other such occasions, an epic. The 26-year-old Sammy Walker led his young team out at Ellis Park, which was bulging with some 36,000 spectators, a record crowd for South Africa in those days. The Lions had won 11 and lost three of their previous games, losing twice to Western Province and once to Transvaal. The week before the first Test, they had beaten Transvaal at their second meeting, so there were high hopes in both camps.

The match lived up to expectations, producing fast and thrilling rugby which delighted the crowd, who afterwards agreed that it was one of the best Test matches South Africa had ever played. They had, after all, won by 26–12.

The game was also memorable for some prodigious goal kicking from Brand and Jenkins. The Lions took the lead three times in the first half, but trailed 13–9 at half-time, and in the end the Springboks were emphatic winners by scoring four fine tries, two from D.O. Williams, and one each from Fanie Louw and Tony Harris. In contrast, all the Lions' points came from penalties, with Albert Taylor kicking the first and Vivian Jenkins three, one of them a huge kick from eight yards inside his own half. Gerry Brand's 14 points equalled Benny Osler's record and it included a huge drop from a penalty wide out on the touchline in his own half. It was a fitting way for him to end his Test career.

The next Test in Port Elizabeth saw South Africa winning easily by 19–3 in a game that was played in sweltering heat, as the temperature reached 93 degrees. Danie Craven always called this the tropical Test, and once told me that it was a terrible ordeal. His tactics were to hit hard early on, both in the first and second halves, and this the Springboks achieved. The result was never in doubt as Ben du Toit, Flappie Lochner and John Bester scored tries, with Turner adding two conversions and two penalty goals. The only Lions score came from a try at the very end by Laurie Duff, who had got up in support of a fine run by Jeff Reynolds.

The Lions travelled from Port Elizabeth to Cape Town by boat, arriving at the last Test with the usual long list of injuries, which meant that the side had a make-do-and-mend appearance. The Lions were long odds against and were the recipients of polite sympathy, but the bulldog breed lived up to its reputation and produced one of those marvellous surprise moments, when the underdog finally has his day. Perhaps it was the presence of eight devil-may-care Irishmen in the team which wrought the miracle.

Furthermore, South Africa played with a strong wind, because the groundsman had told Craven that the wind would drop in the second half. Therefore, when Craven won the toss with his lucky ten-shilling gold coin, given to him by the Mayor of Johannesburg at the start of the series, he took the advantage to run up what was a considerable lead in those days, of 13–3 at half-time. Tries by Turner, which brought up the 500 points scored by South Africa in their first 50 Test matches, and by Bester and Lotz, with Turner converting the first two, against a first try for the Lions by Elvet Jones, seemed to put South Africa in an unassailable position.

The wind failed to die as predicted, however, and the Lions took full advantage and played with enormous spirit. Their forwards gradually got on top, and a converted try by Dancer followed by a penalty kicked by McKibbin brought them to within two points of the lead. Then Bob Alexander, the Irish forward later killed in the war, added another try and the Lions led by a point. The Springboks regained their lead with a penalty by Turner, but Charlie Grieve then kicked the last four-point drop goal to be scored in South Africa, which might not have been given had not the Springboks sportingly indicated that it was over, and so the Lions were back in a precarious lead. Laurie Duff then hammered his way over for a try and, with the score at 21–16, South Africa were in trouble, especially when the players were told by the referee, Nick Pretorius, that the next scrum would be the last of the match.

The Springboks won the ball and Danie Craven spurted round the blind side and passed to Johnny Bester, who put D.O. Williams – a Welsh South African answering to the name of Dai – over under the posts, for what seemed to be a score to draw the match. The referee, however, ruled that Bester's pass was forward, so the Lions redeemed their pride and scored a famous victory. Captain Sammy Walker was carried shoulder-high off the field. It was a result that few at home believed, including, apparently, a reporter who knew a thing or two about rugby, in a London news agency. On seeing the result after the half-time score, he took it on himself to change the final score to Springboks 21, Lions 16! It was, after all, the first Lions win in South Africa since 1910.

It was the end of all international rugby between the two hemispheres for the duration of the war. Many young players on both sides lost the best years of their lives and some never came back. It took 17 years before another Lions team was to visit what, in the meantime, had become the Republic of South Africa.

World War II saw South African rugby thrown into terrible turmoil, as the pro- and anti-war factions fought bitterly concerning support for the war effort. Clubs like Stellenbosch, Paarl, Gardens, Maitland and Bellville broke away from Western Province, but Griqualand West, who avoided any breakaways, Eastern Province, Natal and Western Province remained loyal to the Crown. Fortunately, although political turmoil was to envelop South Africa until the present day, the wounds of wartime healed and, with the South African Rugby Board acting in the role of peacemakers, rugby adopted the concept of reconciliation and reunification, to become a moderating force in politics. In the same way, rugby has been a unifying force in the politics of Ireland today.

# Results of the 1938 Lions in South Africa

P 24   W 17   L 7   D 0   F 414   A 284

| | | | |
|---|---|---|---|
| Border | W | 11 | 8 |
| Griqualand West | W | 22 | 9 |
| Western Province (Town & Country) | L | 8 | 11 |
| South Western Districts | W | 19 | 10 |
| Western Province | L | 11 | 21 |
| Western Transvaal | W | 26 | 9 |
| Orange Free State | W | 21 | 6 |
| Orange Free State (Country) | W | 18 | 3 |
| Transvaal | L | 9 | 16 |
| Northern Transvaal | W | 20 | 12 |
| Cape Province | W | 10 | 3 |
| Rhodesia | W | 25 | 11 |
| Rhodesia | W | 45 | 11 |
| Transvaal | W | 17 | 9 |
| South Africa (Johannesburg) | L | 12 | 26 |
| Northern Province | L | 8 | 26 |
| Natal | W | 15 | 11 |
| Border | W | 19 | 11 |
| North Eastern Districts | W | 42 | 3 |
| Eastern Province | W | 6 | 5 |
| South Africa (Port Elizabeth) | L | 3 | 19 |
| South Africa (Cape Town) | W | 21 | 16 |
| Combined Universities | W | 19 | 16 |
| Western Province (Country) (unofficial) | L | 7 | 12 |

## Sammy Walker's 1938 Lions team

**Full-backs**

| | | |
|---|---|---|
| C.F. Grieve | Oxford University | Scotland |
| V.G.J. Jenkins | London Welsh | Wales |

**Three-quarters**

| | | |
|---|---|---|
| C.V. Boyle | Dublin University | Ireland |
| W.H. Clement | Llanelli | Wales |
| E.L. Jones | Llanelli | |
| R. Leyland | Waterloo | England |

87

| H.R. McKibbin | Queen's University Belfast | Ireland |
| D.J. Macrae | St Andrews University | Scotland |
| B.E. Nicholson | Harlequins | England |
| E.J. Unwin | Rosslyn Park | England |

**Half-backs**

| G.E. Cromey | Queen's University Belfast | Ireland |
| J.L. Giles | Coventry | England |
| G.J. Morgan | Clontarf | Ireland |
| F.J. Reynolds | Army | England |
| H. Tanner | Swansea | Wales |

**Forwards**

| R. Alexander | North of Ireland | Ireland |
| S.R. Couchman | Old Cranleighans | |
| G.T. Dancer | Bedford | |
| P.L. Duff | Glasgow Academicals | Scotland |
| C.R.A. Graves | Wanderers | Ireland |
| W.G. Howard | Old Birkonians | |
| R.B. Mayne | Queen's University Belfast | Ireland |
| M.E. Morgan | Swansea | Wales |
| A.G. Purchas | Coventry | |
| A.R. Taylor | Cross Keys | Wales |
| W.H. Travers | Newport | Wales |
| S. Walker (capt.) | Instonians | Ireland |
| J.A. Waters | Selkirk | Scotland |
| I. Williams | Cardiff | |

Manager: B.C. Hartley
Assistant Manager: H.A. Haig-Smith

# The Buccaneers

This was the decade which was to reignite the popularity of Lions tours in the southern hemisphere after World War II, and the players made a good job of it. Although the Lions didn't win a Test series in the 1950s, the 1955 team went close and were the first to break the stranglehold of the Springboks on British Isles touring teams which had existed since South Africa lost their last series to the British Isles team of 1891. As even the mighty All Blacks had never won a series in South Africa until 1996, this was some achievement, bettered only by the magnificent 1974 Lions. In the 1950s, British back play became the talk of the southern hemisphere as the Lions, on two tours of New Zealand and one of South Africa, played glorious, open and adventurous rugby to earn the admiration and, indeed, the respect and affection of the rugby supporters in both those rugby-mad countries. You cannot do much better than that.

## KARL MULLEN'S 1950 LIONS

The first post-war tour by the Lions was to New Zealand in 1950, and they were the last team to travel in the more gracious and leisurely manner of passenger boat. They went out via the Panama Canal and home through the Suez Canal, thus circumnavigating the world. My eye-witnesses of that tour are no less than the captain, the quietly spoken Karl Mullen, who had led two Irish Triple Crown teams in 1948 and 1949 and later became a distinguished gynaecologist in Dublin; and the vice-captain, that prince of Welsh centres, Bleddyn Williams.

It was the year when England lost 1–0 to America in the World Cup.

Senator McCarthy launched his anti-communist crusade, and India was declared a republic. North Korea invaded the South and Britain decided to send troops. Labour remained in office and the Liberals lost a record 314 deposits. The French declared their plans for the federated states of Europe. George Orwell died and Richard Dimbleby made the first live television broadcast from overseas, when he spoke from Calais.

The Lions knew that they were going to the friendliest of all the Commonwealth countries and, after the dreadful austerity of the war and post-war years (remember that food rationing remained in force until 1954), they were determined to have a good time. That started on the voyage, when they discarded post-war sobriety and most of them put on a stone in weight, despite all the physical training and jogging around the decks. They were the first British team to visit the 'Land of the Long White Cloud', as the Maoris called it, since Doug Prentice's side in 1930, and the welcome which awaited them in that beautiful country was so overwhelming that it is a wonder they were able to perform at all. It was to become known as the 'Friendly Tour', and the bonds between the two teams who represented their countries during that tour have endured to this day. The great New Zealand centre, Fred Allen, will tell you that never has he made finer friends than with the Lions of 1950.

The manager was Surgeon-Captain L.B. ('Ginger') Osborne, who was well liked by tourists (perhaps a primary requirement for success), and the secretary or assistant manager was E.L. (Ted) Savage. Karl Mullen's cheery spirit and the presence of eight other Irishmen set much of the tone for enjoyment, the Irishmen including one of the finest of all fly-halves, the legendary J.W. (Jack) Kyle. He, along with Ken Jones, was recognised by the *Rugby Almanack of New Zealand* as being one of the five players of the year, together with New Zealanders Tiny White, Pat Crowley and Lester Harvey. George Norton was at full-back and the delightfully relaxed Irish centre, Noel Henderson, was a powerful back-up for the centre pairing of Bleddyn Williams and Jack Matthews, and he won a Test cap on the wing, as did young M.F. Lane. The powerful flanker Bill McKay was one of the bravest of forwards on the tour and was to return to New Zealand for the rest of his life as a doctor. In the front row were the genial Tommy Clifford and Jimmy Nelson. Jim McCarthy, who had made such a contribution to winning those Irish Triple Crowns in 1948 and 1949, found it hard going because he was relatively small; he later became a respected executive in Tony O'Reilly's business empire, which meant he must have been good!

Scotland had five players including Doug Smith, who was injured and did not play until the 18th game of the tour, but who was to make a considerable impact in another role on another occasion in New Zealand. He was, however, to play only two games in New Zealand and three in Australia, including one Test. Ranald Macdonald, a relaxed player and personality who played as a wing or centre, won two caps as a winger and scored 24 points on tour.

Angus Black was the most experienced of the three scrum-halves; he had a lovely service and played in the first two Tests against the All Blacks. In the forwards, Scotland was represented by Graham Budge, a Canadian-born Scot, who became the soul-mate of the Welsh prop, Cliff Davies. The other was Peter Kininmonth who, in 1951, was to drop a goal from the touchline, about 45 yards out, to beat Wales; an Oxford Blue, he was another of so many of these Lions to make a name for himself in business.

There were only three Englishmen, which reflected the fact that they finished bottom of the European Championship in 1950 and 1951. Two were half-backs; one was Ivor Preece, a strong fly-half, who was a powerful kicker of the ball and a good link. I played with him for Coventry the year after the tour, and I always respected his composure on and off the field, and his strength of character. He was, however, up against the greatness of Jackie Kyle and, therefore, was destined, like so many other talented players on Lions tours, to be a bridesmaid rather than the bride. Gordon Rimmer was in a similar position but did well to make the tour, considering he was playing at the heels of an England pack which invariably was beaten, but he played in only one Test. The sole English forward was the immensely likeable and popular Cornishman Vic Roberts who, although he too never made the Test team, played in ten games in New Zealand. Vic was later to be a dedicated Baa-Baa 'alickadoo'.

Wales, as Grand Slam winners in 1949–50, provided the bulk of the touring party with 14 players and there were no fewer than nine of them playing in every Test. On paper it was a great Lions team, particularly from the Welsh point of view, and with Kyle at fly-half, why did they not sweep all before them? The answer probably lies in the different standard of northern and southern hemisphere rugby, and the far higher and tougher level of forward play in the latter. It must also be remembered that the All Blacks had been whitewashed the year before by South Africa, yet they won this series 3–0.

Only Bob Scott of that New Zealand back division had any claim to rugby immortality, although Ron Elvidge was another magnificent player. While the Lions back division bristled with great names – some of the best in the world at the time – they failed to win a Test match.

This suggests that forwards win matches, especially in New Zealand, and that the Lions pack of 1950 simply failed to match them.

Billy Cleaver, or 'Billy the Kick' as he was known in Wales, was chosen as utility man, and at centre there was Bleddyn Williams, who missed the first Test with an injury. Bleddyn was one of the finest centres with whom I ever played. Another was Jeff Butterfield, and these two, together with Mike Gibson and Danie Gerber, were the best centres I ever saw play and I would not want to choose between them. Bleddyn was the trusty henchman for Cardiff and Wales, and Dr Jack Matthews, known as the iron man of Welsh rugby, was a tower of strength alongside him in the centre. A measure of Jack's quality and durability was that he played in all six Test matches on tour.

At scrum-half there was the resilient and brave Rex Willis, a man who was prepared to die for his fly-half, who finally played in the last three Tests, while on the wing was the Olympic sprinter, the superlative Ken Jones. Ken was my accomplice as we contrived a try with a cross kick when Wales managed to beat the All Blacks for the last time, in 1953. Ken was immensely fast, but was also a marvellous footballer in both defence and attack. His record of 44 caps for Wales has only been surpassed by Ieuan Evans of Llanelli, in an era when caps were far easier to come by; nowadays, a player in a World Cup year can win as many as a dozen or more caps. In 16 appearances Ken scored 16 tries, which was a record for a tourist in New Zealand. The only other Welsh wingers in his class were Gerald Davies and Ieuan Evans, and both, much later, also became Lions.

Another fine Welsh back of the 1950s, who was chosen as centre or wing, was the young Malcolm Thomas, who became the top scorer with 96 points in 15 appearances. He was to return nine years later with the Lions of 1959. When George Norton broke his arm in the fifth match of the tour, they sent out the baby of the tour, Lewis Jones, who at 19 was a prodigy, and in 11 games he scored 92 points. He was the first British Lion to go on tour by air from the UK. Lewis was later destined to make a name for himself in rugby league, as a magnificent runner and a prodigious kicker of goals.

Among the Welsh forwards was one of the greatest characters in the game, whose naivety and sense of humour were of enormous value on such a campaign. Cliff Davies was a miner from Kenfig Hill who, on the outward journey on the *Ceramic*, typically struck up a friendship with the High Commissioner for New Zealand, Mr William Jordan; they played cribbage together throughout the voyage, and it was always 'Bill and Cliff'. His inseparable buddy, however, was Graham Budge, who was Cliff's best man when they returned to the UK. Another Welsh prop was John Robins, who played in the first three New Zealand Tests. He was a quiet but purposeful man, who was to become a Lions coach in 1966.

Neath contributed those two fine locks, the incomparable Roy John, the best all-round forward of his day with superb technique in the lineout, and that strong, durable forward, Rees Stephens, who was regarded by French forwards of his time with some awe. Another Welsh lock was Don Hayward, later to be converted by Wales into a prop when confronted by the 1951 Springboks. There was no more powerful a forward or scrummager at that time than this huge man from the Monmouthshire valleys, who had hands as big as hams and was as hard as nails. He was to return to New Zealand in 1952 and then went to play rugby league in England, before returning to Wellington for good. His big pal on tour was the Somerset policeman and Welsh hooker Dai Davies, who was never lost for a word, on or off the pitch. The only man who could handle him and Hayward together was the Welsh Triple Crown captain, John Gwilliam, who used to treat them like naughty boys – which at times they were! But they were the type of players you wanted on your side. Finally, there was the Newport flanker, R.T. Evans, who worked as a CID officer. He was a powerful, intelligent player with fine anticipation, and he played in all the Tests.

The tour started well enough and the Lions piled on 80 points to 15 in their easy first three games in South Island, where they began the tour after an acclimatisation period at Nelson. In the first match against Nelson and Marlborough district, Malcolm Thomas set a Lions record of six penalty goals in New Zealand, a feat since emulated both by the All Black Don Clarke in 1959 and by Gavin Hastings in 1993 in Test matches. Malcolm also scored a try, to give him 21 out of the 24 points.

They then went to pot against Otago, even though they had put out what they considered their strongest team with an all-Welsh three-quarter line, Norton at full-back, and Kyle and Willis at half-back. Otago scored a decisive win, scoring three tries to one by wiping out the Lions forwards, so the first lesson of the tour was learned. Even more disappointingly, they now lost to a lesser team, Southland, at Invercargill, and again the standard of play was low, despite the fact that over half the Test team was playing. Nothing went right for them in this game, as Norton broke his arm.

The 1966 Lions were also to lose to Otago and Southland, but the 1950 Lions never lost another provincial match on the tour. Nevertheless, you could have got long odds against the Lions winning the first Test in Dunedin, as all the critics had written them off as not having a ghost of a chance. However, on the day, the Lions forwards rose to the challenge of the fierce rucking of the All Blacks, which most of them, with the exception of those who had watched or played against the 1945–46 Kiwis' army side in Britain just after the war, had never seen, let alone experienced.

The Lions could have won that first Test but for a late try by Ron Elvidge, the New Zealand second five-eighth, who created havoc against them for Otago, and who captained the All Blacks in the first three Tests. Late in the second half, the Lions led by 9–3. John Robins had kicked a first-half penalty, and Kyle scored a try after a super break which left Bob Scott for dead. Roy Roper beat four men to score a try for the All Blacks, and Ken Jones scored in the corner by using his exceptional pace to chase a kick by Kyle. Scott then closed the gap with a penalty midway through the second half and it was anybody's game. In the last minutes, Scott came into the line and punted high for the posts, and although Roy John and Clifford held the rush by the All Blacks forwards, Elvidge scored a try from the resultant scrum and New Zealand had scraped a 9–9 draw.

As Bleddyn Williams said: 'We were pleased to have held the All Blacks in the first Test, when our forwards showed their claws. What a pity the forwards did not play again with the same tigerish tenacity! It was as if they had burnt themselves out in that one game.'

The Lions went on to win their next three games, including the usual tough game against Canterbury, which gave morale a big lift. They made two changes for the second Test, bringing in Malcolm Thomas on the left wing in place of Macdonald, and Bleddyn Williams, recovered from injury, in place of Ivor Preece, who had played at centre in the first Test. New Zealand also made two changes, bringing in Laurie Haig at first five-eighth, or fly-half, and Peter Henderson, who had recovered from injury, on the left wing.

In the second Test, the All Blacks were 8–0 up at half-time from a try by Pat Crowley, who was the outstanding loose forward of the series. The Lions then lost Bill McKay with a broken nose and concussion, and the gaps developed for Roper to get the second try, which Haig converted. The second half became a dour struggle and there were no further scores. Jackie Kyle had another fine game and so did Ken Jones, whose defensive qualities proved to be invaluable.

Again, as Bleddyn Williams tells us, 'The Otago style rucking in the second Test upset our forwards. In all the Tests, the All Blacks rucked viciously in a manner we had never before experienced. Pat Crowley proved to be a merciless and destructive scrum-half killer. He concentrated on the scrum-half, thus disrupting the supply of the ball at source. He hammered Gus Black with relentless persecution in this second Test, and the Scotsman's usually immaculate service became completely disjointed. Crowley was killer number one and the All Blacks owed more to him than to any other player for victory in the rubber. In one strategic blow, the All Blacks threw a spanner into our attacking machinery. I also resented their midfield obstruction, as the New Zealand centres ran across us with deliberate intentions, but Crowley's spoiling was legitimate. That practice of obstruction in midfield has spread and is now, unhappily, widely used.'

After another important win over Wellington, the Lions approached the third Test totally unabashed and not at all in awe of the All Blacks. They made two changes in the backs, with Noel Henderson coming in for the injured Ken Jones and Gordon Rimmer being given the unenviable task of absorbing the batterings of Pat Crowley. Karl Mullen was unfit, so Dai Davies played, and Bleddyn Williams took over the captaincy. Roy John replaced Peter Kininmonth at number eight, and J.E. Nelson joined Hayward in the second row. The New Zealand team was unchanged.

Like its predecessors, this Test was another close-run thing, and again it was Elvidge who scored the vital try, after being seriously injured in the face and chest following a tackle by Jack Matthews. He came back on the field with a stitched eyebrow and a bruised collarbone, merely as an extra full-back and just to make a nuisance of himself, but, in the event, he came into the line to score a winning try in the second half. Once again it was the All Blacks forwards who won the game, even when they were reduced to six men, as Simpson also went off the field with an injured leg which finished his career. They were still too much for the Lions forwards and went on winning the ball. The Lions had managed to lead at half-time with a Robins penalty, but in the second half Elvidge got his try, and a few minutes later Bob Scott kicked a penalty to win the match.

The Lions had now lost the Test rubber but refused to be depressed, for they knew that so little separated them from the All Blacks. They had lost two Tests by the narrowest of margins and the fourth was also to be lost by only three points. In the meantime, they continued to thrill the New Zealand provinces with their delightful back play and won the next six games before the final Test, including a crushing of Auckland, who had Bob Scott at full-back, by 32–9.

They were still without the injured Mullen for the final Test, so Bleddyn Williams again captained the side. The Lions made sweeping changes and brought in two new props, Graham Budge and Cliff Davies. Roy John reverted to second row with Nelson, and Peter Kininmonth returned as number eight, or lock, as it was known in

Britain in those days. Cleaver gave way to Lewis Jones at full-back, Rex Willis took over at scrum-half and Ken Jones, recovered from injury, was back on the right wing.

New Zealand brought in J.M. Tanner for the injured Elvidge, and in the pack Graham Mexted, father of Murray, came in at number eight, moving Johnstone to the flank and captaining the side.

The Lions lost again, but the game was always remembered in New Zealand for a magnificent try scored by Ken Jones. It came from a scrum on the Lions' line and a quick heel saw Willis feed Kyle, who went to pass to Bleddyn Williams, only for the precocious young Lewis Jones to intercept the pass, leaving Kyle and Williams flabbergasted. Finding Ken Jones in support, he gave him the ball and the winger side-stepped Scott to race three-quarters of the length of the field and score under the post. Lewis Jones converted. It was one of the finest tries ever seen at Eden Park.

New Zealand had scored first, when Crowley kicked the ball away from a Lions heel and Wilson fell on it for a try, which Scott converted. Lewis Jones replied with a penalty, and then Bob Scott produced one of his specials, a glorious drop goal from a long way out and on the touchline, to give the All Blacks a half-time lead of 8–3. Henderson then gathered a diagonal kick by Roper to score and make it 11–3, but next came the Jones try. The Lions had about five minutes to snatch the match and they almost did. Only a tremendous tackle by Henderson on Bleddyn Williams, after Roy John had dummied his way through the All Blacks forwards before passing to Bleddyn, prevented the captain from scoring at the death, and apparently he was inches from the line. It had been one of the best internationals seen in New Zealand.

There was no denying the superiority of the All Blacks forwards throughout the series, and every Lion who has toured what the Australians like to call 'the Shaky Isles', because of all the volcanic tremors, will know about that. They were, as ever, worthy winners, but they had taken great pleasure in the brilliance of the Lions backs and the 1950 Lions remain one of the most popular teams ever to visit New Zealand.

The Lions went on to play six games in Australia, where they found the rugby nothing like as hard as it had been in New Zealand, evidenced by their scoring 150 points in six games. They rattled off five convincing victories, including the two Test matches and the New South Wales state side, before surprisingly losing to a New South Wales XV in their last match. B.H. ('Jaika') Travers OBE, who was a colonel in the Australian army during the war, and then played for Oxford University, Harlequins and England, was the captain of that side, and his astute rugby brain had much to do with the defeat.

After Malcolm Thomas had given a repeat performance of his 21 points in the opening match in New Zealand against Combined Country, with six conversions and a penalty goal, the Lions played New South Wales on the Sydney Cricket Ground. Like many other sides, they were astonished when they played across the Test pitch and churned it into a morass where, six weeks later, Freddie Brown's English team was to play.

Although New South Wales was virtually the Australian Test team, they were dispatched by 22–6 and the Lions left for Brisbane, where the first Test was to be played, in a fairly relaxed mood. Again they won comfortably, with a score of 19–6 before 20,000 spectators in typically humid Queensland conditions. The new prodigy, Lewis Jones, scored 16 of the points with a 50-yard drop goal, a try, two penalties and two conversions, with Bleddyn Williams, still captain in the absence of the injured Mullen, getting another try. Burke kicked two penalties for Australia. The Lions pack had three changes from the last Test in New Zealand and, in the backs, Doug Smith won his first Test cap of the tour.

Playing against them was that great character Nick ('Sudden Death!') Shehadie, who had toured Britain with the 1948 Wallabies and would later tour with the 1958 team. He was to become Sir Nicholas Shehadie OBE, Lord Mayor of Sydney and President of the ARFU. He was the epitome of the interesting personalities one encountered in rugby, especially on Lions tours.

The Lions also won the second Test comfortably by 24–3, and had the unusual experience of being watched by a 25,000 Test crowd while on the adjoining ground there was double the number making more noise watching a rugby league cup-tie. Nelson scored two tries and John, Kyle and Macdonald also scored, with Lewis Jones kicking a penalty and a conversion and Robins converting two. Burke scored Australia's try.

Coming home through the Suez Canal, they played one match *en route* – an unofficial game against Ceylon, now Sri Lanka, which they won 44–6 to end a Lions tour whose success was better measured by its friendship than in stark statistics. They gave untold enjoyment to a generation of Kiwis and Aussies by the manner in which they played the game.

Notably, this was the first Lions team to consist entirely of capped players.

# Results of the 1950 Lions in New Zealand and Australia

P 30   W23   D 1   L6   F 614   A 220

| | | | |
|---|---|---|---|
| Nelson, Marlborough, Golden Bay & Motueka | W | 24 | 3 |
| Buller | W | 24 | 9 |
| West Coast | W | 32 | 3 |
| Otago | L | 9 | 23 |
| Southland | L | 0 | 11 |
| New Zealand (Dunedin) | D | 9 | 9 |
| South Canterbury | W | 27 | 8 |
| Canterbury | W | 16 | 5 |
| Ashburton County– North Otago | W | 29 | 6 |
| New Zealand (Christchurch) | L | 0 | 8 |
| Wairarapa–Bush | W | 27 | 13 |
| Hawke's Bay | W | 20 | 0 |
| East Coast, Poverty Bay & Bay of Plenty | W | 27 | 3 |
| Wellington | W | 12 | 6 |
| New Zealand (Wellington) | L | 3 | 6 |
| Wanganui | W | 31 | 3 |
| Taranaki | W | 25 | 3 |
| Manawatu–Horowhenua | W | 13 | 8 |
| Waikato, Thames Valley & King Country | W | 30 | 0 |
| North Auckland | W | 8 | 6 |
| Auckland | W | 32 | 9 |
| New Zealand (Auckland) | L | 8 | 11 |
| New Zealand Maoris | W | 14 | 9 |
| | | | |
| Combined Country | W | 47 | 3 |
| New South Wales | W | 22 | 6 |
| Australia (Brisbane) | W | 19 | 6 |
| Australia (Sydney) | W | 24 | 3 |
| Metropolitan Union | W | 26 | 17 |
| New South Wales XV | L | 12 | 17 |
| | | | |
| Ceylon (unofficial) | W | 44 | 6 |

## Karl Mullen's 1950 Lions team

**Full-backs**

| | | |
|---|---|---|
| W.B. Cleaver | Cardiff | Wales |
| B.L. Jones* | Llanelli | Wales |
| G.W. Norton | Bective Rangers | Ireland |

**Three-quarters**

| | | |
|---|---|---|
| N.J. Henderson | Queen's University Belfast | Ireland |
| K.J. Jones | Newport | Wales |
| M.F. Lane | University College Cork | Ireland |
| R. Macdonald | Edinburgh University | Scotland |
| J. Matthews | Cardiff | Wales |
| D.W.C. Smith | London Scottish | Scotland |
| M.C. Thomas | Newport | Wales |
| B.L. Williams | Cardiff | Wales |

**Half-backs**

| | | |
|---|---|---|
| A.W. Black | Edinburgh University | Scotland |
| J.W. Kyle | Queen's University Belfast | Ireland |
| I. Preece | Coventry | England |
| G. Rimmer | Waterloo | England |
| W.R. Willis | Cardiff | Wales |

**Forwards**

| | | |
|---|---|---|
| G.M. Budge | Edinburgh Wanderers | Scotland |
| T. Clifford | Munster | Ireland |
| C. Davies | Cardiff | Wales |
| D.M. Davies | Somerset Police | Wales |
| R.T. Evans | Newport | Wales |
| D.J. Hayward | Newbridge | Wales |
| E.R. John | Neath | Wales |
| P.W. Kininmonth | Richmond | Scotland |
| J.S. McCarthy | Dolphin | Ireland |
| J.W. McKay | Queen's University Belfast | Ireland |
| K.D. Mullen (capt.) | Old Belvedere | Ireland |
| J.E. Nelson | Malone | Ireland |
| V.G. Roberts | Penryn | England |
| J.D. Robins | Birkenhead Park | Wales |
| J.R.G. Stephens | Neath | Wales |

Manager: Surgeon-Captain L.B. Osborne     * Replacement

## ROBIN THOMPSON'S 1955 LIONS

I now come to my own Lions tour, which I intend to cover in some depth, in an attempt to give you a more intimate insight into the mechanics and character of such a tour, and my own thoughts on some of the pleasures and problems encountered.

First came the extreme delight I felt at being selected for such an adventure, and then crept in the personal doubts about taking on a country who were the undisputed world champions, and whether I was good enough to measure up to the challenge and make the Test team. I was given huge support by my club and my parents. The Swansea Rugby Club, in their generous Welsh fashion, gave Billy Williams and me a suitcase and £50, a handsome sum of money in those days, which, in fact, contravened the International Rugby Board's laws on amateurism. The Welsh, like the dominions, were always pragmatic in such matters.

I left with the rest of the Welsh Lions by coach for Eastbourne, where we were to meet our fellow adventurers, to be kitted out for our four months' trip of a lifetime and to be instructed on what would be expected of us. I had not a care in the world apart from the prospect of the huge challenge which faced us, for the Springboks had not been beaten in a Test series by any country, either home or away, for 59 years.

When we congregated at Eastbourne, we were unaware of any problems, and our first rude awakening came when we were addressed by a man from the Foreign Office. He told us that we were to be careful how we behaved with non-white people in the recently formed Republic of South Africa, which had embarked on the disgraceful path of apartheid which was to bring them so much grief for over 40 years. We were instructed that on no account should we invite these people into our hotels and warned that any sexual contact with people of a different colour would put us in grave danger of imprisonment. We were surprised, even astonished, but at the time, made light of it. On the whole we were a bunch of politically agnostic young men, who had not thought too deeply about politics either at home or abroad and, being more or less apolitical, we were determined to go ahead and enjoy ourselves.

At that time, immigration from the West Indies into the UK was increasing, the Mau Mau were being offered an amnesty in Kenya and 60,000 blacks were evicted from their homeland west of Johannesburg. We were probably more interested in other things, such as Joe Davies making the first 147 break on television, and Marlon Brando winning an Oscar for *On the Waterfront*. Churchill resigned that year and

Albert Einstein, James Dean, Thomas Mann and Henri Matisse all died. The Warsaw Pact was created and Tito and Krushchev made up. Ruth Ellis was sentenced to be the last woman hanged in Britain, and independent commercial television was launched, with toothpaste as the first advertisement.

Later in our week at Eastbourne, we were told by our big bluff manager, Belfast man Jack Siggins, what was expected of us in terms of behaviour, and we thought that the ground rules he set out were pretty generous. Basically, he said that we were to be well dressed at all times, particularly at official functions, that we were adult and that we should keep our own hours, but that the two nights before a game he expected us to be in the hotel and in bed before midnight. He also told us, more enigmatically, that we should always make sure the water was clean before we dived in. All good advice which, on the whole, we heeded.

It was amusing to recall how we were on our best behaviour with Jack and each other for the first week. Nobody misbehaved, we went to bed reasonably early, no one had much to drink and our fitness level improved considerably. We were kitted out with two pairs of boots each from a well-known manufacturer, but a couple of us had hand-made boots by one of the finest makers of football boots, Law of Wimbledon. They were as light as a feather and, seeing their quality, a number of players immediately made phone calls and arranged details for measuring and having the boots sent out to them. We had all given the outfitters our measurements but, when we tried on our blazers, it was apparent that somebody had paid insufficient attention to detail, so, amid ribald comments about shapes and sizes, the next couple of days saw fitting sessions with the tailors, who were kept working flat out.

The training sessions began, and it was quickly evident that there were as many as half a dozen players who simply were not up to the standards required for such a hard tour, an assessment which was borne out by subsequent events. I have also asked members of many other pre- and post-war tours whether they experienced the same problem. Invariably the answer was an unequivocal 'Yes'. Therefore, there has always been a problem with selection on Lions tours, which is not surprising considering the horse trading that goes on between selectors drawn from four different countries. Wild horses would not drag the names of these inadequates from me, but I remember hearing that mighty Lions forward, Rhys Williams, saying 'Some of these guys could not get into Llanelli seconds'. It meant, of course, that these players had to be used sparingly, thus causing huge problems for team selection during the tour. From the start, that delightful man and great centre Jeff Butterfield assumed the responsibility of fitness coach and he took over the training sessions.

In terms of tactics and strategy, there was soon established a natural pecking order of those who really knew their rugby and those who did not, and a sort of senior unofficial committee evolved, to which, wisely, the management and the captain listened. People like the hard-bitten Scot Angus Cameron, the elegant and brilliant Jeff Butterfield, those 100 per cent forwards Rhys Williams, Jim Greenwood, Bryn Meredith and the irrepressible Welsh wizard Cliff Morgan were among the better rugby minds of the tour and set the agendas to follow.

Another feature of a Lions tour was that you were able to assess a player's ability and, by the end of the tour, you knew every player's strengths, weaknesses and capabilities, both on and off the field, to the nth degree.

It was soon apparent, in that first week spent training at Eastbourne College, that there were some remarkably talented players and people of considerable substance on the tour. There was also an immediate sense of fun, emanating mostly from the Irish and that remarkable man Cliff Morgan, who became a household name. We were highly amused when, at a team meeting, the ubiquitous Trevor Lloyd, the third scrum-half, suddenly said in his high-pitched Welsh accent, 'Hey, Jack!' (which was very brave, for we were still thinking in terms of Mr Siggins). 'What if a player has a girl and somebody tries to muscle in? Now, that could cause a great deal of trouble on a tour. I think that we should have a rule that nobody interferes with another player's girl.' Jack Siggins, for once, seemed lost for words, but the laughter relieved him from making a response. Thus 'Lloyd's Law' was born, which was invoked, more in jest than seriously, throughout our tour and has entered into the vocabulary of most Lions tours ever since.

I remember, too, that great character Reg Higgins creating another catchphrase of the tour. As we were walking along the tarmac to our plane at Heathrow, a gorgeous air hostess wiggled her way past us and, as we all stopped to admire her as young men will, he suddenly said in his broad Lancashire accent, 'Eh, Dad! Buy me that!' Again, it was to be used many times in a country so rich in wildlife and lovely girls!

We left our shores virtually unheralded and unnoticed, and the next morning the papers only had the briefest accounts of our departure for what turned out to be an experience of a lifetime. We were the first Lions team to travel by air, thus shortening a tour to South Africa by about a month. We flew in a Lockheed Constellation and the flight took 36 hours, stopping at Zurich, Rome, Cairo, Khartoum, Nairobi, Entebbe and, finally, Johannesburg.

It was the first time that most of us had been to Africa and one will never forget the thrill of that flight, the humidity of Cairo and looking forward to getting out at Khartoum for a breath of air, only to feel the blast of oven-hot air as the 140-degree heat rolled into the aircraft off the tarmac and one was immediately drenched in sweat. On the flight onwards to Nairobi, we finally cast off our deference to the management and, in the ladies' powder room at the tail of the aircraft, half a dozen of us started a small party, and proceeded to drink the plane dry. In no time we were joined by others, and eventually there were about 20 of us crammed into an area designed for a quarter of that number. Finally the captain of the aircraft appeared and breathed a huge sigh of relief, because for the last hour he had been trimming the aircraft as it gradually became increasingly tail-heavy.

There were 30 players, none of whom were aged over 30, because Jack Siggins made that the criterion of his selection policy. Consequently, some famous players such as Jack Kyle, Bleddyn Williams, Ken Jones, Noel Henderson, Rees Stephens and Don White were left at home. Our captain, Robin Thompson, was, frankly, not sufficiently experienced. The vice-captain was Angus Cameron, a strong character with a fine football brain who, fully fit, would have been a tremendous asset, but he came on tour with a wrecked knee and he really should not have played. Angus was finally rumbled by the Springboks in the second Test, when they played on him with disastrous results. The captain of the tour should have been the immaculate Jeff Butterfield.

The stars of the tour were Cliff Morgan, Jeff Butterfield and the precocious baby of the team, Tony O'Reilly, who had his 19th birthday in the Kruger National Park and who was the most mature teenager I have ever seen, both in intellect and in playing ability. The friendship of the Dubliner with the equally amusing Northerner Cecil Pedlow was one of the features of the tour, particularly as they conducted a friendly running battle with the Ulster hard-liner, Jack Siggins. O'Reilly said of Pedlow, when he was late for his 50th birthday lunch at the O'Reilly mansion in Kildare many years later, 'Did you know that Pedlow is a rear-gunner on a bread van in Belfast?' He also related the story of Pedlow asking a guy at a cocktail party, 'What do you do?' the reply to which was that he was a writer, currently writing a book about Belfast. 'Then you'd better hurry up,' said Pedlow.

Another find on the tour was the uncapped Dickie Jeeps, who was really Cliff Morgan's choice, for he knew that you could not have two conductors in the band. He got four Tests for the Lions before he played for England. Danie Craven, however, always maintained that had the Lions played Johnny Williams, a reserve scrum-half, in the Tests, then the Lions would have won the series.

It was the forwards, for my money, who were the unsung heroes of this tour: that remarkable front row who sounded like a firm of solicitors, Meredith, Meredith and Williams (the last only 6ft 3ins tall but a giant), backed up by Tom Reid and splendid back-row men like Jim Greenwood, Russell Robins and Reg Higgins, the last until he got injured. I also loved the play of Johnny Williams and the admirable Douglas Baker, and, in the background, the young Arthur Smith was learning the trade which was to make him into a fine player and goal kicker.

The South Africans were kindness personified to us. No people are prouder of their country, which is not surprising considering its great beauty and enormous variety of climates and contrasting regions, from the tropical North East Transvaal and east coast to the Indian Ocean, to the Savannah of the Karoo and the temperate Cape. They were always, in my view, aware of the flaws in their politics and were, as a nation, uneasy with their politicians and their appalling policy of apartheid. They wanted us to ignore the bad element and love them for themselves, their country and their great hospitality, which has been the hallmark of the Afrikaner since his trekking days. It was not surprising, therefore, that so many rugby people were beguiled by them and became so ambivalent over their racial policies.

It was to have a profound effect on many of us, and the first time that I really began to think about apartheid and worry about our role in it was when a number of United Party women, who had organised themselves into an anti-apartheid organisation called 'The Black Sash Women', picketed our hotel in Port Elizabeth. I also observed at the games how the black people were segregated behind the goalposts, and I saw how they were treated in so many other aspects of normal life.

I learned recently from Tony O'Reilly, who is a good friend of that marvellous South African leader Nelson Mandela, that Mandela was one of those who stood in support of the Lions under the huge advertisement for Quinn's bread at Ellis Park, as a gesture of defiance towards the nationalist regime. When we won that unforgettable first Test, and at other times, our black supporters lit newspaper bonfires whenever we scored. We would always run over and applaud them at the end of a game, in recognition of their support.

After our exhausting flight from the UK, we arrived at Jan Smuts airport in Johannesburg and were astonished at the number of people who had come to the airport simply to see us. In turn, we surprised and delighted them when we sang *Sarie Marais* in Afrikaans, which we had bothered to learn under our choirmaster, Cliff Morgan. We were then taken by coach to Vereeniging on the Saturday night, for ten days acclimatisation before the first game. I was so tired after the flight that I fell on my bed fully clothed and was woken the following morning by Angus Cameron, to be told that I was expected on the first tee at nine o'clock against some of the locals. Once again, we had an insight into how rugby-mad the country was, as thousands came out from Johannesburg to see us, and they lined the fairways of the golf course as if it were the British Open.

That week, the details of touring were worked out, the duty boy rosters were organised and the policy of changing room-mates every week or fortnight was put in place. On the following Wednesday, we were taken to Pretoria to see Northern Transvaal beat Western Province. It was our first glimpse of provincial rugby in South Africa and we were shocked and appalled at the power and the pace of it all, together with the liveliness of the ball, which bounced like a mad thing on those hard grounds. We could not believe how far the ball travelled in the thinner air of the high veldt. I can still remember Tony O'Reilly, who was to score a record number of 16 tries on the tour, sitting behind me in the stand and whispering in my ear, 'When does the next plane leave for home and shouldn't we be on it?' We were pretty quiet that evening, and the next day in training it was apparent that everybody was working twice as hard.

We were fortunate that we were a fast side, with quick-thinking backs in Cliff Morgan at fly-half, the peerless Jeff Butterfield at centre with the powerful Phil Davies, and fast and intelligent wingers in Cecil Pedlow, Tony O'Reilly and Gareth Griffiths, with quick back-row forwards and a mobile front row.

The hospitality was overwhelming. One farmer, whose wife was the daughter of my tutor at St John's College, Cambridge, actually kept a leopard, which had been decimating his cattle, alive for a couple of weeks so that I could shoot it! Jack Siggins, the manager, heard about it and decided to ban my involvement, but the farmer shot it anyway and gave me the cured skin. It was not so politically incorrect in those days but, alas, the skin was stolen from my hotel room in Nairobi on the way home. On another occasion, a farmer pitched up at our hotel, the old Carlton in the centre of Johannesburg, and again, to the chagrin of the management, presented me with a lion cub. Siggins insisted on my donating it to a local zoo, which I did with some relief. South Africa was unsophisticated in those days and there were still some dirt roads between Johannesburg and Pretoria.

For the first time, the Lions were accompanied throughout the tour by two journalists, Vivian Jenkins of *The Sunday Times* and J.B.G. Thomas of *The Cardiff Western Mail*. They were both popular with the team and were virtually accepted as members of the party, as was the equally likeable Roy McKelvie of *The Daily Mail*, who arrived in time for the first Test. As the press contingent grew to astonishing levels on later tours, they were never able to enjoy the same intimacy that these early journalists achieved, particularly when the tabloids began examining aspects of the tour other than those connected with rugby.

We were to play 25 matches in 15 weeks with 19 wins, one draw and five defeats and, in the process, we drew the series at two–all. Strangely, we gave the lie to the theory that it is difficult to perform at altitude, for we won both our Tests at altitude (Johannesburg and Pretoria are over 5,000 feet) and lost the two at sea level. We got off to the worst possible start as we lost the first game against Western Transvaal, a team of no consequence at the time and one that we should have been able to put away quite comfortably. They won 9–6 after the Lions had led by two tries to nil, but a drop goal by Peters, and the Lions' first encounter with the prodigious kicking by van der Schyff, who dropped a huge goal and then kicked a penalty, both from the half-way line, severely dented the Lions' confidence.

I had been selected for that first game, but I was feeling poorly, and spent the day in bed with what seemed an upset stomach. Picked again for the Saturday game against Griqualand West, I was determined to play but, again, felt desperately ill on the morning of the game. The manager saw me and, realising that I was in a bad way, asked Norman Weinberg, the president of Griqualand and a prominent surgeon, to have a look at me. He promptly diagnosed appendicitis and shipped me off to Kimberley hospital where, after attending the match dinner, he arrived to perform the operation – but not before I had questioned his sobriety. He laughed and said that I had ruined his evening, because he was unable to drown the sorrow of his side's defeat by 24–14. He did a great job on me, for I missed only the first ten matches of the tour and returned to play against Rhodesia five weeks later.

It was a pretty bleak moment when the manager and a few players came to see me the next day, before they left for Johannesburg to play the Northern Universities and then on to Orange Free State and Windhoek in South West Africa, before I was to join up with them again in Cape Town. That night, however, two men arrived in my private ward with a crate of beer and announced that they would leave only when it was finished. They were Sailor Malan, the World War II ace fighter pilot who shot down the record number of 32 enemy aircraft, and a local businessman called Sam Armstrong, who was a dead ringer for Victor McLagan, the film star. They came in every night for five nights and, on the fifth, Sailor told me that the next day I was going to convalesce on his farm. In the meantime, the town of Kimberley avalanched my ward with crates of booze, cartons of cigarettes and dozens of boxes of chocolates, enough to open a large shop. Such was the hospitality of those South Africans, both English- and Afrikaans-speaking.

I had a week's convalescence with Malan, who had led the Torch Commandos for Oppenheimer in opposition to the nationalist policies and, as a reward, had been given the lease on this showpiece property, a de Beers farm of some 600,000 acres which was as much a game farm as anything else. Almost every day we went out shooting the high-flying partridges coming into the dams, or shooting other game such as springbok, and I was as fit as a fiddle when I rejoined the team in Cape Town some 12 days later.

Meanwhile, the Lions had begun to show their quality with strong wins over Northern Universities, Orange Free State, whom they shattered by 31 points to three, when they became angry after a Free Stater had knocked out two of Rhys Williams's front teeth, and South West Africa, now known as Namibia. Wins over Western Province and South Western Districts followed, before the Lions were brought down to earth with their biggest provincial defeat of the tour. They lost by 20 points to nil against Eastern Province, but the result was pre-ordained, because by now the Lions had accumulated a dreadful list of injured and sick players. We played Tony O'Reilly at full-back and Bryn Meredith was unfit, so we had to play Robin Roe with two cracked ribs at hooker. We lost 35 out of the 41 scrums, as Amos du Ploy bored in on Roe, thus winning a Test cap which he had not really earned in light of the circumstances. He was not to survive after playing in the first Test at Ellis Park.

The Lions bounced back and won the next eight games in a row, including the first Test. That Test was never to be forgotten by all who saw it, and it attracted the biggest gate in the history of the game. An official record 95,000 spectators paid to see the match, many from the most rickety scaffolding stands thrown up for the occasion which, nowadays, would give any building inspector or ground safety officer a nervous breakdown. They also estimated that another 10,000 got in with forged tickets, or one way or another. The black market got up to £100 a ticket, a fortune in those days, but the sheep farmers coming in from the Karoo would pay anything to see that match. The Lions sold their surplus tickets to the hotel barber at £50 a time and everybody made a killing.

The selling of tickets was, for some, their only income during a four-month tour, apart from the one pound and ten shillings a week pocket-money, so they had no compunction in breaking the amateur laws. In future Lions tours there would be a team fund organised by the players, which was shared out at the end of the tour, and it usually amounted to enough to buy presents for their families and wives or girlfriends.

Those hard Afrikaner cases, from Transvaal and throughout the high veldt, had come to see the Lions thrown to the Christians, but were astounded when 45 points, the most ever in a Test in South Africa at the time, were scored and the Lions got one more than their beloved Springboks. To add insult to injury, the Lions had lost Reg Higgins with a knee injury soon after half-time, and played most of the second half with only 14 men.

The Lions won 23–22, and it was, without question, one of the greatest Test matches ever played anywhere in the world, in any era. There is a famous photo of van der Schyff letting his head drop in dejection, when he failed with the last kick of the game to convert a last-ditch try. Like most of the team and their supporters, O'Reilly could not look at the kick, and when somebody asked him in the dressing-room what he was thinking of at the time of van der Schyff's kick, he said, 'I was merely in direct communication with the Vatican.'

Ernie Michie, immaculately turned out in his kilt, had led the Lions on to the field with his bagpipes wailing what some thought was a lament for the Lions, and Robin Thompson, clutching our tour mascot, a large toy Lion named Elmer, had run the team out to the huge roar of a crowd waiting to see the first British side play their invincible Springboks for 17 years.

It was a nail-biting thriller of a game, and it was no wonder that a total of 678,000 flocked to see all 24 matches during the tour. The hallmark of these Lions was their direct, simple play, their speed of pass, their speed of running, and their philosophy of ignoring whether it was good or bad ball; they merely used whatever was available. Above all, they were adventurous and ran everything they could.

The Lions scored a dazzling opening try, when Butterfield, or 'Buttercup' as Cliff Morgan called him, collected a poor pass and classically broke on the outside and drew the full-back, to put Pedlow over in the corner. Van der Schyff then kicked two penalties with two superb kicks, which people forgot in the recriminations which were to follow. The diminutive scrum-half Tommy Gentles, the smallest ever Springbok and the smallest player I ever saw in Test rugby at 5ft 3ins, broke and Stephen Fry, the Springboks captain, put Theunis Briers, a Paarl farmer, away on one of his powerful runs for a try. It was converted by van der Schyff, and South Africa led 11–3. An eight-point lead was never safe from these Lions and Butterfield now contrived another try, scoring at the post with a clever change of direction, and Cameron converted to make it 11–8 at half-time.

Immediately after the restart, the Lions lost Reg Higgins for the rest of the tour with torn knee ligaments, but this misfortune only seemed to inspire them, and the pack played like men possessed. In a ten-minute period, the Lions scored 15 points, to roar into a commanding 23–11 lead. First, from a strike against the head by Bryn Meredith, Cliff Morgan weaved some of his magic and I can still see him sticking his neck out and rocketing past the great Basie van Wyk with a devastating outside break, to score an inspirational try. Two more tries swiftly followed when, from two kicks ahead, the bounce deceived van der Schyff, and the indefatigable Greenwood and the alert O'Reilly went over. Angus Cameron converted all three and the Johannesburg crowd were stunned. In the last quarter, the seven Lions forwards inevitably began to tire and the Springboks began to get back into the game.

The Lions continued to hold until the last few climactic minutes when, with only a couple of minutes to go, that mighty forward Chris Koch picked up and stormed his way over from 20 yards out and van der Schyff banged over the conversion. Then, late into injury time, with the massive crowd screaming deliriously, Stephen Fry picked up a loose ball and flipped it to Briers, who beat both Pedlow and Cameron with an inside swerve to score about half-way out. Agonisingly, the Lions stood there waiting for a conversion, which was difficult only because of the pressure. The scoreboard read 23–22 and the last number then disappeared, as the scorer prepared to put up 24. That photograph will remain a monument to van der Schyff's despair, as the ball swung to the left of the posts. It was van der Schyff's last game for South Africa and he turned to making a living by crocodile hunting in Rhodesia.

Danie Craven put the defeat of his beloved Springboks down to the fact that they were not motivated. 'You must be keyed up for the big occasion, and the belief among old Springboks that a team which sings before a Test is destined to weep afterwards is not a silly superstition.' He was to ban singing by the team on the way to future Tests.

It was the match of that generation and all who saw it will never forget it. The Lions were jubilant, for they knew they had achieved the minor miracle of putting South Africa on the back foot in a Test series in their own country. One man in the crowd dropped dead from excitement. The South Africans took it very well and it was to revive back play in the Republic, as the Lions quickly found to their cost.

Three more games were won against Central, Boland and Western Province Universities, the last providing one of the best games of the whole tour, which was not surprising as 11 of the students subsequently won Springboks colours. I happened to be captain that day, and I remember that they matched us try for try at four each, and that I was sweating. Only a try by Tom Reid in the dying moments saw us through by 20–17. I recall they had a lovely pair of half-backs in Richard Lockyer and Brian Pfaff and they had Butch Lochner, later to become a Springboks selector, in the back row. At the time Butch was a farmer, but on subsequent visits to that country I found that, in turn, he became a lecturer at Stellenbosch and then a colonel in the army.

The great Johannes Claassen, who played against us that year, had a similarly chequered career, first in the university, then the army, and at one time he even became a bishop. I often wondered about this, and I concluded that it was a system by which the Afrikaner brotherhood rewarded their famous sons.

For the next Test, South Africa dropped five of the team. Wilf Rosenberg, a really sharp centre, came in to partner Des Sinclair in the centre and van Vollenhoven was switched to the wing. Swart and van der Schyff were the backs dropped, with Roy Dryburgh drafted in at full-back. The three forwards dropped were Amos du Ploy, C. Kroon and the legendary Basie van Wyk, who had played his last game for the Springboks. In their place came the immensely strong Northern Transvaal prop Jaap Bekker, Bertus van der Merwe, and the fast flanker Dawie Ackermann, who had played so well for Southern Universities against us. The Lions made only two changes; Gareth Griffiths, flown in as replacement after Arthur Smith had broken his thumb in the first game, was preferred to Pedlow, and Russell Robins was moved to flanker, to accommodate Tom Reid at number eight.

Apparently Stephen Fry, the Springboks captain, was too nervous to address his team before the kick-off and asked Danie Craven to do it for him. The Lions on the other hand were cheerful, but the back row and the unfit Angus Cameron were to be our Achilles' heel, and we lost by the resounding margin of 25–9, a big score in those days. Van Vollenhoven had found his spiritual home on the wing, as Gerald Davies did a couple of decades later, and the Springboks wing, later to play rugby league for St Helens, scored three magnificent tries.

The seven tries scored by the Springboks at Newlands constituted a record for a Test in South Africa. There was no hint in the first 20 minutes of the avalanche to come and, at that stage, the Lions led with a penalty goal by Cameron. Jeeps and Morgan were unhappy at half-back and the Lions pack was far from its best. Nevertheless, it was not until three minutes before half-time that the Springboks scored, when Sinclair kicked hard across field for van Vollenhoven to steal the ball from under O'Reilly's nose and score. At half-time it was 3–3.

The Springboks had now spotted how slow Cameron was at getting into the corners with his crook knee and they played on him, in what was to be his last game of the tour. Inexorably the tries came as the Lions, for the only time on tour, really cracked. Van Vollenhoven got two more quick tries for his hat-trick, and Rosenberg, Dryburgh, Briers and Ackermann all added tries, although Dryburgh converted only two of them. The only response by the Lions was a couple of tries by Butterfield and Bryn Meredith, two of the most outstanding players of the tour.

It was the Lions' turn to lick their wounds, as the South Africans had picked up the gauntlet of running rugby and had beaten us at it. We journeyed north, sadder and wiser men, for what should have been an easy game against Eastern Transvaal at Springs but, with a side mostly composed of the midweek 'dirt-trackers', as they are called in Lions parlance, we nearly came to grief again and only scraped a draw at 17–17. We only had 14 men in the second half, for Doug Baker pulled a muscle and, as he was needed for the Test as a makeshift full-back, he could not be risked. To make matters worse, Doug lost his contact lenses the next day and we had to enlist the aid of the British High Commission to get a new pair flown out from Germany.

There was now the prospect of the hardest week of the tour, as we had to play Northern Transvaal one Saturday and the Springboks the next, which was almost the same as playing back-to-back Tests. I was fully fit again and I was delighted to be included in the team against the Blue Bulls, as Northern Transvaal are known. I was renewing my 1951 Swansea confrontation with Hansie Brewis, that great Springboks fly-half. He was now at the end of his fine career, as was Fonnie du Toit, his scrum-half in the fantastic Springboks side which toured Britain in 1951. In addition, Northern Transvaal had van Vollenhoven in the centre and Bekker, Retief and 'Salty' du Rand, their captain, in the pack.

The Lions were expected to lose, but we won another famous victory by only the narrow margin of 14–11. I shall never forget Butterfield's try that day when, with a couple of minutes to go, he juggled the ball from somewhere behind his back inside his own 25, and shimmied his way through a gap to race 80 yards to score, with the local hero, van Vollenhoven, chasing him every step of the way, but unable to make up an inch of his three- or four-yard lead.

So we had set the scene for another battle of the giants in the third Test. The Lions made four changes, with Doug Baker coming in for Cameron, and I came into the pack at flanker, for Tom Reid to revert to the second row in place of the injured Thompson, and for Russell Robins to return to number eight. Cliff Morgan was given the captaincy and Billy Williams, the indestructible prop, was given the leadership of the forwards and the vice-captaincy.

South Africa made only one change, bringing in the Free Stater Coenraad Strydom, known as 'Popeye', for the tiny Tommy Gentles. Later, Dan Retief withdrew with an injury and he was replaced by Butch Lochner at number eight.

This Test became known in South Africa for a remarkable training session as Danie Craven, obsessed by the idea that the British press were spying on him, took his players off the field and, when they had gone, took them back again for a session under bright moonlight. The press dubbed it 'the moonlight sonata'.

It did them no good, as the Lions now changed their tactics and decided to attack the Boks where they least expected: through the forwards, with heavy support kicking from the backs. We made a few mistakes, but we were well worth our 9–6 margin at Loftus Versveld, another of those magnificent grounds which abound in South Africa.

There were 63 lineouts, which illustrated how we decided to make it a kicking and not a running game and took the Springboks forwards on up front. It was a hot, enervating day and some of the forward exchanges were particularly fierce. The scrummaging of our front row of Meredith, Meredith and Williams was quite magnificent, and I well remember Jappie Bekker talking to Chris Koch and swapping places for a few scrums. I asked Chris Koch at the after-match function what happened, and he told me that Bekker was having trouble with Courtney Meredith and asked him to change. After a couple of scrums, Koch said he told Bekker to do his own dirty work.

During this match, Courtney Meredith picked up one of the worst mouth injuries I have ever seen. He came up to me at half-time and, with blood streaming from his mouth, showed me his tongue, which was almost severed half-way back to the root, and asked me, 'How bad is it?' I said, 'It's bloody terrible, but keep your mouth shut and stay on the field for the second half or we are done for.' He was in great pain but, to his undying credit, he did just that and, after the game, was rushed to hospital to have it stitched. He was in trouble with this injury for a couple of weeks and did not play again until the final Test.

As often happened on these Lions tours, players like Courtney Meredith and Rhys Williams were, in the Orange Free State match, victims of what is known as 'the cheap shot'. It became necessary to have a fixer to stop such unprovoked attacks. Tony O'Reilly became the principal spotter from the safety of the backs and I was made the avenging angel. Tony would come up to me and say, 'Number four' or whatever, and I was supposed to go in and mete out the punishment at the next opportunity, preferably at a nice loose maul. I don't know how I got such a difficult job! It was merely, as Tony often explained, that I could hit harder than the others, even though I was one of the smallest forwards at about 14 stone. It was all about having been taught to fight on the coal tips in Brynamman during the school holidays and having boxed a bit at school.

The first Test ever to be held in Pretoria was an unpretty, dour game and out of character with the normal style of the 1955 Lions, because our strategy was to win at all costs, to go one up in the series with one to play. In a grimly fought first half, the only score was a left-footed drop goal by Jeff Butterfield. Twelve minutes into the second half, Baker increased our lead with a penalty, before Dryburgh replied with a huge 50-yard drop goal from a penalty. Sustained Lions pressure finally brought reward, when I managed to pick up a loose ball and gave to Butterfield, who crashed over for a try. Although Dryburgh then kicked an orthodox penalty, the Lions finished strongly and were attacking fiercely at the end. Everybody, including Danie Craven, said that they deserved a win, a fact which shook South Africa and, indeed, the world of rugby, to the core.

After the enormously successful fortnight in Pretoria, we then took off in high spirits to the Kruger National Park for a well-deserved break. On the way, we lunched at Crocodile River at the home of Ivan Solomon, a millionaire citrus grower, who typified the massive hospitality we received wherever we went in the new Republic by laying on a *braai* or barbecue of such quality that it was something to remember. We spent the next four days in this extraordinary game reserve which is the size of Wales, and most of us saw lions, leopards, elephants, buffalo, crocodiles, hippopotamuses and almost every type of game. It was magic, and I will never forget the first night, for we were celebrating O'Reilly's and Danny Davies's birthdays. Remarkably, it was only the former's 19th, for his maturity of mind and body was equal to anyone on tour. What a grand party it was! The next day we had to send our truck, which accompanied us full of cases of beer, back to Nelspruit for new supplies.

We had three matches to play before the final Test, and the first was against Natal in Durban which, in many ways, was the most English of all the provinces we played. Unthinkingly, we offended them by resting most of the Test team and trotting out the dirt-trackers, including none of our stars like Morgan, O'Reilly and Butterfield. The local press, *The Natal Mercury*, called us the 'Insult XV', but then we had to rest our top players who had just finished a tough campaign in Northern Transvaal.

I was made captain of what was considered to be a rag-bag side and, frankly, we played as though we were, although there was no criticism of the forwards, for it was the backs who squandered one opportunity after another. I remember we snatched our 11–8 win against a very lively and young Natal team only in the closing seconds of the game, when Tom Reid, bless his big heart, picked up and fed me, so that I put Tug Wilson over for the try.

We now played the Junior Springboks at Bloemfontein, which was virtually as hard as any Test match and, again, the temperature reached 80 degrees. It was also evident that the Lions were beginning to get travel and tour weary, and we struggled to win a dour game by 15–12. Worse was to come, for next we lost 14–12 to Border in East London, who were a really tough outfit. They were a bit like the Llanelli or Swansea of South Africa: always guaranteed to give any touring team a hard time.

It is easy to make excuses, and some of them were true, for we were by now a tired side and beleaguered with injuries, and some of the selections for the final Test were disastrous. Tom Reid should have been retained after his great game in the third Test, but tour politics saw the captain, Robin Thompson, brought back, and O'Reilly, who played on the wing for most of the tour, was brought into the centre in place of Phil Davies. Cliff Morgan was not really fit to play after an ankle injury sustained against the Junior Springboks but, as it was unthinkable both in his own mind and those of the other members of the team that we should take the field without him, he decided to play.

The only changes made by the Springboks selectors, Chairman Frank Mellish, W.C. Zeller, Danie Craven, Maurice Zimmerman and Basil Kenyon, who refused to panic after Pretoria, were to bring back Tommy Gentles at scrum-half and the formidable Daan Retief into the pack.

The major factor in the final disappointing defeat was, of course, the Springboks spirit, which dictated that they were not going to lose a Test series at home and, on the day, they were magnificent. The Lions had the chance of being the first team since the turn of the century to win a Test series, but were simply not good enough, on that day, to do it.

The Lions threw everything they had at the Springboks in the first 20 minutes and scored first when, from a sweeping three-quarter attack, Gareth Griffiths kicked ahead; the always energetic Greenwood won the race with Tommy Gentles, and Pedlow converted. In the first half, the Lions looked good to win and created many scoring chances which were not taken. Ulyate then began to ply Pedlow with high balls where his eyesight was suspect and Briers, chasing up, stole a ball from under his nose to score a try. At half-time it was 5–3 to the Lions.

In the second half, Ulyate applied the same tactic and, again, Briers stole in for a try. A break by Gentles brought a try from Ulyate, converted by Dryburgh, and the Lions had no petrol left in their tank, as van Vollenhoven scored a try in the corner and Ulyate dropped a goal to make it 17–5. The Lions showed that they could still bite back when O'Reilly scored, breaking his shoulder in the process; but, with a minute to go, Retief scored under the posts and Dryburgh converted, to make the final score 22–8.

And so ended a dream, and a tour which was measured as much by its friendliness, great humour and comradeship as by the standard of play, among one of the finest bunches of players to represent the British Isles. They were popular wherever they went and Danie Craven, who, in his famous office in Stellenbosch University, granted me the last interview he gave to a pressman shortly before he died in 1992, said they were the team he always admired most for their attitudes both on and off the field.

The South African media were no less flattering. One newspaper said that they were grateful to these Lions for reminding them that the skull was still a receptacle for brains, rather than being just a battering ram.

No wonder thousands of South Africans turned up to say *Tot Siens* (goodbye) to us, and as we walked out on to the tarmac we turned and sang *Sarie Marais*, *Sospan Fach* and *Now is the Hour* for them, before heading home, via one game in Nairobi.

After leaving the UK unheralded all those weeks ago, we were to arrive home to a fanfare of plaudits, as far finer players and better men for such an amazing and fulfilling experience. We had enjoyed a crash course in the University of Life.

## Results of the 1955 Lions in South Africa

P 25   W 19   D 1   L 5   F 457   A 283

| Western Transvaal | L | 6 | 9 |
|---|---|---|---|
| Griqualand West | W | 24 | 14 |
| Northern Universities | W | 32 | 6 |
| Orange Free State | W | 31 | 3 |
| South West Africa | W | 9 | 0 |
| Western Province | W | 11 | 3 |
| South Western Districts | W | 22 | 3 |
| Eastern Province | L | 0 | 20 |
| North Eastern Districts | W | 34 | 6 |
| Transvaal | W | 36 | 13 |
| Rhodesia (Kitwe) | W | 27 | 14 |
| Rhodesia (Salisbury) | W | 16 | 12 |

| South Africa (Johannesburg) | W | 23 | 22 |
| Central Universities | W | 21 | 14 |
| Boland | W | 11 | 0 |
| Western Province Universities | W | 20 | 17 |
| South Africa (Cape Town) | L | 9 | 25 |
| Eastern Transvaal | D | 17 | 17 |
| Northern Transvaal | W | 14 | 11 |
| South Africa (Pretoria) | W | 9 | 6 |
| Natal | W | 11 | 8 |
| Junior Springboks | W | 15 | 12 |
| Border | L | 12 | 14 |
| South Africa (Port Elizabeth) | L | 8 | 22 |
| East African XV (Nairobi) | W | 39 | 12 |

## Robin Thompson's 1955 Lions team

**Full-backs**

| A. Cameron | Glasgow HS FP | Scotland |
| A.G. Thomas | Llanelli | Wales |

**Three-quarters**

| J. Butterfield | Northampton | England |
| W.P.C. Davies | Harlequins | England |
| G.M. Griffiths* | Cardiff | Wales |
| H.T. Morris | Cardiff | Wales |
| A.J.F. O'Reilly | Old Belvedere | Ireland |
| A.C. Pedlow | Queen's University Belfast | Ireland |
| J.P. Quinn | New Brighton | England |
| A.R. Smith | Cambridge University | Scotland |
| F.D. Sykes | Northampton | England |

**Half-backs**

| D.G.S. Baker | Old Merchant Taylor | England |
| R.E.G. Jeeps | Northampton | |
| T. Lloyd | Maesteg | Wales |
| C.I. Morgan | Cardiff | Wales |
| J.E. Williams | Old Millhillians | England |

**Forwards**

| T. Elliot | Gala | Scotland |
| J.T. Greenwood | Dunfermline | Scotland |
| R. Higgins | Liverpool | England |

| H.F. McLeod | Hawick | Scotland |
|---|---|---|
| B.V. Meredith | Newport | Wales |
| C.C. Meredith | Neath | Wales |
| E.T.S. Michie | Aberdeen University | Scotland |
| T.E. Reid | Garryowen | Ireland |
| R.J. Robins | Pontypridd | Wales |
| R. Roe | Lansdowne | Ireland |
| R.C.C. Thomas | Swansea | Wales |
| R.H. Thompson (capt.) | Instonians | Ireland |
| R.H. Williams | Llanelli | Wales |
| W.O.G. Williams | Swansea | Wales |
| D.S. Wilson | Metropolitan Police | England |

Manager: J.A.E. Siggins
Assistant Manager: D.E. Davies

* Replacement

This team believed in open rugby and revived the whole concept of back play in South Africa, whose teams had been becoming too engrossed with forward power. They never differentiated between good or bad ball and they played some of the most direct running rugby ever seen, unsurpassed until those great Lions teams of 1971 and 1974.

## RONNIE DAWSON'S 1959 LIONS

This was another tour which committed itself to all-out attack, but which never got its just deserts. It scored more points than any other Lions team, 842 in 33 games, 25 of which were in New Zealand, six in Australia and two in Canada. They won only one of the four Tests in New Zealand, and were robbed of the title of the most successful team so far in this century only by the boot of Don Clarke. He kicked six penalty goals in the first Test, which was enormously depressing, as the Lions scored four tries, only to lose 18–17. Clarke also deprived them of victory in the second Test, with a late try and conversion. Without Clarke, the Lions' record would surely have been played four, won three, lost one, instead of lost three, won one.

Nevertheless, they played brilliant rugby and scored a remarkable 165 tries. Tony O'Reilly got 22 of them, 17 in New Zealand, establishing a record which may never be broken, while the mercurial Peter Jackson scored 19. Thus, it was one of the most attractive and effective sides ever to tour New Zealand and they drew huge gates everywhere, because of their propensity for attacking from anywhere. If they had a weakness, it was in defence and in the giving away of too many penalties. It is interesting to note that, in the first Test at Dunedin, they drew a record crowd of 41,500, and the match takings were £20,500. It seems a far cry from today's big gates, which in some cases fetch well over a million pounds.

In that last year of the 1950s, we saw the phenomenon of Teddy boys and girls, and the juke-box; Cliff Richard sang his hit song *Living Doll*; cinemas were closing due to television, with 57 closing that year; Hugh Greene became governor of the BBC; duty-free booze was approved at airports; the first Mini was produced; and they began building the first hovercraft. Overseas, Buddy Holly was killed in a plane crash; mobs rioted in Little Rock, USA, against the schooling of blacks in mixed schools; and Castro took power in Cuba.

Although unsuccessful in New Zealand, some tremendous players went on that Lions tour, six of whom had been on the 1955 tour. These were Tony O'Reilly, Jeff Butterfield, Dick Jeeps, Bryn Meredith, Hugh McLeod, and Rhys Williams. All of them made a big contribution to the Test team, apart from that star of 1955, Jeff Butterfield, who was plagued by a thigh injury. There was also one player from the 1950 Lions side which toured New Zealand, Malcolm Thomas, who was an invaluable source of information as well as being a very experienced player.

For once, the Irish were the most predominant of the home nation teams on the tour, with ten players; England and Wales had nine apiece, and Scotland five. As ever, there were some terrific, fun guys and characters like Andy Mulligan and O'Reilly, Ray Prosser and David Marques, who became unlikely buddies, hard cases like Gordon Wood of Limerick, and city slickers like John Young, the AAA champion of 1956, who had recorded a best time of 9.6 seconds for the hundred yards, and who later became secretary of the London Stock Exchange. It was the sort of perfect blend of gentlemen of all classes which always epitomised a Lions tour, and which made a nonsense of that British disease of class distinction and privilege. Such a tour can only sustain a meritocracy and a bond of fellowship arising from the soldiering which is a fact of life when touring the southern hemisphere.

Once again, the team had men like Rhys Williams, an automatic choice at lock on both his tours, as durable as they ever came, and Roddy Evans, who played so well in the first two Tests but missed the latter stages of the tour due to injury. Hughie McLeod, that prop from the Scottish Borders, had now grown into a magnificent player. Ronnie Dawson claimed the hooker position and this was a contentious argument before and after the tour, for it was always claimed by the *cognoscenti* that Bryn Meredith was one of the greatest hookers of his or any other era and it was therefore considered a mistake to make Ronnie captain, which meant Bryn would be left out of the Test team. It was another example of poor selection by those secretive men in the East India Sports Club in St James's Square. That is not to say that Ronnie Dawson was a poor player; far from it, and he was also a hard-working captain. His conscientious work for rugby later saw him become the coach to the 1968 Lions, a leading administrator, the president of the Irish Rugby Union, and chairman of the IRFB. A man and a player of some consequence.

This tour also heralded the arrival on the scene of another of the illustrious men in the Lions' history who was to make a tremendous contribution to the concept as a player, coach and manager, and who, together with his Northern Irish colleague, remarkably also from Ballymena, Willie John McBride, became one of the most highly regarded and respected Lions of all time. He played in ten Tests on three Lions tours in 1959, 1962 and 1968; he coached the unbeaten pride of them all, the 1974 team to South Africa, and managed Billy Beaumont's 1980 team to South Africa. This truly marvellous and much-loved man was Sydney Millar.

Another person who reached the dizzy heights of influence in the game and became chairman of the IRFB was Ken Smith, who came in as a late replacement for that magnificent England flanker Peter Robbins who, sadly for the tour, because he would have been the life and soul of the party (and there was never a funnier man in rugby), broke his leg on the Barbarians' Easter tour against Newport. Ken seized his chance with both hands, and played in two Test matches in both Australia and New Zealand.

In the back row, there were big men in every sense of the word in John Faull and Noel Murphy, whose fathers had played for Wales and Ireland respectively. The more I list these players, the more I realise what a fine body of men they were.

At half-back, they had the durable and ever-reliable Dickie Jeeps, whom Cliff Morgan had selected as his partner for that reason on the previous tour. Cliff wanted a man who would deliver the ball come hell or high water, and that was the sort of player Jeeps was. His fly-half was Bev Risman for four Tests and Horrocks-Taylor and Malcolm Price for the other two, when Risman was injured. Bev was the son of the famous Great Britain rugby league captain, Gus Risman, and was himself to turn pro in 1961.

Dave Hewitt, one member of a whole family of Hewitts who have played for Ireland, was the outstanding centre of the tour, closely followed by Malcolm Price of Wales. The efficiency of their three-quarter play was evidenced by the remarkable fact that O'Reilly and Jackson scored an astonishing 41 tries between them. Bill Patterson, Malcolm Thomas and Ken Scotland also played a Test match each in the three-quarter line.

There were two superb full-backs on tour in Ken Scotland and Terry Davies. They had contrasting styles, with Ken being the first in what is now a long line of running Scottish full-backs, and Terry a strong defensive full-back. In the event, they shared the Tests in New Zealand two each, with Ken being preferred for the earlier two Tests against Australia.

The undoubted stars of the tour were the two magnificent wings, O'Reilly and Jackson. The Lions won their tests in Australia fairly comfortably by 17–6 and 24–3, but came a cropper in the first game against New South Wales, losing 18–14. In the first Test at Brisbane, O'Reilly and Ken Smith scored tries, with Risman kicking a conversion, Hewitt kicked two penalties and Ken Scotland dropped a goal to Australia's two penalties. In the second Test at Sydney, Malcolm Price scored two tries and O'Reilly, Risman and Dawson got one each, with Hewitt getting two conversions, and Ken Scotland a penalty goal and a conversion, to Australia's penalty goal.

After winning all their provincial games in New Zealand except Otago, where they got a familiar beating by 26–8, the Lions were in pretty good shape for the fateful first Test in Dunedin.

The first points came from Clarke, who kicked a penalty after 20 minutes and, two minutes later, repeated the performance. Hewitt replied with a penalty for the Lions, and then O'Reilly levelled the scores with an unconverted try in the corner, after Risman made the break. Malcolm Price scored another try at the end of the half from a cross-kick by Risman, and the Lions changed ends, leading 9–6. Jackson then scored in the corner, after Roddy Evans had intercepted a pass. After Clarke had kicked another penalty, the Lions went into what, in those days, was a comfortable lead, 27 minutes into the second half, when Risman picked up a loose ball and kicked ahead for Ken Scotland to pick up and pass to Price, who got his second try of the match, converted by Risman.

The game seemed won, but then, to the disgust of the Lions, Clarke kicked three more penalties to set a New Zealand record in a Test match, the last two minutes from full-time, and to snatch what was considered the cruellest defeat ever sustained by the Lions. This was to precipitate a huge world-wide debate as to the value of a penalty goal against a try, and had much to do with the future change in scoring values. The Lions also disputed the role of the referee, Mr A.L. Fleury of Otago.

The Lions lost only one of their next seven games, against Canterbury at Christchurch on the Saturday following the first Test. This is always one of the tough fixtures on a tour of New Zealand and this game was no exception, as the Lions went down 20–14. On the credit side, they beat that other major province, Wellington, by 21–6, and so they were not too unhappy, except for the rising injury toll which caused key players like Risman, Hewitt, Jackson and Scotland to be unavailable. Their places were taken by Malcolm Price at fly-half, and Malcolm Thomas was brought into the centre together with Bill Patterson, the uncapped replacement player. John Young came in on the wing and Terry Davies played full-back.

It was the first appearance of another New Zealand legend against a British side, for the All Blacks brought back Colin Meads, who had played against Australia the previous season, and Kel Tremain played his first Test. In the centre was T.R. Lineen, whose son Sean was to play for Scotland.

Again, the Lions had the desperate misfortune to lose in the closing minutes of the game and, once more, it was that man Don Clarke who was to be their executioner by scoring and converting a try in the dying minutes.

Ralph Caulton, on his All Blacks debut, scored two tries to provide a half-time lead of 6–0. Ten minutes into the second half, Don Clarke blatantly obstructed O'Reilly after he had kicked ahead, and instead of awarding a penalty try, as he ought to have done, the referee merely awarded a penalty, which Terry Davies kicked. The Lions then took the lead with a try by Young, after a marvellous run by Price and a lovely scissors with Thomas, which Davies converted. However, McCullogh, with a minute to go, broke down the blind side and passed to the supporting Clarke, who scored the winning try with a massive dive over the line and converted it, to make the score 11–8 and to give the All Blacks a two–nil lead in the series.

The third Test in Christchurch saw the All Blacks forwards in one of their most devastating moods. After three easy provincial wins, the Lions had Scotland, Hewitt and Jackson fit again. They played Phil Horrocks-Taylor, who had flown out as a substitute for the injured Mick English and who had had only one game on the Tuesday as preparation, at fly-half. A new back row was tried, with Smith and Faull regaining their places, and Haydn Morgan getting his first Test. Gordon Wood also came in for Millar at prop.

Urbahn scored the first try for New Zealand and John Faull kicked a penalty for the Lions. There followed a penalty and a remarkable left-footed drop goal by Don Clarke, who had become the scourge of these

Lions and, with four minutes to half-time, Hewitt scored a magnificent try for the Lions after a half break by Horrocks-Taylor. Faull converted and the Lions were within a point of the All Blacks but, with a minute to go to the interval, Colin Meads swept through for a try and Clarke converted, to make it 14–8 at half-time. There was no further score for the first 30 minutes of the second half, and then Urbahn and Caulton scored tries, with Clarke adding the last conversion, to give New Zealand their only convincing win, 22–8, in the series which they now could not lose.

The Lions registered four more wins before the final Test and were still in good heart, as their popularity was as big as ever with the New Zealand public, who loved their style both on and off the field. This was reflected in the fact that the biggest crowd to watch a rugby match, 63,000, gathered at Eden Park, Auckland, for the final Test.

Jeeps was unfit, so the selectors brought in Irishman Andy Mulligan, who had flown in as replacement for Stan Coughtrie. After the embarrassment of having had a scrum-half too many in 1955, the selectors had cut the number down to two, but it is a vulnerable position and Sod's Law operated. However, the easy replacement by air travel has meant that nowadays the Lions still take only two. Ken Scotland was brought into the centre and Terry Davies came in at full-back. In the forwards, Ray Prosser was preferred to Gordon Wood and Roddy Evans, who had gone home with a knee injury and homesickness, was replaced by Bill Mulcahy, another great Irish character in the side.

Happily, for they earned it, these Lions finished their tour with a victory. It was fitting that they should win by three tries, scored by the three most outstanding backs of the tour. The first came after a Don Clarke penalty, through that 'Jack in the box' Peter Jackson, who enchanted the New Zealand crowds with his elusive running. Tony O'Reilly came in from the other wing and broke the midfield before passing on to Ken Scotland who, in turn, put Jackson over for the try, which made it 3–3 at half-time. The second came from O'Reilly, in the fourth minute of the second period, when he was put away on the narrow side by his great pal and fellow entertainer on the tour, Andy Mulligan. After Don Clarke had levelled the score with another penalty, Bev Risman scored a fine blind-side try. Don Clarke, who had scored 39 points in the series, had one final chance to level the score in the closing minutes, but he missed what, for him, was a comparatively easy penalty and justice was done.

It was the first Test won by a British team in New Zealand since the initial Test of the 1930 tour, and only the second Lions victory over

New Zealand in 60 years. It was a popular win by an immensely popular side. There was, however, some retrospective criticism about the team selections before the tour, and their erratic nature during the tour itself, but then many of these were dictated by injury. The team played two games in Canada on the way home.

## Results of the 1959 Lions in Australia, New Zealand and Canada

P 33   W 27   D 0   L 6   F 842   A 353

| | | | |
|---|---|---|---|
| Victoria | W | 53 | 18 |
| New South Wales | L | 14 | 18 |
| Queensland | W | 39 | 11 |
| Australia (Brisbane) | W | 17 | 6 |
| New South Wales Country Districts | W | 27 | 14 |
| Australia (Sydney) | W | 24 | 3 |
| | | | |
| Hawke's Bay | W | 52 | 12 |
| East Coast–Poverty Bay | W | 23 | 14 |
| Auckland | W | 15 | 10 |
| New Zealand Universities | W | 25 | 13 |
| Otago | L | 8 | 26 |
| South Canterbury, North Otago & Mid Canterbury | W | 21 | 11 |
| Southland | W | 11 | 6 |
| New Zealand (Dunedin) | L | 17 | 18 |
| West Coast–Buller | W | 58 | 3 |
| Canterbury | L | 14 | 20 |
| Marlborough, Nelson, Golden Bay & Montueka | W | 64 | 5 |
| Wellington | W | 21 | 6 |
| Wanganui | W | 9 | 6 |
| Taranaki | W | 15 | 3 |
| Manawatu–Horowhenua | W | 26 | 6 |
| New Zealand (Wellington) | L | 8 | 11 |
| King Country–Counties | W | 25 | 5 |
| Waikato | W | 14 | 0 |
| Wairarapa–Bush | W | 37 | 11 |
| New Zealand (Christchurch) | L | 8 | 22 |
| New Zealand Juniors | W | 29 | 9 |

| New Zealand Maoris | W | 12 | 6 |
| Thames Valley–Bay of Plenty | W | 26 | 24 |
| North Auckland | W | 35 | 13 |
| New Zealand (Auckland) | W | 9 | 6 |
| | | | |
| British Columbia | W | 16 | 11 |
| Eastern Canada | W | 70 | 6 |

## Ronnie Dawson's 1959 Lions team

### Full-backs
| | | |
|---|---|---|
| T.J. Davies | Llanelli | Wales |
| K.J.F. Scotland | Cambridge University | Scotland |

### Three-quarters
| | | |
|---|---|---|
| N.H. Brophy | University College Dublin | Ireland |
| J. Butterfield | Northampton | England |
| D. Hewitt | Queen's University Belfast | Ireland |
| P.B. Jackson | Coventry | England |
| A.J.F. O'Reilly | Old Belvedere | Ireland |
| W.M. Patterson* | Sale | |
| M.J. Price | Pontypool | Wales |
| M.C. Thomas | Newport | Wales |
| J.R.C. Young | Harlequins | England |

### Utility
| | | |
|---|---|---|
| G.H. Waddell | Cambridge University | Scotland |

### Half-backs
| | | |
|---|---|---|
| S. Coughtrie | Edinburgh Academicals | Scotland |
| M.A.F. English | Bohemians | Ireland |
| J.P. Horrocks-Taylor* | Leicester | England |
| R.E.G. Jeeps | Northampton | England |
| A.A. Mulligan* | Wanderers | Ireland |
| A.B.W. Risman | Manchester | England |

### Forwards
| | | |
|---|---|---|
| A. Ashcroft | Waterloo | England |
| A.R. Dawson (capt.) | Wanderers | Ireland |
| W.R. Evans | Cardiff | Wales |
| J. Faull | Swansea | Wales |
| H.F. McLeod | Hawick | Scotland |

| | | |
|---|---|---|
| R.W.D. Marques | Harlequins | England |
| B.V. Meredith | Newport | Wales |
| S. Millar | Ballymena | Ireland |
| H.J. Morgan | Abertillery | Wales |
| W.A. Mulcahy | University College Dublin | Ireland |
| N.A.A. Murphy | Cork Constitution | Ireland |
| T.R. Prosser | Pontypool | Wales |
| G.K. Smith | Kelso | Scotland |
| R.H. Williams | Llanelli | Wales |
| B.G.M. Wood | Garryowen | Ireland |

Manager: A.W. Wilson
Assistant Manager: O.B. Glasgow

* Replacements

W.M. Patterson was the only uncapped player, but later played for England in 1961

# The Toilers

The Lions never won a Test match against New Zealand or South Africa in the 12 Test matches played against them in the 1960s; their only wins were the two Tests in 1966 against Australia, whose rugby had reached a low ebb. This reflected the generally poor standards of British rugby at that time, when there was a shortage of inspiring players such as Jack Kyle, Cliff Morgan, Tony O'Reilly, Jeff Butterfield and Bev Risman, who could catalyse attacking concepts in the teams they played with in the previous decade. Many players of this era were too defensively orientated, in my view because they were becoming increasingly exposed to media influences. The advent of television coverage of sport was to have a massive influence on the individual, who began to be afraid of making mistakes.

They were also having to contend with the continuing mistakes made by the Four Home Unions' selectors, who not only seemed inexpert, but were too often wanting the face to fit their ideas of what was required, without any knowledge of, or regard for, the need for specialisation in positions such as the forwards. They obviously had little idea of the difference between a tight-head and loose-head prop, or an open-side or blind-side flanker.

The failure to provide strong blind-side flankers for the tour of South Africa in 1962 was a case in point. They seemed totally unaware of the propensity of the southern hemisphere countries to drive the blind side for long periods. The first instinct of any New Zealand team, when it is in any sort of trouble, is to close it up and go down the narrow side, and the same is true in South Africa.

The year 1962 was a fateful year in South Africa, for the nationalist government imprisoned Nelson Mandela. In other parts of the world, Decca Records rejected a group called the Beatles; more US soldiers were sent to Vietnam; the Cuban missile crisis ended when Krushchev agreed to dismantle missile sites; astronaut John Glenn orbited the earth; Polaris missiles were agreed for British submarines; Selwyn Lloyd fuelled the consumer boom by cutting purchase tax on cars and domestic appliances, and a Mini cost from £459 19s 3d; the first colour supplement was launched by *The Sunday Times*, and Peter Cook rescued *Private Eye*; Pop Art was created by Andy Warhol, who unveiled his painting of a Campbell's soup can; William Vassall was convicted of spying; James Hanratty was sentenced to death; the Liberals won Orpington; and Marilyn Monroe was found dead.

## ARTHUR SMITH'S 1962 LIONS

Arthur Smith was a truly delightful man and a player with great erudition, having achieved a first-class degree in mathematics at Glasgow and then a Ph.D. at Cambridge. He was a fine, quiet man and therein lies a tale, for on the 1955 tour, Arthur was put to share a room with a player who shall remain nameless. Suffice to say that he was a fairly nervous individual, and found that Arthur was prone to long silences and to ignoring him whenever he entered or left the room. He became so upset that he asked the manager to move him, which caused a minor crisis, for it would seem odd to change room-mates in the middle of a week. The player insisted, so the management decided to put a harder-headed person in with him, to discover what the problem was. I was elected and so I moved in and said, 'Hello, Arthur. I'm your new room-mate,' only to be greeted with an absent-minded shrug of the shoulders. That evening, I went up to the room to see Arthur sitting on the bed and he was in a world of his own, so I snapped my fingers under his nose and said, 'A penny for them.' He seemed to wake with a start and said, 'I'm sorry. I was working out a maths problem, as I am studying for my Ph.D.' He could not understand my amusement and was a little startled when I explained what it was about, while Jack Siggins sighed with relief to discover there was no problem after all.

Arthur was a wing of extraordinary ability, and few have ever had his remarkable control of pace. He was a brainy rugby man, who never really shone on his first Lions tour in 1955, because he broke a bone in his wrist at the start and played only four matches. He did not, however, waste the time when he was unable to play but used it to practise, becoming a first-class goal kicker.

Following Avril Malan's 1961 Springboks team to Britain and Ireland, when they lost only their last match against the Barbarians, the

Home Unions' selectors chose the biggest Lions pack ever to leave the British Isles. The 1955 Lions had only three forwards over 15 stone, while Smith's team had nine, including Keith Rowlands (who became secretary of the International Board in 1987), Willie John McBride, Mike Campbell-Lamerton, Bill Mulcahy, David Nash, Syd Millar, Peter Wright, Kingsley Jones and John Douglas. They also had the magnificent Bryn Meredith, restored as hooker, and some fine back-row forwards, including Alun Pask who, although he was in his prime as a number eight, was made to play on the blind side. This was because of the tactical decision of the manager, Brian Vaughan, to go for power and he therefore wanted Campbell-Lamerton, his biggest forward, locking the scrum in the middle of the back row.

As a result, the Lions were never able to dominate the loose play around the scrum, at the back of the lineout, or in the tackle situation and broken play. The ignoring of non-specialist players in key positions can often make the difference between success and failure. Furthermore these Lions, although they had some splendid backs in their captain Smith, Richard Sharp, a tremendous and elegant player on his day, Ken Jones, Dewi Bebb, and the durable Jeeps, a combative rather than a perceptive scrum-half, they had no one, especially at half-back, to light the spark. The solid Gordon Waddell and Mike Weston, who played in all four Tests at centre, but were often pressed into service at fly-half, were more strong tactical kickers than sharp runners, which is what is required on the hard grounds of South Africa.

The manager, Brian Vaughan, a naval commander who was involved in the commissioning of the first nuclear submarines, did not have the benefit of a coach, so he took the job on himself. A man of excellent rugby pedigree, being a former England forward, he was convinced that they could beat South Africa by winning possession. However, they gained a reputation for being a static team, unable to dominate in loose play, and therefore failed to produce any flair in attack, which was a traditional feature of previous Lions teams in the Republic. These Lions lacked nothing in commitment, especially in tight forward play, where they stretched the Springboks to the limit. The hugely experienced rugby correspondent Terry O'Connor thought that Vaughan was one of the very best managers he had toured with and that he never got the recognition he deserved.

They lost five matches, including three Test matches, and drew four. Their only provincial defeats were against Northern Transvaal and Eastern Transvaal, but they also drew with two provinces, Griqualand West and Orange Free State, and with Northern Universities.

Nevertheless, the Test matches, except for the fourth, were very closely contested. Richard Sharp was not available for the first two Tests, because of that *cause célèbre* which is still talked about, when Mannetjies Roux, playing for Northern Transvaal, hit him with a high tackle which saw his head inflict a broken cheekbone on the luckless Sharp who, in the manner of the perfect gentleman (which was one of his hallmarks), never made a complaint. The British camp were incensed, for they had seen other examples of Roux's recklessness in this respect, including a similar tackle on Alun Priday in Cardiff the year before. Many South Africans also protested, but Roux was still included in the first Test.

The first Test was drawn, and the second lost 3–0. The third was at 3–3 when a blunder cost the Lions the series, and it was only in the final one that the Springboks came out firmly on top and won by a large margin.

The first Test at Ellis Park was a poor affair, memorable only for two tremendous tries, one scored by each side, and also for the fact that Johannes Claassen was preferred to Avril Malan as captain. The great South African wing, Jannie Engelbrecht, withdrew with injury and Mof Myburgh, the huge Northern Transvaal prop, made his debut.

The problem was that the two packs were so evenly matched that neither side could achieve ascendancy. A few minutes before half-time, Ken Jones kicked for touch, Roux fielded and, switching direction, put Johnny Gainsford, the superlative Springboks centre and one of their all-time greats, away on a decisive run for a try in the corner. Ken Jones made amends for his earlier error when he scored the equaliser ten minutes from the end. John Wilcox gathered a kick ahead in his own 25 and counter-attacked; when he was tackled, the ball went loose and Waddell picked up and gave to Jones, who jinked his way through the defence and raced 60 yards to score. Alas, Smith's conversion attempt failed.

The second Test, in Kings Park, Durban, brought another of those hugely controversial refereeing decisions, which often coloured tours abroad and which ultimately led to the production of neutral referees in 1980. It was another tight, undistinguished and close-run affair, with the Springboks leading 3–0 from a 35-yard penalty by Keith Oxlee, kicked five minutes from time. In the last minute, the Springboks were penalised for a crooked throw at a lineout on their own line and, as the scrum went down, Mulcahy called for a hold and a wheel which went like a dream and, as had been the plan, Keith Rowlands fell on the ball. The referee, Ken Carlson of East London, declared that he was unsighted and disallowed the try, to the intense annoyance of the Lions forwards, who were certain that the try should have stood. Keith

Rowlands claimed that he scored the try and, as he is a man of integrity, I believe that the referee made a grave error of judgement.

The score stood at 3–0, at the final whistle of a Test which had seen the dropping of Avril Malan and the moving of Frik du Preez, one of South Africa's mightiest forwards, from flank to lock. It also saw the introduction at scrum-half of another Springboks legend, Dawie de Villiers, who was to become South Africa's ambassador to London and a minister in the South African government. The Lions made two changes: Dewi Bebb at left wing for Niall Brophy, and Haydn Morgan for Budge Rogers.

Richard Sharp recovered to play in the third test and Tom Kiernan came in for Wilcox. The interest was so intense that the largest crowd in the history of Newlands in Cape Town up to that time (54,843) were shoe-horned into the ground and another 4,000 were locked out. This set the scene for another grim struggle between the two packs. Bryn Meredith showed that he was the best hooker of his era and the Lions dominated the set pieces, but in the loose play the Springboks had the edge, with Doug Hopwood, that immense number eight, always in the vanguard of the Springboks forward onslaughts.

Sharp drew first blood with a 30-yard drop goal, but this was nullified with a penalty from Keith Oxlee when the Lions were penalised for hands in a ruck, to make it 3–3 at half-time. The score stood until eight minutes from the end of a dour game, enlivened only by a fine run by Engelbrecht from his own 25, but he was called back as the pass from Gainsford was deemed forward. Next came an ill-advised attempt by Sharp to open up from his own line, from a heel against the head by Meredith. The Springboks defence closed in and Ken Jones, receiving a hospital pass, was flattened in a tackle and the ball went loose. It was Oxlee who scooped it up to weave his way over for a try, which he also converted for the Springboks to win the match 8–3. The conversion was a milestone, for it brought up 1,001 points in South African Test history.

The mobility of the Lions pack suffered further as Pask broke a rib when flung into touch in that third Test and the selectors made a few strange decisions. They brought Bill Mulcahy onto the flank in his place and D.P. Rogers, who was to win 34 caps for England, took over from Haydn Morgan. Wilcox regained his place at full-back and Hewitt played in the centre in place of Jones, while Brophy replaced Dewi Bebb, and Dickie Jeeps took over the captaincy from the injured Arthur Smith.

Although the series was lost, there was a capacity crowd at Bloemfontein for the final Test, which the Springboks won by 34–14, the most points scored by them in a Test in South Africa. Keith Oxlee, the Natal fly-half, after scoring all the points in the third Test, finished as the star of the series with a record 16 points in this final Test, one more than Okey Geffin's 15 points against the All Blacks in 1949.

The score was only 10–6 to the Springboks at half-time from tries by Roux and Wyness, both converted by Oxlee, to a penalty by John Wilcox and a try by Ronnie Cowan. In the second half, Gainsford proceeded to slash open the Lions' defence and scored a try, before Rowlands replied with one for the Lions, converted by Wilcox. It was still anybody's game at 13–11, before the Springboks went on a scoring spree of 13 points in six minutes. Oxlee kicked a penalty and a typically thrilling run by Frik du Preez, for van Zyl to score and Oxlee to convert, began the rot. This was quickly followed by a try by Claassen, again converted by Oxlee, and the Lions were undone. A further penalty by Oxlee and a great try by Roux, with an Oxlee conversion, completed South Africa's scoring and Campbell-Lamerton got a consolation last try for the Lions.

History should not judge the 1962 Lions harshly, for they could quite easily have won the series with better selection, a bit more luck and different tactics.

## Results of the 1962 Lions in South Africa

P 25  W 16  D 4  L 5  F 401  A 208

| | | | |
|---|---|---|---|
| Rhodesia | W | 38 | 9 |
| Griqualand West | D | 8 | 8 |
| Western Transvaal | W | 11 | 6 |
| Southern Universities | W | 14 | 11 |
| Boland | W | 25 | 8 |
| South West Africa | W | 14 | 6 |
| Northern Transvaal | L | 6 | 14 |
| South Africa (Johannesburg) | D | 3 | 3 |
| Natal | W | 13 | 3 |
| Eastern Province | W | 21 | 6 |
| Orange Free State | D | 14 | 14 |
| Junior Springboks | W | 16 | 11 |
| Combined Services | W | 20 | 6 |
| Western Province | W | 21 | 13 |
| South Western Districts | W | 11 | 3 |
| South Africa (Durban) | L | 0 | 3 |
| Northern Universities | D | 6 | 6 |

| Transvaal | W | 24 | 3 |
|---|---|---|---|
| South Africa (Cape Town) | L | 3 | 8 |
| North Eastern Districts | W | 34 | 8 |
| Border | W | 5 | 0 |
| Central Universities | W | 14 | 6 |
| Eastern Transvaal | L | 16 | 19 |
| South Africa (Bloemfontein) | L | 14 | 34 |
| East Africa | W | 50 | 0 |

## Arthur Smith's 1962 Lions team

**Full-backs**

| T.J. Kiernan | University College Cork | Ireland |
|---|---|---|
| J.G. Wilcox | Oxford University | England |

**Three-quarters**

| D.I.E. Bebb | Swansea | Wales |
|---|---|---|
| N.H. Brophy | University College Dublin | Ireland |
| R.C. Cowan | Selkirk | Scotland |
| J.M. Dee | Hartlepool Rovers | England |
| D. Hewitt | Queen's University Belfast | Ireland |
| W.R. Hunter | CIYMS | Ireland |
| D.K. Jones | Llanelli | Wales |
| A.R. Smith (capt.) | Edinburgh Wanderers | Scotland |
| M.P. Weston | Durham City | England |

**Half-backs**

| H.J.C. Brown* | Blackheath & RAF | |
|---|---|---|
| R.E.G. Jeeps | Northampton | England |
| A. O'Connor | Aberavon | Wales |
| R.A.W. Sharp | Oxford University | England |
| G.H. Waddell | London Scottish | Scotland |

**Forwards**

| M.J. Campbell-Lamerton | Army & Halifax | Scotland |
|---|---|---|
| G.D. Davidge* | Newport | Wales |
| J. Douglas | Stewart's College FP | Scotland |
| H.O. Godwin* | Coventry | England |
| S.A.M. Hodgson | Durham City | England |
| K.D. Jones | Cardiff | Wales |
| W.J. McBride | Ballymena | Ireland |
| B.V. Meredith | Newport | Wales |

| S. Millar | Ballymena | Ireland |
| H.J. Morgan | Abertillery | Wales |
| W.A. Mulcahy | Bohemians | Ireland |
| D. Nash | Ebbw Vale | Wales |
| A.E.I. Pask | Abertillery | Wales |
| D.P. Rogers | Bedford | England |
| D.M.D. Rollo | Howe of Fife | Scotland |
| K.A. Rowlands | Cardiff | Wales |
| T.P. Wright | Blackheath | England |

Manager: Commander D.B. Vaughan RN
Assistant Manager: H.R. McKibbin

* Replacements

## M.J. CAMPBELL-LAMERTON'S 1966 LIONS

They may have been the 'Swinging Sixties', but the 1966 British Lions never really got in on the mood. London was declared the swinging capital of the world, with Carnaby Street the centre of the new young fashion. England beat West Germany to take the soccer World Cup; Mao Tse-tung proclaimed the Cultural Revolution with his little red book and Brezhnev became the Soviet leader; the Moors murderers were sentenced to life imprisonment and Verwoerd, father of apartheid, was knifed; Arkle won the Cheltenham Gold Cup; the Pope and the Archbishop of Canterbury met officially for the first time in 400 years; Freddie Laker formed a new cut-price airline; Gwynfor Evans became the first Welsh nationalist MP; Australian troops were sent to Vietnam; Lord Thomson bought *The Times* newspaper; and an unmanned spaceship landed on the moon.

Although they went unbeaten in the eight matches of the Australian first leg of their tour and beat Australia by 31–0 in the last Test in Brisbane, the 1966 Lions, once they crossed the Tasman Sea, gained a reputation for being an indifferent side. Having come to New Zealand with a name for playing fast open rugby during the Australian leg of the tour, they then seemed to go into a shell. In New Zealand, they lost all four Test matches in a series for the first time, three of them by a large margin, and stumbled raggedly through their provincial games, where they lost four and drew two. On the way home, they were also to lose to British Columbia.

It was the first Lions tour to have a coach, instead of an assistant manager, in J.D. Robins. There was considerable surprise and controversy, especially in Wales, when the team was announced and Mike Campbell-Lamerton was made captain instead of Alun Pask, who had skippered Wales to the Five Nations Championship that season. This was exacerbated when Campbell-Lamerton came under considerable pressure from the New Zealand press for his lack of form, and failed to win a place in two of the Tests. However, it must be said that he was a man of considerable courage, and to agree to leaving himself out was a measure of his quality as an individual and as a captain. Not many of his predecessors would have done that, except for Douglas Prentice.

If they were not good enough players, they were, like most Lions teams, good tourists, and remained popular with the New Zealand public. It must be remembered, too, that it was an immensely long and arduous tour, sharing with the first British party of 1888 the record for the longest tour, comprising 35 matches. They got off on the wrong foot before they left the UK because of press controversy, and they became an unhappy touring party, failing to adjust to New Zealand conditions and attitudes.

According to Vivian Jenkins, the vastly experienced *Sunday Times* rugby correspondent at that time, 'There is also the question of whether a team has enjoyed itself on tour. I regret to report that, while nearly every one of the touring party said he would love to come back to New Zealand again as an ordinary visitor, not one of them (and this was confirmed to me by the manager, Des O'Brien) wanted to return there to play rugby.

'Competition taken to extreme, as it is in New Zealand, produces things that, to our own players, are not worth the ends involved. Dirty play is one of them and there was more than enough of this on tour. Kicks on the head, which necessitate stitches, or broken noses from stiff arm tackles, do not come under the heading of hard play, to which no rugby man objects. Instead, they are just plain dirty. No doubt we will be accused of squealing, the usual New Zealand comeback, but the only alternative is to stay silent and respond in kind, and what kind of a game does that make rugby?'

One wonders whether these words, and the outburst by Jim Telfer after he captained them in a provincial match, were the catalyst for the two later tours of 1971 and 1974, when the Lions coined those emotive phrases of 'Get your retaliation in first' and 'Take no prisoners'.

There was constant criticism by the New Zealand press concerning the lack of leadership at all levels. Terry McLean, the great New Zealand rugby journalist, said, 'The British, at times, played shamefully badly, but nobody really cracked the whip. I must be blunt – the trouble was leadership. The discipline within the party was not sufficiently strong for the demands and rigours of the tour. The manager and assistant manager were both charming men, but neither had much taste for cracking the whip. They both preferred quietness and the appeal to the intellect. The series represented a clash between style and method, the classic style of the Lions and the powerful workaday method of the All Blacks. Method, as it so often does, triumphed, but style at its best, as portrayed by Mike Gibson with the breadth and quality of his attack, is superior to method.'

Wilson Whineray, the illustrious All Blacks captain, said, 'It is clear in retrospect that the Lions' decision, made early in the tour, to play the All Blacks up front was wrong. They suffered from battling to narrow wins, or not winning at all, and the spectators suffered from watching dreary rugby.' He went on to say: 'I believe a team should play to its strength, and the Lions' greatest strength was their backs. Their outstanding back was Mike Gibson, who played in 19 of the 25 games in New Zealand. Stewart Wilson, Dewi Bebb and David Watkins all had good tours, and A.J. 'Sandy' Hinshelwood and Colin McFadyean were strong elusive runners. Of the forwards, W.J. McBride was a giant in every sense of the word; Roger Lamont and Noel Murphy were outstanding loose forwards, but there was a need for a quick flanker. The front row were strong and durable, while both hookers, Ken Kennedy and Frank Laidlaw, were splendid players.'

The manager was castigated for taking a holiday in Fiji during the tour, but this was at the suggestion of the New Zealand Rugby Union, who were concerned at the pressure which Des O'Brien was put under. Make no mistake, the demands of a British Lions tour are intense, and unquestionably some tour managements have cracked, or at the least showed signs of buckling, under it all.

There was no problem on the Australian part of the tour, which the Lions sailed through, winding up unbeaten, an achievement no team had matched since Bedell-Sivright's team in 1904. It was a pretty good effort, considering that Australia had Ken Catchpole, one of the greatest of all scrum-halves, with Hawthorne at fly-half and Peter Ryan at full-back, not to mention Tony Miller, John Thornett, Peter Crittle, Ron Heming, Jules Guerassimoff and Greg Davies in the forwards. The only real resistance to them came from New South Wales, where a Combined Country XV held them to 6–3, and the New South Wales team itself, then the heart of Australian rugby, held them to a 6–6 draw in the ten days before the first Test in Sydney.

There was an Australian record crowd of 42,303 for a rugby union game at the Sydney Cricket Ground, which was probably due to the

League cancelling a big match on an adjoining ground in deference to the tourists. Although it was an open and exciting game, it was marked by too many mistakes by the Lions backs and, in the end, it was the pack which won the game for them. It was this which perhaps clouded judgement for the New Zealand part of the tour. Australia held the lead at half-time by a bullocking try from the 37-year-old veteran Tony Miller, converted by George Ruebner, who also kicked a penalty, to give Australia a useful lead at the interval.

In the second half, Don Rutherford, later to become England's technical director through their glory days of the early 1990s and who played a large part in shaping these events, then kicked a penalty for the Lions. This was followed by a try, when Ray McLoughlin went around the front of a lineout and got the touchdown, which Rutherford converted to make it 8–8.

The Lions' winning try was spectacular, started again by McLoughlin going around the front of the lineout with the forwards interpassing, before the ball was flung out to the elegant Mike Weston, who wrong-footed the defence with a weaving run before throwing out a long pass for Ken Kennedy to get over in the corner.

Easily disposing of Queensland, who in those days were a minor force, the Lions then, horror of horrors, were forced to play their final Test at Lang Park, the rugby league ground, for there was no suitable union venue. My, how times have changed! For without the special dispensation of rugby union's Vatican, the International Rugby Board, which was in keeping with other irregularities allowed in Australia in order to combat rugby league, the players would have professionalised themselves. It is hard to believe that such nonsense existed until very recently.

The Lions ran away with the game, which was astonishing, considering that the Wallabies had recently beaten the Springboks and the All Blacks, and were to beat Wales at Cardiff a few months later. Remarkably, these Lions recorded the biggest winning Test match score of 31–0 against any country in their whole history.

The first half gave no indication of the deluge to come, as they reached the interval leading by a mere three points from a penalty in the first minute by Stewart Wilson. Soon after the restart, David Watkins dropped a goal and then, after 18 minutes of the half, the Lions scored 25 points in 22 minutes. Ken Jones, Noel Murphy, Dewi Bebb, David Watkins and Ken Jones again scored the tries and Wilson, who had the game of his life, converted all five, as well as having a major hand in a few of them. Pask had lived up to his reputation as the world's finest number eight, and Wilson, David Watkins, Ken Jones and Dewi Bebb all appeared class players.

The Lions were quickly brought down to earth by losing their first provincial game in New Zealand against Southland, which was a bit like losing to the North of Scotland, for Invercargill is to New Zealand what Inverness is to Scotland. (Incidentally, Chris Rea, the 1971 Lion who became a well-respected commentator on the game, once accused an English journalist of sitting on every fence from Invercargill to Inverness.) They went on to lose their next two Saturday games against Otago and Wellington, and the writing was on the wall.

The Lions arrived at Dunedin for the first Test with three losses and a draw from nine games, and a tally of 113 points for to 106 against, a clear indication that they were not playing fluent rugby. It is true that never at any time in New Zealand were they going well. They failed to put up a score over 20 points, apart from the game against the universities and the games at Nelson and West Coast–Buller against the up-country sides, when you usually expect a big win or two.

The omens were bad and, when you consider that the New Zealand pack contained forwards of the quality of the incomparable Colin Meads in his tenth season for the All Blacks, and all-time greats like Ken Gray, Waka Nathan, Brian Lochore and Kel Tremain, with Chris Laidlaw at scrum-half, then you have to feel some sympathy for those 1966 Lions. On the other hand, the Lions pack contained many fine forwards like McBride, McLoughlin, Kennedy, Murphy, Pask, Price, Telfer, Thomas and Williams, and some very useful backs. It seems that they failed tactically and by vacillation in selection.

In the first Test, the first half was even, but ended with New Zealand leading 8–3, following a try by McLeod converted by Williment. Wilson replied with a penalty for the Lions and 'Mac' Herewini put over a drop goal. In the second half, Williment and Lochore scored tries, but Williment missed both conversions. He did, however, kick two more penalties to make it 20–3.

It was in this match that the Lions encountered the new catchphrase, 'second-phase possession of the ball', which has become ensconced in rugby vocabulary. This consisted of a midfield player, usually the second five-eighth or inside centre, allowing himself to be tackled, and turning in order to set up the feed from the subsequent ruck and, having drawn some of the defence, being able to attack again against a disorganised defence. Ian MacRae was the arch exponent of this ploy.

The Lions pulled themselves together and won the next five games, including those against Canterbury and Auckland, who were two of the big four provincial teams.

The matter of dirty play continued to haunt the tour and, on the eve of the second Test at Athletic Park, Wellington, no less than the

Governor General was called upon, together with the chairman of the New Zealand Rugby Union, to have a talk with the captains of the two teams.

The Lions made six changes for the match, including their captain: out went Ken Jones and Roger Young in the backs, and Alun Pask, Brian Price, Ken Kennedy and Campbell-Lamerton in the forwards; while in came Sandy Hinshelwood and Alan Lewis behind the scrum, and Delme Thomas, Noel Murphy, Willie John McBride and Frank Laidlaw in the forwards.

It was to be the closest affair and, on a typical Wellington winter's day of wind, rain and mud, the Lions led 9–8 at half-time. Wilson kicked a penalty and Tremain scored a try for the All Blacks, converted by Williment, before a drop goal by Watkins and another penalty by Wilson took the Lions ahead. In the second half, Colin Meads crashed over and Williment converted, then an unconverted try by the Canterbury winger Steel and another penalty by Wilson saw the All Blacks home by 16–12. The game was almost saved in the dying moments, when Delme Thomas made a 50-yard run, but his pass within yards of the line went astray.

The third Test in Christchurch, in cold and slippery conditions, saw the Lions, after being 6–6 at half-time with two penalties by Williment to two tries by Ronnie Lamont and David Watkins, committing too many errors, just as they seemed to have the legs of New Zealand. Consequently, the All Blacks won 19–6, with Steel scoring a try and Waka Nathan getting two tries from his formidable support and backing up, with Williment adding a final conversion to give the All Blacks another comfortable win.

Even though the All Blacks had already won the series, there was a crowd of 58,000 at Eden Park for the final Test, which at the time provided record gate receipts of £43,000 for any match in New Zealand's rugby history. It was a perfect day, with a firm ground and plenty of sunshine.

Again the Lions, after losing Pask with a broken collarbone after 27 minutes, were outplayed by the superlative All Blacks pack and had no answer to the aggression of their forwards in the loose. Nathan opened the scoring with a try from a quick throw-in at a lineout and Williment converted. Malcolm Dick then scored a try, converted by Williment, but then a fine try by Hinshelwood and another by McFadyean, after a brilliant run by Gibson and converted by Wilson, made it 10–8 at half-time. Twenty-four minutes into the second period, MacRae scored a try, converted by Williment, and it was followed by a drop goal by Herewini and a try by Steel. Although Wilson got another penalty for the Lions, the final points came from Williment's boot with a penalty, to make it another decisive win for the All Blacks. It was the first four-match whitewash New Zealand had ever recorded against a touring team.

To add to their woes, the Lions lost to British Columbia on the way home from this punishing and wearisome tour, which took over five months in total. They then won the final game against Canada, none too convincingly, by 19–8. It will be hard to believe in future times that the team did all this soldiering, putting their bodies on the line, without any recompense and simply for the love of the game.

## Results of the 1966 Lions in Australia, New Zealand and Canada

P 35   W 23   D 3   L 9   F 524   A 345

| | | | |
|---|---|---|---|
| Western Australia | W | 60 | 3 |
| South Australia | W | 38 | 11 |
| Victoria | W | 24 | 14 |
| Combined Country XV | W | 6 | 3 |
| New South Wales | D | 6 | 6 |
| Australia (Sydney) | W | 11 | 8 |
| Queensland | W | 26 | 3 |
| Australia (Brisbane) | W | 31 | 0 |
| | | | |
| Southland | L | 8 | 14 |
| South Canterbury, North Otago & Mid Canterbury | W | 20 | 12 |
| Otago | L | 9 | 17 |
| New Zealand Universities | W | 24 | 11 |
| Wellington | L | 6 | 20 |
| Marlborough, Nelson, Golden Bay & Motueka | W | 22 | 14 |
| Taranaki | W | 12 | 9 |
| Bay of Plenty | D | 6 | 6 |
| North Auckland | W | 6 | 3 |
| New Zealand (Dunedin) | L | 3 | 20 |
| West Coast–Buller | W | 25 | 6 |
| Canterbury | W | 8 | 6 |
| Manawatu–Horowhenua | W | 17 | 8 |
| Auckland | W | 12 | 6 |
| Wairarapa–Bush | W | 9 | 6 |

| | | | |
|---|---|---|---|
| New Zealand (Wellington) | L | 12 | 16 |
| Wanganui–King Country | L | 6 | 12 |
| New Zealand Maoris | W | 16 | 14 |
| East Coast–Poverty Bay | W | 9 | 6 |
| Hawke's Bay | D | 11 | 11 |
| New Zealand (Christchurch) | L | 6 | 19 |
| New Zealand Juniors | W | 9 | 3 |
| Waikato | W | 20 | 9 |
| Thames Valley–Counties | W | 13 | 9 |
| New Zealand (Auckland) | L | 11 | 24 |
| | | | |
| British Columbia | L | 3 | 8 |
| Canada (Toronto) | W | 19 | 8 |

## Campbell-Lamerton's 1966 Lions team

**Full-backs**

| | | |
|---|---|---|
| T.G. Price* | Llanelli | Wales |
| D. Rutherford | Gloucester | England |
| S. Wilson | London Scottish | Scotland |

**Three-quarters**

| | | |
|---|---|---|
| D.I.E. Bebb | Swansea | Wales |
| F.P.K. Bresnihan* | Wanderers | Ireland |
| A.J.W. Hinshelwood | London Scottish | Scotland |
| D.K. Jones | Cardiff | Wales |
| C.W. McFadyean | Moseley | England |
| K.F. Savage | Northampton | England |
| J.C. Walsh | Sunday's Well | Ireland |
| S.J. Watkins | Newport | Wales |
| M.P. Weston | Durham City | England |

**Half-backs**

| | | |
|---|---|---|
| C.M.H. Gibson | Cambridge University | Ireland |
| A.R. Lewis | Newport | Wales |
| D. Watkins | Newport | Wales |
| R.M. Young | Queen's University Belfast | Ireland |

**Forwards**

| | | |
|---|---|---|
| M.J. Campbell-Lamerton (capt.) | London Scottish | Scotland |
| D. Grant | Hawick | Scotland |

| K.W. Kennedy | CIYMS | Ireland |
|---|---|---|
| F.A.L. Laidlaw | Melrose | Scotland |
| R.A. Lamont | Instonians | Ireland |
| W.J. McBride | Ballymena | Ireland |
| R.J. McLoughlin | Gosforth | Ireland |
| N.A.A. Murphy | Cork Constitution | Ireland |
| C.H. Norris | Cardiff | Wales |
| A.E.I. Pask | Abertillery | Wales |
| D.L. Powell | Northampton | England |
| B. Price | Newport | Wales |
| G.J. Prothero | Bridgend | Wales |
| J.W. Telfer | Melrose | Scotland |
| W.D. Thomas | Llanelli | |
| D. Williams | Ebbw Vale | Wales |

Manager: D.J. O'Brien
Coach: J.D. Robins

\* Replacements

## Tom Kiernan's 1968 Lions

1968 was another troubled year for the British Lions, as it was nationally and internationally. The economy was in trouble and five typists from Surbiton began an 'I'm backing Britain' campaign, promising to work an extra half-hour a day for nothing. George Brown resigned as Foreign Secretary; Yuri Gagarin died in a plane crash and Russian tanks crushed Prague. D'Oliviera was dropped from the South African cricket tour because of his colour; student strikes and demonstrations disrupted Paris and other French cities; and there was a state of anarchy in colleges in Britain. The 22-storey building Ronan Point collapsed; and the first sextuplets were born in Britain. Martin Luther King was assasinated and Bobby Kennedy was shot. Tony Hancock committed suicide and *The Forsythe Saga* gripped television audiences.

The 1968 Lions were the 20th British team to tour abroad and were under the management of the irrepressible David Brooks. The coach was Ronnie Dawson and the captain Tom Kiernan. This tour actually did much better than their Test record suggests. They managed to draw the second Test, but lost the other three, two of them by the narrow margin of five points. Had the third Test been won, then they would have been hailed as a fine side, because their provincial record was superb; they lost only to Transvaal. The main blot on their copybook was that of the 38 points they scored during the Test rubber, 35 came from penalties and they scored only one try. Those 35 points were all scored by Kiernan, which gave him the record for the most points in a series until Gavin Hastings broke it in 1993 with 38.

The Tours Committee took more care than usual in choosing their management and David Brooks was appointed a season in advance of the tour. He was fond of saying that there was no truth in the rumour that he was the first computer appointment. Ronnie Dawson was selected because he had knowledge of South African conditions, having toured there twice before.

There was more than a smattering of illustrious players in the side, with forwards such as the ever-present Willie John McBride and Syd Millar, together with Ken Goodall, Jim Telfer, Rodger Arneil, John Pullin, Tony Horton, Bob Taylor and Peter Stagg, who at 6ft 8ins was the tallest man ever seen in the home internationals up to that time. Behind the scrum they had the burgeoning talents of Gareth Edwards and Barry John; this tour was their finishing school, before they were let loose to become the scourge of the other Home Unions and the All Blacks in 1971. The Lions also had Gerald Davies, still a centre in those days, the magnificent wing Maurice Richards and, of course, the superb Mike Gibson, who on the tour became the first British player to win an international cap as a replacement when he came on for Barry John in the first Test. Behind them, they had the unwavering Tom Kiernan, who was a good captain and another fine ambassador for Irish rugby.

Rugby in the British Isles was at a low ebb at the end of the 1967–68 season, and although the Lions did far better than people expected, they were not strong enough to beat the Springboks, who scored eight tries to one in the series. Nevertheless, Danie Craven said of them, 'The Lions were a good team, well prepared and well coached. How near they came to beating us in the series is something we are inclined to overlook. It is true that we beat them convincingly in the first and last internationals, but in both those matches the important turning points came our way. The Lions gave us grey hairs and it was a great achievement to have beaten them in the internationals.'

A major criticism of the tour was that, in common with most Lions teams of the past, they did not take matters too seriously, and that enjoyment of the experience of touring was the primary consideration, with rugby of secondary importance. This is perhaps an over-simplification, but in essence it had an element of truth, for there can be no question that most British teams overseas did not have the same inner driving force and commitment which seems to impel and activate the psyche of the antipodeans or the South Africans. In the dressing-room of the Australian cricket team in the Sydney Cricket Ground, known as the SCG, there is written in letters about nine inches high 'We shall not fail on the score of determination', which just about sums it up.

On the 1968 tour, there was a growing media presence as the tabloids, who used to treat rugby like the plague until its popularity forced them to sit up and take notice, began reporting those matters which the players regarded as sacrosanct, namely their social activities. Very quickly the 1968 team became dubbed 'the wreckers', due to their inclination for a good party, and David Brooks became regarded as the gang foreman. Anyone who knows David as I do, will understand that he regards life as fun and thinks that nothing should stand in the way of letting it be lived amusingly and to the full.

The parties were, on occasions, fairly riotous and I gather that Willie John and a few others were not averse to giving it a crack, as they say in Irish. At the party after the first Test, Willie John slipped and needed eight stitches in his leg and two in a finger. Having lost the first and drawn the second Test, the third in Cape Town was critical for the series. Consequently, when they lost, the scene was set for a really big party. They were staying in Cape Town Hotel, run by the delightful Jeff Reynolds, himself a 1938 Lion. To cut a long story short, it turned out to be quite a night and, as they left the debris surrounding them the next morning, Jeff presented a bill for the damages, which he had halved and halved again, for he is that sort of man. It still came to about £900, but apparently Brooky, as the team called him, did not turn a hair. Instead he signed the account with a flourish, accompanied by the remark, 'Huh! It couldn't have been a very good party!' which, one has to admit, had a bit of style about it. For all that, David Brooks was a first-class manager and he engendered an excellent spirit in the team and, despite coming from four different nations, they were as united as any Lions team has ever been or will ever be. His players were fond of him and, had they won that second or third Test, Brooks would have been remembered as one of the great managers.

One South African newspaper headline said of them, 'No angels, but no oafs'. There was no criminal damage done; it was all horseplay and whooping it up. The only things that got broken were glasses and a few items of bedroom furniture, with beds being particularly prone to damage, seeing as one of the purposes of the wreckers was to tip sleepers out of their beds. The Loyal Order of Wreckers was launched at Mossel Bay, but Gareth Edwards reckoned that they were formed on a long train ride to the Kruger Park, and officially recognised at Salisbury.

After being presented with some fancy cigarette lighters as presents, they also formed a splinter group called 'the burners'. They held a symbolic burning of shirts belonging to players and members of the press, and of girls' knickers, outside the hotel in Cape Town after the Boland match, probably in disappointment at having lost Gareth Edwards that afternoon with a badly pulled hamstring, which was to keep him out of the third and fourth Tests. As an antidote to both groups, that marvellous man Bob Hiller, who was destined to be a 'dirt-tracker' for two tours because of the presence of Kiernan as captain in 1968 and of the peerless J.P.R. Williams in 1974, formed an alternative pacifist group called 'the kippers'. Bob was one of those essential men who led the midweek team and helped to keep them motivated; tours without a leader of the 'dirt-trackers' usually struck problems in the provincial games.

Once again the back play of these Lions, as it was throughout the 1960s, became too stereotyped. They continually used the ploy of the kick ahead, which was so prevalent in British rugby at that time. Consequently, there was no way they could be creative and this showed up in the Test matches. Another weakness was bad finishing. They never found themselves in the backs and again a long injury list, endemic on the hard and fast grounds of South Africa, must take some of the blame. But for the excellent goal kicking of Kiernan and Hiller, their problems would have been far worse.

Apparently, Mike Gibson had a disappointing tour at fly-half, which suggests that his true position was at centre, where he was to excel in 1971. The injury to Barry John in the first Test was, perhaps, one of the tragedies of the tour.

Having won their first six games leading up to the first Test at Loftus Versveld in Pretoria, the Lions were in good heart and optimistic. It was a disappointing match, however, considering the perfect conditions and the hard ground. Although the Lions lost by a mere five points, they were well beaten and only 17 points from Kiernan's boot kept them in the game. The loss of Barry John midway through the first half, when he was upended by Jan Ellis and broke his collarbone, was critical, for he was the only player who looked likely to open up the middle. History was being made, as the International Board allowed four replacements to be nominated to take the place of injured players. Why, again, they took so long to make this decision is one of life's great mysteries.

Seventy-five thousand spectators jammed themselves into those towering stands at Loftus and watched 45 points being scored, the same as that first Test in 1955, but the game had none of the drama or the running skills of the earlier occasion. Instead, it was a game ridden with error and the Springboks were simply too good for the Lions. The score was hardly a reflection of how the game went and, as Tom Kiernan remarked afterwards, 'Fancy me scoring 17 points and being on the losing team!'

Tiny Naude, Dawie de Villiers and Frik du Preez scored tries for the Springboks, and Visagie added two penalty goals and two conversions. Willie John scored the only Lions try and Kiernan slammed over five penalties and a conversion, to establish a record of the most points scored by an individual in a Test against South Africa. It was a typical try by Frik du Preez which was the highlight of the game when, like a rhinoceros at full gallop, he steamed through the front of a lineout and through about six defenders for an unstoppable try. The Lions had made much use of the short three-man lineout, but mistakes and the looseness of their play worked against them, and the Springboks won easily.

Two more wins, and their only defeat in the provincial games, preceded the second Test in Port Elizabeth, which produced a huge controversy over the referee, J.P. Schoeman, who was appointed by the South African Board from outside the panel. The refereeing was bizarre, as he allowed the Springboks to double-bank at the lineouts, and he penalised the Lions so mercilessly in the scrums that, in the end, Gareth Edwards was afraid to put the ball in. The order was then given by the senior prop, Syd Millar, not to strike for the ball. There followed a week of recriminations and negotiations, because the Lions knew that the admirable John Pullin of England was a totally fair striker of the ball, and they felt that they could not compete with such eccentric refereeing. Terry O'Connor, in *The Daily Mail*, suggested that the Lions should go home in protest against the refereeing.

It finally blew over, as such matters usually do, but when touring in those days you always had to be on your toes over such matters. It was amazing how often they seemed to occur.

The game was drawn 6–6, as the Lions gave an impressive impersonation of the thin red line holding out against huge odds. The back row of Telfer, Arneil and Bob Taylor tackled like demons and so did all the backs, while Tom Kiernan had another good day. The Springboks did most of the attacking, but were thwarted by a remarkable Lions defence which, in itself, earned them a draw. Visagie and Naude each kicked a penalty for the Springboks and Tom Kiernan put over two for the Lions to keep the series alive.

Moving on to the battle of Springs, as it became known, John O'Shea was the first British Lion to be sent off for foul play, when he threw a punch after a general warning from the referee following a number of incidents and skirmishes. Apparently he was not the first Lion to take an early bath, as Eddie Waring used to put it, for another Lion, David Dobson of England, was sent off in Australia in 1904 for mouthing an obscenity to the referee. O'Shea was pelted with oranges and all sorts of objects, and was then struck in the face by a spectator as he left the field. This precipitated the biggest punch-up of the tour, at the mouth of the tunnel, while the game went gaily on. It made Eric Cantona's altercation with a Crystal Palace fan look like a minor disagreement at a Sunday School outing, as everybody pitched in, including the Lions reserves, officials, police and Lions supporters. Apparently, the best blow struck was by Willie John McBride on the offending spectator, who was later arrested.

To their satisfaction, the Lions won the match 37–9 and went on to defeat Northern Transvaal, always an important side to win against, together with Griqualand West and Boland, before the third Test in Cape Town.

The Lions were considerably weakened by the absence of Gareth Edwards. Roger Young, his great mate, deputised for him, and Maurice Richards, Gerald Davies, who scored the try of the tour at Boland, and Peter Stagg were brought into the side. The Springboks were without their great wing, Jannie Engelbrecht, who was injured.

South Africa won the series with a try by Thys Lourens. It was converted by Visagie, who also kicked a penalty, as did Tiny Naude with one of his outfield specials. Kiernan, as usual, scored the Lions' points with two well-struck penalties.

The Lions won their last three provincial games before the last Test in Johannesburg. Although there was no significance, as the series was already lost by the Lions, 60,000 packed Ellis Park for the last game and were rewarded with the best rugby of the tour by Dawie de Villiers's Springboks. With both scrum-halves, Edwards and Young, out with injury, the Lions played their third scrum-half replacement, Gordon Connell. Bresnihan came back in for Davies, and Pullin, who had flu, should never have played. Mannetjies Roux gave South Africa an early lead with a superbly taken try, and Kiernan levelled with a penalty midway through the first half, but Gould gave the Springboks a half-time lead of 6–3, with a left-footed drop goal.

There was no holding the Springboks in the second half, as Jan Ellis and Tommy Bedford in particular cleaned up the loose ball and linked with their backs. Tries were added by Ellis, Olivier and Nomis, with Visagie converting two. Kiernan had the last word with a final penalty, to beat Okey Giffen's record, and end an undistinguished series.

The Lions lost through no failure by the forwards, who played splendidly and gave their best performance of the series. The backs, however, failed dismally and missed taking their chances, making far too many errors and the game was lost 19–6.

## Results of the 1968 Lions in South Africa

P 20   W 15   D 1   L 4   F 377   A 181

| Western Transvaal | W | 20 | 12 |
|---|---|---|---|
| Western Province | W | 10 | 6 |
| South Western Districts | W | 24 | 6 |
| Eastern Province | W | 23 | 14 |
| Natal | W | 17 | 5 |
| Rhodesia | W | 32 | 6 |
| South Africa (Pretoria) | L | 20 | 25 |
| North West Cape | W | 25 | 5 |
| South West Africa | W | 23 | 0 |
| Transvaal | L | 6 | 14 |
| South Africa (Port Elizabeth) | D | 6 | 6 |
| Eastern Transvaal | W | 37 | 9 |
| Northern Transvaal | W | 22 | 19 |
| Griqualand West | W | 11 | 3 |
| Boland | W | 14 | 0 |
| South Africa (Cape Town) | L | 6 | 11 |
| Border | W | 26 | 6 |
| Orange Free State | W | 9 | 3 |
| North East Cape | W | 40 | 12 |
| South Africa (Johannesburg) | L | 6 | 19 |

## Tom Kiernan's 1968 Lions team

**Full-backs**

| R. Hiller | Harlequins | England |
|---|---|---|
| T.J. Kiernan (capt.) | Cork Constitution | Ireland |

**Three-quarters**

| F.P.K. Bresnihan | University College Dublin | Ireland |
|---|---|---|
| T.G.R. Davies | Cardiff | Wales |
| A.J.W. Hinshelwood | London Scottish | Scotland |
| K.S. Jarrett | Newport | Wales |
| W.K. Jones | Cardiff | Wales |
| W.H. Raybould | London Welsh | Wales |

| M.C.R. Richards | Cardiff | Wales |
| K.F. Savage | Northampton | England |
| J.W.C. Turner | Gala | Scotland |

**Half-backs**

| G.C. Connell* | London Scottish | Scotland |
| G.O. Edwards | Cardiff | Wales |
| C.M.H. Gibson | North of Ireland | Ireland |
| B. John | Cardiff | Wales |
| R.M. Young | Queen's University Belfast | Ireland |

**Forwards**

| R.J. Arneil | Edinburgh Academicals | Scotland |
| M.J. Coulman | Moseley | England |
| M.G. Doyle | Blackrock College | Ireland |
| K.G. Goodall* | City of Derry | Ireland |
| A.L. Horton | Blackheath | England |
| P.J. Larter | Northampton | England |
| W.J. McBride | Ballymena | Ireland |
| S. Millar | Ballymena | Ireland |
| J.P. O'Shea | Cardiff | Wales |
| J.V. Pullin | Bristol | England |
| P.K. Stagg | Sale | Scotland |
| J. Taylor | London Welsh | Wales |
| R.B. Taylor | Northampton | England |
| J.W. Telfer | Melrose | Scotland |
| W.D. Thomas | Llanelli | Wales |
| B.R. West* | Northampton | England |
| J. Young | Harrogate | Wales |

Manager: D.K. Brooks
Coach: A.R. Dawson

* Replacements

# Gloria in Excelsis

Throughout the twentieth century, and for over 70 years, the Lions had lived more in hope than in glory, as the southern hemisphere became increasingly hard to beat. The Lions of 1971 and 1974 destroyed this aura of invincibility and once more made British rugby respected throughout the world, not only because they had defeated both New Zealand and South Africa, but for the style of rugby which they employed.

It is my view that these two dazzling successes, which were no flukes but emphatic events as crushing as anything that New Zealand or South Africa had achieved, can be traced back to the disastrous Wales tour of South Africa in 1964. Those events began the thinking behind an explosion of coaching and organisation, such as the squad system and the appointments of Ray Williams of Wales and Don Rutherford of England as technical advisers to their Unions. There was also a considerable influence exerted on the 1971 tour by the Welshmen who had failed in their tour of New Zealand in 1969, and were burning to go back and gain their revenge.

## JOHN DAWES'S 1971 LIONS

The 'Swinging Sixties' were over. In 1971, the 'Angry Brigade' bombed the house of the Employment Secretary, Robert Carr, and postmen went on strike for the first time, for a 19.5 per cent wage rise. Idi Amin took power in Uganda; the Provisional IRA broke from the Officials and the first British soldier was killed in Ulster. *The Daily Sketch* newspaper closed after 62 years; Arsenal won the League and Cup double, and George Best was sent off in the referees' revolution against persistent arguing. Margaret Thatcher stopped free school milk, Charles Manson was sentenced to death, and Louis Armstrong died. Decimal currency was introduced in February of that year.

It was propitious that, at the time, there emerged a generation of some of the greatest backs in Welsh history, such as Gareth Edwards, Barry John, Gerald Davies, John Dawes, J.P.R. Williams and John Bevan, backed up by superlative players from the other Unions, like David Duckham and Mike Gibson, playing in his best role as a centre. They were the finest set of backs since the 1955 team in South Africa, and they became such renowned names in the rugby world that many are referred to only as Gareth, Barry, Gerald or JPR.

I am often asked, and indeed I often ask myself, which was the greater team, 1971 or 1974? The jury is out for all eternity on this issue, and you cannot get any group of rugby people who witnessed both to agree on the subject. It is my opinion, however, that the 1971 Lions had backs who were without equal in my experience. Never did I see more consummate play from backs, with such unparalleled mastery of the basic skills.

The 1974 Lions had the better record, for they never lost a game, and had the best pack of forwards ever put on the field by the British Lions. They were able to defeat the Springboks forwards, whereas the 1971 Lions were praised merely for matching the All Blacks forwards. I for one refuse to take sides on this issue, for there is no conclusive answer. Suffice to say that they were the two best British Lions teams ever to take the field, and we will be fortunate if we ever see their like again. Perhaps if you had the 1971 backs and the 1974 forwards, you would be close to creating the perfect Lions team.

Before the 1971 tour started, the forwards appeared more suspect than the backs but, in the event, they performed superbly and gave the lie to the theory that British packs could not hold a candle to an All Blacks pack. Among them were forwards who were, or who were to become giants in the game: Willie John McBride, Mervyn Davies, Ian McLauchlan, John Pullin, Sean Lynch, Peter Dixon, John Taylor and Derek Quinnell.

Doug Smith, an old Lion himself in 1950, was the right sort of man to manage such a party. He was a tough guy with extremely strong points of view, and suffered fools not at all gladly, but he was charismatic and popular. He also made the most amazing and awesome prediction of all time when he said, before and during the tour, that the Lions would win the Test series 2–1 with one match drawn. He was a good listener and, as he says, 'In the early part of the tour, Ray McLoughlin was invited into our daily meetings and contributed enormously to the success of the Lions forwards, and latterly Willie John McBride and Mike Gibson were also part of our "Brains Trust".'

The Tours Committee confidently predicted that Carwyn James would lose his bid to become the Welsh Nationalist MP for Llanelli in the forthcoming general election, and in him they had the most imaginative and brilliant coach of all time. He understood the secret of quietly motivating the players under his command, with no fuss or bother, using the carrot rather than the goad. Merely by a quiet word here and there, he allowed all their natural talents to develop. He was also a master at handling the media, giving them what they wanted to know, without telling them too much. He had all the hard-bitten New Zealand journalists like Terry McLean, and the Brits such as Terry O'Connor and John Reason, eating out of his hand.

Doug Smith, the manager, said of him in the report to the Tours Committee after the tour, 'I cannot praise my assistant, Carwyn James, too highly. From the day of our appointment, we began to think alike as far as the tour and its preparation was concerned. He was an outstanding coach, who did things in a simple, methodical way, which made each member of the team realise that the player is an integral member of a great side. He was held in the greatest esteem by the team and the New Zealand officials.'

Above all, Carwyn was determined that the Lions should express themselves. He was not averse to the barbed comment about such matters as dirty play and poor refereeing. He was determined that a certain referee should not handle the final Test, even though the New Zealand Council tried desperately to get him to agree. Carwyn showed an iron will and refused point blank, pointing out the man's grave deficiencies as a referee. He remembered that in one Test in 1969, this referee had thrown both hands in the air in triumph when McCormack dropped a goal against Wales.

Carwyn was a close personal friend of mine. He came to see me about a week before leaving to ask my opinions on various matters, and suddenly asked me how I thought his Lions team would do. Having been in New Zealand and Australia with the Welsh team in 1969, and knowing that a third of the team was made up of the same Welshmen, I was unable to offer him much encouragement. Subsequently, when I pitched up in Wellington halfway through the tour, where he was having dinner in the team hotel with a delightful half-Maori girl, he gleefully gave me a hard time for a minute or two over the results so far. I immediately sensed a quiet confidence in him, as if he held a royal flush and, as the ace coach holding the 'king', Barry John, he certainly did.

Carwyn was a very complex man and a wise man who, after matches, liked a quiet corner. He was certainly the greatest rugby intellectual I ever knew and, after his untimely death in 1983, I sorely missed those fascinating post-mortems we held in the BBC Club after every international at Cardiff.

We were lifelong friends, and I was his captain when he played for the Welsh Schools Under-19 group in 1947, and again when he won his two Wales caps against Australia and France in 1958, first as a centre and then in his real position of fly-half. Yet strangely, in those early years, he showed none of his remarkable qualities as a rugby thinker, but then perhaps he was a little too shy and diffident in those days. He was unfortunate that his playing career coincided with Cliff Morgan's.

Doug Smith, assisted by a selector from each country but, ridiculously, not officially by his coach (who, in truth, should have been the chairman of selectors), spent the 1970–71 season selecting the team. A very busy season it was, being England's centenary year, with various celebration matches and a World Rugby Congress attended by some 49 countries, which did much to accelerate the expansion of the game world wide. A combined England and Wales side played Scotland and Ireland at Twickenham; then a Wales XV played a European team in Cardiff, and Fiji came and toured England. In fact, when the Fijians destroyed a powerful-looking Barbarians team at Gosforth, they also demolished the aspirations of some players to tour with the Lions. At the end of the tour, there was a very strong recommendation by Doug Smith and Carwyn James, in their reports to the Four Home Unions Tours Committee, that the coach should in future be a member of the selection committee.

At the time, the Wales team, which had been steadily evolving since 1968, won the Triple Crown and the Grand Slam under the captaincy of John Dawes, so it was inevitable that Welsh representation would be strong. Thirteen of them were chosen, together with six each from Ireland and England and five from Scotland. John Dawes also got the captaincy, and what a marvellous job he made of it! Dawes had already made an enormous impact when he helped develop London Welsh into one of the best clubs in the land. He did it by first of all creating a strong defence, and then developing a tremendous attacking ethic, which certainly had its influence, not only on the Grand Slam Wales side, but on his British Lions team, which contained no fewer than six London Welsh players, with another flown out as a replacement.

Doug Smith was to say of him in his end-of-term report, 'The appointment of John Dawes was probably one of the main reasons for the success of the tour. A charming and knowledgeable man who held the respect of everyone in the team, not only for his own outstanding ability as a player, but for his friendliness.'

John Dawes played more games than anyone else, and his team always looked better when he was in it. He also had some excellent and intelligent senior 'pros' around him, men like Willie John, Ray McLoughlin, Ian McLauchlan and, of course, those terrific Welsh half-backs, Gareth Edwards and Barry John. The latter became the major individual star and genius of the tour, which saw him called 'the King' by those around him, in deference to his authority and effrontery on the field. Everybody thought he was too young to retire as he did at the age of 26. Gareth was no less a star, and remains one of the very greatest and most popular of players to have worn a Wales and a Lions jersey. He once said, 'The Lions experience is a step ahead of home internationals. You have more wise men around you; no one is distracted from the game; you learn to play with judgement rather than pure emotion.' This is so true, because the Lions are the distillation of the best in our four countries and, therefore, everything that happens is that much faster and more skilful.

The drink of the tour was an LGT, or a large gin and tonic, a tipple that some of the players were perhaps to embrace all too fervently in the years ahead, but that has nothing to do with the events of the time.

John Dawes's opposing captain was none other than the legendary Colin Meads, aptly known as 'Pinetree'. He was one of the very greatest forwards of all time and the ultimate competitor, being totally uncompromising, as All Blacks forwards usually are. A New Zealander to the core, he took enormous pride in the All Blacks and he believed more than anybody that forwards won matches. Carwyn understood this, and his tactic was not to allow much opportunity for second-phase possession, in which the All Blacks were better versed than any. His tactics were, therefore, to move the ball wide as quickly as possible, and this was why he used to coach his backs into fast fingertip passing.

Carwyn also coined the now famous phrase 'Get your retaliation in first', which was originally intended to combat the illegal lineout play of the All Blacks but which, in the end, was to cover a much wider field! This, together with Willie John's slogan in 1974 of 'Take no prisoners', was to become another part of Lions folklore.

Two other important elements of Carwyn James's strategies for the tour were the use of the counter-attack and the way in which he targeted as a danger that other All Blacks powerhouse, Sid Going, more noted for his strong breaks and linking with his forwards than for his passing to his backs. Derek Quinnell was selected, in the third Test, to look after him.

I have many lasting memories of that side. The first is of the athleticism, intensity and service of Gareth Edwards, mixed with his ability to break, and this, with the sheer genius of Barry John in the midsummer of his all-too-short career, when he became the focal point for praise by the Lions and the New Zealand public, were essential to the Lions' high morale. The emergence of Barry John as a goal kicker, scoring an amazing 170 points from kicking alone, was really what won the series. He scored in every game he played in.

Another memory is the timing and unerring skill of John Dawes in drawing men, and in his perfect passes to those better placed to run. One of those tremendous runners was Mike Gibson, also in the salad days of his career, whom many New Zealanders, including Colin Meads, chose ahead of Barry John as the finest of the Lions backs, largely because they could understand the strong positive running of Gibson and they also admired his defensive qualities. Their philosophies of hard play could not accept the almost supernatural ghosting of Barry John, which Norman Mair once so beautifully captured in a match preview in *The Scotsman* when he wrote, 'What a relief it was to see Barry John leaving by the door, rather than simply drifting through the wall!' They preferred the directness of Gibson, because that was something they could come to grips with, whereas the ethereal quality of Barry John's play was something totally alien to the All Blacks philosophy of power rugby.

There was also the full bloom of Gerald Davies's flair for running with the grace and speed of a gazelle. Even when in full stride, he was apparently in full control and able to swerve or sidestep or do whatever was necessary to create a score for himself or others. He was the consummate running machine and a highly intelligent and charming man. He was converted, totally against his will, from a centre to a winger on the 1969 Welsh tour in New Zealand for he had played there for Cambridge University and for the 1968 Lions.

On the other wing, there was the equally likeable David Duckham, whose elegant running belied his size. He was a big man who could also run on top of the ground, and was extraordinarily nimble in being able to change pace or direction. The Welsh public loved him and called him Dai Duckham, in recognition of his high skills as a runner; they would gladly have given him Welsh citizenship. Neither must we forget another powerhouse wing on that tour, John Bevan, who played in the first Test. I can remember Doug Smith pointing him out to me on the first night I arrived in New Zealand and saying, 'That boy is terrific and he would do anything I asked of him for the team.' John was to prove that point in his distinguished career in rugby league.

Behind all these magnificent players was the incomparable J.P.R. Williams, a veritable rock of a player. He was the sort of full-back which every pack of forwards dreams of having behind them, a competitor beyond compare, in a land which was full of them. He was the only full-back that made the All Blacks forwards think twice about following up a high kick, by being underneath it. I can see him now in my mind's eye, taking a high ball and, with that little touch of madness which seemed to be a part of his courage on the field, picking out an unfortunate All Blacks forward to charge at. The look of triumph on his face when he dropped the critical goal to draw the final Test and win the series was worth going a long way to see.

If these were the stars, the supporting cast of men like Chris Rea, Arthur Lewis, Alistair Biggar, John Spencer, Chico Hopkins and Bob Hiller, who always kept the scoreboard going in Barry's absence, made equally valuable contributions to the tour. So did many of the forwards, some of whom, such as Gordon Brown and Fergus Slattery, were on a learning curve which was to hold them in good stead in 1974.

It all began disastrously when they had to play two matches within five days of flying half-way round the world. The first was some 58 hours after arrival on a night flight, against Queensland who, not surprisingly, beat them by 15–11. This caused Des Connor, the Queensland coach who had played for New Zealand and Australia, to say that this was the worst Lions team to be sent to New Zealand. How wrong first impressions can be! They also only scraped home 14–12 against New South Wales, before moving on to New Zealand, where they won all ten games before the first Test, including taking the valuable scalps of Otago, Wellington and Canterbury. They thus alerted New Zealand to the fact that there were real problems ahead of them.

Of these, it was the Canterbury game which became the main talking-point of the tour outside the Tests, for its totally disgraceful violence and downright dirty play. Nobody there at the time, or the many millions who saw the photographs in the papers of Sandy Carmichael, who had suffered a multiple fracture of the cheekbone, will ever forget what was the unacceptable face of rugby football as played by some. The Lions laid the blame squarely where it belonged, which was on the attitudes of the Canterbury players, and on Hopkinson and Wyllie in particular.

It was not only Carmichael who was a victim; Fergus Slattery had two teeth loosened by a punch and suffered bad concussion; John Pullin was felled from behind at a lineout by a punch from behind, and Gareth Edwards was floored by a rabbit punch. The referee, at one point during the battle in the second half, bizarrely called the captains together and told them that from that moment on he was going to follow the ball, and if anything else happened, it was up to the captains to sort it out.

The Lions continued to try and play some rugby throughout, and their far superior back play saw them home by 14–3, but they had lost their two Test props. Ray McLoughlin broke his thumb while hitting back, and both he and Carmichael, under the ruling of the Tour Agreement, were, sadly, sent home. Strangely, the Lions flew out another lock, Geoff Evans, so that Mike Roberts, one of the now five second rows, had to play a number of games at prop. They also sent out the Cornish prop, 'Stack' Stevens.

Canterbury had shown how schizophrenic New Zealand rugby could occasionally be. There was a considerable backlash in New Zealand, as *The Christchurch Press* called it 'The Game of Shame', while *Truth*, a weekly journal, said, 'New Zealand rugby has become as grotesque as a wounded bull', and named three of the Canterbury villains. The All Blacks coach, Ivan Vodanovich, warned the Lions that if they did not get off the ball in the rucks, then the forthcoming first Test match at Dunedin would resemble the battle of Paschendael. Happily, the chairman of the New Zealand Council issued a statement saying, 'There will be no battle at Carisbrooke next Saturday.'

Because of the damage done in Christchurch, the Lions were left with what were considered their second-string props, Ian McLauchlan and Sean Lynch, for the first Test, but, as so often happens, they more than rose to the occasion and played superbly in all the Tests, to make a reputation for themselves as fine players. The Lions were, unusually, to play six Welshmen and an Irish man, Mike Gibson, in their back division in that first Test.

The All Blacks included six new caps and, therefore, in the last five matches had played 33 players, a sure sign of an unsettled team. Nevertheless, they attacked the Lions from the start, only for the Lions to score first, entirely against the run of play, when Ian McLauchlan charged down a clearance kick by Sutherland in his own 25 and stormed on, to score what was not only a crucial try but his only one of the tour. A minute from half-time, McCormack equalised with a penalty. In the space of a few moments, McLauchlan himself acknowledged that he had made the jump from 'Mickey' to 'Mighty Mouse', by which pseudonym he thereafter became known. The Lions had lost Gareth Edwards with a leg injury early in the half, and he was replaced by his admirable deputy, Chico Hopkins. In the second period, Barry John kicked two penalties in the 12th and 36th minutes to win the match 9–3. Beaten in the lineouts, the Lions had done well in the scrummaging, and a big feature of the match was the way that Barry John tortured and tormented McCormack with his kicking for the corners, which saw him floundering and dropped for the subsequent Tests.

Willie John still recounts how he sat in the dressing-room afterwards, wondering how on earth they had won as, for much of the game, the Lions were simply not in it. It did wonders for the Lions' morale, for they had shown that the All Blacks could be beaten and they were no longer afraid of them. It also did Willie John a power of good, for he had previously played nine Tests for the Lions and had never won before.

McCormack was replaced in the second Test by Laurie Mains of Otago, later to become an outstanding coach who took New Zealand to the final of the 1995 World Cup. The All Blacks also dropped Carrington and moved Brian Williams, their magnificent Samoan, out from centre to wing, and Howard Joseph from Canterbury was brought into the centre. Sutherland had broken his leg in a charity match and was replaced by Alex Wyllie. The Lions made only one change, replacing John Bevan by David Duckham.

Lancaster Park was heavy, as it often is, but the weather was fine as the All Blacks forwards had their most impressive day. The All Blacks drew first blood, when Going worked the narrow side and put Burgess through a gap for a try. The Lions levelled when Williams and Gibson put Gerald Davies away on a 50-yard run, only for John to miss the easy conversion. Going then scored a typical powering try from a ruck, which Mains goaled, and John made it 8–6 at half-time with a penalty.

Ten minutes into the second half, referee John Pring awarded a penalty try to New Zealand when Gerald Davies took Brian Williams early in a tackle, and Mains kicked the goal. Burgess then crossed for his second try, similar to the one he scored in the first half, which Mains failed to convert, but he then succeeded with a penalty. Now came that famous try from a memorable run by Ian Kirkpatrick, when he burst away from broken play and, handing off Lions galore, raced 50 yards for a great try in the corner, and the All Blacks were cruising home by 22–6. In the remaining minutes, however, the Lions showed some spirit; Gerald Davies got a second try and John dropped a goal. The All Blacks had won impressively by 22–12 and stopped the Lions' run of 15 games in New Zealand without a defeat, and they were well pleased.

Sid Going and Bob Burgess were their stars behind the scrum, and Meads and Kirkpatrick were the outstanding forwards. The Lions paid a heavy price for not stopping the two All Blacks danger men, Going and Kirkpatrick.

Four more wins included a thoroughly nasty game at Hawke's Bay which was a mini-Canterbury, for John Pullin was badly hurt by a punch, but Mike Gibson's pulled hamstring had nothing to do with the unpleasant events on the field. This was the game when Gerald Davies flew on the wind to score four tremendous tries, and when the Welsh halves, Edwards and John, showed their disgust at the Hawke's Bay tactics. John began to toy with the Hawke's Bay players by standing still in his own 25 and passing the ball behind his back, before offering it to them and taunting them before kicking for touch as they closed in on him. It may have been naughty, but John was not prepared to allow such foul play without a demonstration of disapproval.

New Zealand picked the same team for the third Test at Wellington, but two late changes were forced on them. Brian Williams withdrew with a groin injury, to be replaced by Carrington, and Whiting, who had received a back injury in training, was surprisingly replaced by Brian Lochore, the great All Blacks captain, who was well past his sell-by date for Test matches. The Lions made two changes, with Carwyn James bringing in Quinnell in place of Peter Dixon to look after Sid Going on the blind side, and Gordon Brown making his first Test match appearance for the Lions in place of Delme Thomas. Remarkably, Quinnell played in four winning teams against New Zealand, one on each Lions tour in 1971 and 1977, and for Llanelli and the Barbarians in 1972–73.

Having won the toss, the Lions made good use of the wind in the first half and had the game won by half-time, when John dropped a goal after three minutes, and the All Blacks lost control at the tail of the lineout. Edwards, who had one of his finest matches for the Lions that day, ran around the narrow side and found the gap to put Davies over in the corner, and John's conversion went over via the upright. Another typical burst by Edwards, full of power and purpose, around the tail of a lineout, followed by a hand-off and a quick pass to John, who had come in close to him, brought another critical and smartly taken try. John easily converted, and at half-time the All Blacks were in serious trouble. Although the All Blacks strained every sinew in the second half, they failed to break the well-organised defence and managed only one try by Mains after ten minutes. The Lions had won a handsome victory by 13–3.

Thus, the Lions were in the happy position of being two–one up with one to play, but they still had to win the series. Doug Smith, the manager, was jubilant and referred to Wellington as, 'This wonderful city; we leave it 81 points to the good. We scored 47 here against Wellington, 27 against New Zealand Universities and 13 against New Zealand. What is more, King Jesus John is coming with us!'

Having completed their provincial games without defeat, Willie John captained the side for the first time in four tours against Manawatu–Horowhenua. John Bevan scored his 17th try of the tour in this last provincial match, thus equalling Tony O'Reilly's record in 1959. The Lions now prepared for another big one, knowing that a defeat would spoil all their efforts and the end-of-tour party. The only change in their side for the final Test at Eden Park, Auckland, was the return of Dixon in place of Quinnell. For the All Blacks, Burgess was injured in the third Test and his replacement, Cottrell, was retained, and Phil Gard came in at second five-eighth. Williams and Whiting, fit again, were restored in place of Hunter and Lochore, and Tom Lister was brought in at flanker for McNaughton.

The referee, John Pring, was again chosen to officiate, largely at the behest of Carwyn James, who detected that he was an honest broker. He became the first and last referee to officiate in all matches of a four-match series.

The game was hard and uncompromising and there was too much at stake for it to be a flowing affair, but, by heaven, it was dramatic! The All Blacks started at the gallop and were into a four-minute lead with a try from a set scrum, when Wyllie stood off, took Going's pass and sold a dummy before giving to Gard, who slipped to Cottrell who had looped behind him to score, and Mains converted. A few minutes later, Mains added a penalty and matters looked ominous but, before half-time, Barry John kicked a penalty and converted a try by the indefatigable Peter Dixon, who went over from a lineout, to make it a nail-biting 8–8 at half-time. John kicked another penalty after the break and Lister again levelled the scores with another try from a lineout. J.P.R. Williams then thumped over a marvellous drop goal but, eight minutes from time, Mains kicked a penalty for the game to end in a draw at 14–14. It was enough for the Lions to win their first series in New Zealand and to go home as heroes, and it was a good party! This Test was to end the magnificent career of Colin Meads, and neither did we see Lochore in the All Blacks jersey again, after the third Test.

By becoming the first British team to win a major series abroad in the twentieth century, these 1971 Lions had become the greatest, and had struck a huge blow for the cause of British rugby. Carwyn James had vindicated the new move to coaching and silenced the doubters.

# Results of the 1971 Lions in Australia and New Zealand

P 26   W 23   D 1   L 2   F 580   A 231

| | | | |
|---|---|---|---|
| Queensland | L | 11 | 15 |
| New South Wales | W | 14 | 12 |
| | | | |
| Counties–Thames Valley | W | 25 | 3 |
| King Country–Wanganui | W | 22 | 9 |
| Waikato | W | 35 | 14 |
| New Zealand Maoris | W | 23 | 12 |
| Wellington | W | 47 | 9 |
| South Canterbury–North Otago | W | 25 | 6 |
| Otago | W | 21 | 9 |
| West Coast–Buller | W | 39 | 6 |
| Canterbury | W | 14 | 3 |
| Marlborough–Nelson | W | 31 | 12 |
| New Zealand (Dunedin) | W | 9 | 3 |
| Southland | W | 25 | 3 |
| Taranaki | W | 14 | 9 |
| New Zealand Universities | W | 27 | 6 |
| New Zealand (Christchurch) | L | 12 | 22 |
| Wairarapa–Bush | W | 27 | 6 |
| Hawke's Bay | W | 25 | 6 |
| East Coast–Poverty Bay | W | 18 | 12 |
| Auckland | W | 19 | 12 |
| New Zealand (Wellington) | W | 13 | 3 |
| Manawatu–Horowhenua | W | 39 | 6 |
| North Auckland | W | 11 | 5 |
| Bay of Plenty | W | 20 | 14 |
| New Zealand (Auckland) | D | 14 | 14 |

## John Dawes's 1971 Lions team

**Full-backs**

| | | |
|---|---|---|
| R. Hiller | Harlequins | England |
| J.P.R. Williams | Bridgend | Wales |

**Three-quarters**

| | | |
|---|---|---|
| J.C. Bevan | Cardiff College of Educ. | Wales |
| A.G. Biggar | London Scottish | Scotland |
| T.G.R. Davies | London Welsh | Wales |

| S.J. Dawes (capt.) | London Welsh | Wales |
| D.J. Duckham | Coventry | England |
| A.J.L. Lewis | Ebbw Vale | Wales |
| C.W.W. Rea | Headingley | Scotland |
| J.S. Spencer | Headingley | England |

**Half-backs**

| G.O. Edwards | Cardiff | Wales |
| C.M.H. Gibson | North of Ireland | Ireland |
| R. Hopkins | Maesteg | Wales |
| B. John | Cardiff | Wales |

**Forwards**

| R.J. Arneill* | Leicester | Scotland |
| G.L. Brown | West of Scotland | Scotland |
| A.B. Carmichael | West of Scotland | Scotland |
| T.M. Davies | London Welsh | Wales |
| P.J. Dixon | Harlequins | England |
| T.G. Evans* | London Welsh | Wales |
| M.L. Hipwell | Terenure College | Ireland |
| F.A.L. Laidlaw | Melrose | Scotland |
| J.F. Lynch | St Mary's College | Ireland |
| W.J. McBride | Ballymena | Ireland |
| J. McLauchlan | Jordanhill College | Scotland |
| R.J. McLoughlin | Blackrock College | Ireland |
| J.V. Pullin | Bristol | England |
| D.L. Quinnell | Llanelli | |
| M.G. Roberts | London Welsh | Wales |
| J.F. Slattery | University College Dublin | Ireland |
| C.B. Stevens* | Harlequins | England |
| J. Taylor | London Welsh | Wales |
| W.D. Thomas | Llanelli | Wales |

Manager: Dr D.W.C. Smith
Coach: C.R. James

\* Replacements

## WILLIE JOHN MCBRIDE'S 1974 LIONS

Some critics implied the 1974 Lions embraced only a forward-orientated and kicking game. Furthermore, they suggested that organised violence was part of their creed, after Willie John McBride's philosophy of 'Take no prisoners' was leaked. Unquestionably, at times there was a blitzkrieg philosophy, and it was on this tour that the code '99' was evolved, which meant one in, all in. Both Syd Millar, the coach, and Willie John himself had played there in 1962 and 1968, when the Lions did not win a single Test match, although they managed one draw on each occasion. They were, therefore, conditioned to the concept that you had to be tough to survive in such a physical country, where the white population felt threatened by the sheer weight of numbers of the black population, and reacted by denying dignity to anyone who was not white. Sometimes the Springboks would carry such uncompromising attitudes on to the field into a game which they loved above all others. They knew no way other than wanting to win at any cost.

This was far from the whole story of the 1974 Lions, for Hannes Marais, the South African captain, maintained that these Lions were the best team he had ever played against, including Brian Lochore's 1970 All Blacks. He was also to say that they were unfriendly towards his players.

It is entirely true to say that McBride's Lions were a great side, because of a huge determination to win through a highly organised forward effort; but then, after all, both the captain and the coach were forwards. That is not to say that they did not possess backs who showed tremendous quality, illustrated by the incontrovertible evidence of the huge number of points scored: 729 in their 22 games, more than any other team to visit South Africa. Remarkably, they lost not a single game, which was their passport to recognition of their greatness and of being the most powerful British team of all time. Never had the Springboks suffered a greater humiliation for, as they themselves pointed out, they were not a weak team, as their two Test wins in France at the end of 1974 revealed.

The year of 1974 saw the Heath government fall after the three-day week, and Harold Wilson returned as Prime Minister. There was an attempt to kill Princess Anne, and American heiress Patty Hearst became a bank robber. The boundaries of the English and Welsh counties were reorganised and we saw the demise of Cumberland, Rutland, Huntingdonshire and Westmoreland. There was roaring inflation, with the price of a gallon of four-star petrol rising from 42p to 72p.

The only inflation they saw in South Africa was in the high scoring of this Lions team. In the weeks before the tour, there were the inevitable objections and denunciations by the various anti-apartheid lobbies but, as I have said before, young rugby men are not primarily interested in politics. Some of them were hurt, however, by some local education bodies in Wales refusing to pay them while on tour, which produced financial hardship.

Alun Thomas, the manager, ensured that the discipline on the tour was strong in matters such as dress and behaviour, but when it came to politics he found himself on the defensive from the word go, receiving a hard time from some members of the press and the tour party. The tour was well managed and the playing side was magic, as Thomas left Syd Millar and McBride to run the events on the field.

In his end-of-tour report, Alun Thomas wrote:

> Syd Millar did for the 1974 Lions what Carwyn James had done for the 1971 Lions, in that he motivated and inspired the players to great heights and helped them realise their potential. He was the perfect choice and the perfect companion. His happy nature belied the steel in his character, and whilst very much a players' man, he was broad enough to chide them if they stepped out of line. A 'big' man, yet with a sense of detail about the various problems of South Africa that was uncanny. If there is no substitute for experience, here it was epitomised in one man. He had a clear vision of what was required to win, and to hear him analyse and evaluate tomorrow's problems at the team talks on the eve of a game was an experience. He was so simple, so articulate and yet so masterful. No team has ever gone on the field better prepared.

Willie John's Lions rewrote the record books. They won 21 consecutive matches in South Africa and drew the final Test, to become the first team to beat the Springboks in a four-match series for 78 years. Their aggregate of 729 points was a record for any tour of South Africa, and their 107 tries were a record for British teams in South Africa. Their win by 97–0 against South Western Districts was the biggest win by any touring team in South Africa, with J.J. Williams setting a new try-scoring record with six tries, and Alan Old setting a further points-scoring record in the same match. They were certainly more than merely a forward-orientated team.

So upset did Danie Craven become at the eclipse of his beloved Springboks that, in the presentation of Springboks blazers to six new caps in the 'Ostrich Hall' in Port Elizabeth after the third Test, he turned on them and said, 'It hurts me to be giving you these, because you have not earned them.' Danie, for all his geniality, could be a tough old buzzard at times.

On the playing side, such undreamt-of success was a tribute to those great Irishmen, coach Millar and captain McBride, for to break so many scoring records and to win the only full-scale Test series in South Africa this century was to scale the pinnacle of any rugby man's ambition. These two warriors, for that is what they were and still are, belong at the top of any roll of honour in British rugby.

The tour manager wrote of McBride:

> The captain was another exceptional man, and all the credit for the team's success goes to him and his great ally, Syd Millar. His outstanding qualities as a player and a man are so well known that I can never adequately describe them in print. He was literally worshipped by the players, not only because of his own courage and strength of commitment, but because they saw in him all the things they would like to be. He shielded them, nurtured them and, above all, inspired them. He shirked nothing, and was that 'rare breed', a natural leader of men. He is so obviously a future manager, as too is the assistant manager.

For McBride on his fifth Lions tour (only Mike Gibson has equalled such a feat), it was the perfect fulfilment of a long and distinguished career, and it exorcised those unsuccessful tours of the 1960s in which he had taken part. He will tell you that it was a very tough learning curve, but the reward in the end was well worth waiting for.

As the high scoring suggests, the tour far from belonged entirely to the forwards, for the Lions had some terrific backs in players such as Gareth Edwards, who was the principal strategist following the departure of Barry John. His kicking had South Africa on the rack throughout the tour, as did his long pass, which did much to protect the delightful free-running Phil Bennett. Phil was a marvellous instinctive player who, on his day, could twinkle as brightly as any star, including Barry John, as he showed when he catalysed that unforgettable try for the Barbarians against the All Blacks in 1973. South Africa tried to target him, but Gareth Edwards protected him with his length of pass and by using the option to kick, which was a feature of Wales's golden period of the 1970s. Gareth's running from the base was also a constant threat and produced many crucial tries, and this tour provided some of the finest hours of his illustrious career.

The rock which was J.P.R. Williams was as impregnable as ever. He had physical and mental toughness and courage, which at times seemed to border on dementia, because he was so brave and fearless. J.J. Williams was another to have a fine tour, together with the remarkably talented Andy Irvine, who played on the wing in the last two Tests. The two centres, Ian McGeechan and Dick Milliken, were so consistent that they played together as a centre pairing in all four Tests.

The South Africans made it difficult for themselves by panicking after losing the first Test in the wet at Newlands, and by making wholesale changes. In all they played 33 players in the series, 21 of whom were new caps. Only three of the Springboks, namely captain and prop Hannes Marais, wing Chris Pope and flanker Jan Ellis, played in all four Tests.

Eight changes, one of them positional, were made after that first Test, so it was not surprising that they lost the second Test 28–9. There were also 11 changes for the third Test, one again positional, and once more they lost heavily by 26–9, which speaks volumes for the requirement of continuity and experience if you are to create a settled winning team. In contrast, the Lions played only 17 players in the rubber and one of the changes was due only to an injury to Gordon Brown, who had emerged as one of the best post-war locks in Britain.

Like all Lions teams, they were a fine bunch of men to know, though strangely one of the few criticisms of them by the South African captain, Marais, was that they were unsociable and that his team got the cold shoulder. Perhaps it did not occur to him that there were rather a lot of them to get to know.

These Lions had lots of fun, and apparently their Sunday drinking schools were of university standard. I love the story that Tommy David tells of one of his nights in the Kruger Park, when they were told, while drinking barefoot in the bar, to be careful on their way back because of snakes, poisonous spiders and scorpions. Apparently they left hurriedly, racing back to their rondavels (huts) in huge leaps. He was just drifting off to sleep when there was a thunderous banging on the door, and cries in a Gwent accent of, 'Lemme in! Lemme in!' It was Bobby Windsor and, as Tommy relates, 'He was frighted to death, and it takes a lot to frighten anybody who has been shouted at by Ray Prosser. "Tom," whimpered Bobby, and until you've heard a member of the Pontypool front row whimpering, you ain't heard nothing. "Tom, I'm lost. I can't find my 'ut. Can I sleep with you?"

'So he climbed into my bed. There was more than 30 stone in that single bed, but it didn't seem to worry Bobby – I suppose that anybody who has spent a lot of his time jammed between Graham Price and Charlie Faulkner is used to living rough.

'We lay there listening to the sounds of Africa. Bobby said, "Tom, I can hear lions." So could I, and as we lay there sweating and thinking about those massive jaws and terrible teeth, we heard something bumping against the side of the hut and roaring. By this time I was holding hands with Bobby, so you can tell what a terrible state he was in. Then it happened, and something came hurtling through our mesh window. Instantly, me and Bobby were out of our bed and, shrieking with fear, fought each other to get under the bed, each trying to shove the other into the paws of whatever had pounced through our window.

'At any second I expected to feel his fangs in my rear. The lion's fangs, that is, not Bobby's – although if biting me could have got me out of the way, I wouldn't have put that past my hooker. We were still fighting and screaming when there were some terrific bangs on the door. Christ! I thought, we got gorillas coming in as well. It wasn't, it was Chris Ralston, Mike Burton and Ian McLauchlan; they'd come for the log which they had thrown through the window and they couldn't stand up for laughing. Just the usual sort of prank to relieve the boredom, but enough for me to consider asking Dr Christian Barnard to put me on his waiting list.'

Humour plays a large part on such tours and there are always two or three guys who enliven a tour with native wit, or who can entertain with music and singing. Such people are invaluable on long tours, for they can do so much for morale, whether things are going well or badly. Rarely does one see any real misfits on Lions tours.

Tours are a huge test of character. Apart from training and playing, there are many problems like small beds for big men, noisy rooms and room-mates (there is nothing worse than sharing with a snorer), wrong types of food and bad service or problems with the telephone, with journalists trying to phone out and dozens of girls trying to phone in. Willie John had massive experience of all this and understood that all complaints should be brought into the open, each then being examined and solved on its merits. Man management, including encouraging and sympathising with those who fail to get into the team for the Tests, is all-important.

Willie says that one reason for their success was that they never contemplated the possibility of defeat. His Lions concentrated on the scrummage, because they soon discovered that the Springboks had neglected this area of forward play. Consequently, they achieved consistent forward dominance, which they hadn't done in New Zealand in 1971. Another McBride motto was, 'Never ever take a step back' for, as he said, 'We learned over the years in South Africa and New Zealand that you must always stand up to anything that is thrown at you.'

Syd Millar admits that they often played nine- and ten-man rugby, but they also played 15-man rugby and scored more tries than the 1955 Lions, who were previously regarded as the best running team ever to visit South Africa. Those who thought that the 1974 side should play like the 1971 team failed to understand that they were different, with a midfield that did not have the same ability to transfer ball. It was unfair to compare McGeechan and Milliken with Gibson or Dawes, for they had different approaches, but you never saw a higher work rate than that of the 1974 centres. Another thing which Millar tried to achieve was not to have a midweek and a Test team. He therefore mixed them up as far as he could, but this was possible because he had so many good forwards under his command, these Lions being blessed by having the strongest 16 forwards that ever went on a Lions tour. It was astonishing that some critics failed to understand that they were, sensibly, playing to their strength and not attempting to put back any clocks.

Suffice to say they rattled through the seven provincial matches, including capturing the valuable scalps of Eastern and Western Province before the first Test in Cape Town, which, together with Sydney in Australia and Vancouver in Canada, is one of the best venues in the world for a Test match. Newlands, nestling under Table Mountain, is one of the great rugby shrines, and a Mecca that rugby men the world over should visit sometime in their lives.

Eastern Province was the first big test of the Lions' resolve. Twice Gareth Edwards, the captain for the day, asked Hannes Marais, the Eastern Province captain, to cut out the rough stuff. Nothing happened, so finally Edwards said, 'All right, if that's the bloody way you want it, you can have it.' There were some vicious fist fights, most of which the Lions won, along with the match. The same weekend, the French club Tarbes were involved in another monumental punch-up with Eastern Transvaal, and the match was abandoned 20 minutes from the end, which tells you something about how hard it can be in South Africa.

I have always maintained that Lions tours to New Zealand and South Africa were a bit like going off to the medieval crusades or soldiering with Wellington in the Peninsular campaign. Furthermore, we all did it for nothing; in fact, most of us lost money. It was all for the love of the game and, I must admit, for the opportunity of having a crack at a bit of glory.

The Lions also played a coloured (mixed blood) team called the SAR Federation XV or the 'Proteas', before the first Test. Like so many other such events in the apartheid years, it was largely a cosmetic exercise, because it was not fully representative, as the bigger coloured union stated that there should be no mixed sport in an abnormal society. Furthermore, there was no structure by which the Bantu or coloureds could play against the provincial teams.

The ground for the first Test was like a quagmire after the overnight rain and after two preliminary curtain-raisers. It was, therefore, tailor-made for nine-man rugby, and played into the hands of the Lions forwards. It was quickly evident that the Springboks had forgotten the art of scrummaging and, after ten minutes, the Lions had them in a vice. Nevertheless the Springboks, with the wind behind them, scored first when Dawie Snyman dropped a goal early on, and it was not until nearly half-time that Phil Bennett kicked a penalty, making the score level at 3–3.

In the second half, with the strong wind behind the Lions, it was evident that they would win comfortably and they were rarely out of the Springboks' half, but in such conditions tries were hard to come by. They finally won 12–3, with two more penalty goals and a drop goal by Edwards.

Not a few reputations were made or confirmed in this first Test, as the Lions showed that Syd Millar had made the right decisions with regard to his forward selections. Before the start of the tour many thought, for instance, that Mervyn Davies might be the number two to Andy Ripley, but he showed, with one terrific tackle on Jan Ellis in the first Test which set a pattern for the tour, that he was an absolute hammer, as hard and merciless as they come. With his mobility and basketball skills with the ball in the hand, he was a truly great player. His career ended abruptly when he suffered a sub-arachnoid haemorrhage in the Welsh Cup semi-final in 1976.

Similarly, Fergus Slattery was thought to be in the shadow of Tony Neary, but he showed such a tireless work rate and range of skills, most notably his knack of taking a tackle and riding over it before passing the ball to the support, that he easily held his Test place, and he was to retire as the world's most-capped flanker, with 61 caps.

The third member of this unrivalled back row was Roger Uttley who, on tour, was converted from lock, where he had played for England in 1973 and 1974, into a hard, blind-side flanker. He added considerably to tightening the forward effort and gave another dimension to winning the ball at the tail of the lineout, as he took much of the workload and pressure off Mervyn Davies. Later, he was to be assistant coach to Ian McGeechan on the successful Lions tour to Australia in 1989.

The second row spoke for itself with the big man, Willie John, and Gordon Brown, equally as large and as hard in combat, with a huge personality both on and off the field. He was the brother of the Scottish captain Peter Brown, and created an unusual record by replacing him when he was injured against Wales in 1979.

The front row of Ian McLauchlan, Bobby Windsor and Fran Cotton was not the sort to be intimidated; on the contrary, any intimidation that was going on was going to be by them. Bobby Windsor, a member of the legendary Pontypool front row, was a master at throwing in at the lineout, which is an extremely important art, and it was the reason he pipped Ken Kennedy for the Tests. Fran Cotton, an English hard case from Wigan, rugby league country, was brought to South Africa as a back-up loose head for McLauchlan, only to win his place on the tight head, because of his strength and commitment and his understanding with Windsor. 'Mighty Mouse' was the ideal loose-head prop and the keystone of the Lions pack and, in eight Tests for the Lions, he only once finished on the losing side.

There was only one change in the pack throughout the whole series, when Chris Ralston, a tougher and better lock than his laid-back demeanour implied, came in for the injured Gordon Brown, who had broken a hand in the Port Elizabeth Test brawl, for the last Test. This was a measure of the consistency of their forward play and of their immense durability on such an exacting tour, which was a factor in winning the match and the series. When you look at the reserves of Sandy Carmichael, Mike Burton, Ken Kennedy, Chris Ralston, Andy Ripley, Sean McKinney, Tony Neary and Tommy David, then you can appreciate why they never lost a match.

Returning to the high veldt, the Lions continued to give the provincial teams a pounding. They beat one of South Africa's strongest teams, Transvaal, who were Currie Cup finalists that year, by 23–15 before the second Test at Loftus Versveld in Pretoria, and they also beat Rhodesia handsomely.

The Springboks selectors panicked and made all those inexplicable changes, while the Lions fielded the same team. As expected, the Lions' scrummaging was even more lethal on the hard ground and the Springboks forwards crumbled, as the Lions inflicted on South Africa their biggest-ever defeat. The Springboks managed to hold the line in the first half, when they trailed from two tries by J.J. Williams scored on each side of the field. Bennett converted the second, while Bosch dropped a goal to make it 10–3 at half-time.

In the second half the Lions crushed the Springboks pack, and Phil Bennett, who played the game of his life, cut loose to score a tremendous try when he split the Springboks' defence and sliced through for a twinkle-toed try which had even the partisan Pretoria crowd on their feet in admiration. Further tries were scored by Brown and Milliken, while Bennett kicked a penalty and Ian McGeechan dropped a goal. South Africa's only response was two penalties by

Bosch. The Lions had inflicted the heaviest-ever defeat on the Springboks and had totally given the lie to accusations that they played only nine- or ten-man rugby.

There was now a reaction to this run of unparalleled success and, having peaked, the Lions struggled against the Quaggas, a South African Barbarians-style team, named after an extinct species of zebra. They also only scraped home in the dying moments against the Orange Free State with a try by J.J. Williams, which made it 11–9. They got back into their stride with a 69–16 win against Griqualand West, and then beat Northern Transvaal, who won the Currie Cup that year, before easily beating the Leopards, a Bantu team, in East London before the third Test in Port Elizabeth. It was made evident by the performance of the flanker, Morgan Cushe, that one day South Africa would have black Springboks, even though Danie Craven said in 1976 that it would never happen.

This third Test was South Africa's last chance to save the series, and they had gone into 'purdah' and trained behind closed doors, forbidden by their coach, Claassen, to read the newspapers. They also made further changes and included some hard cases in their pack. Inexplicably, they selected Gerrie Soonekus, a number eight, at scrum-half, although he had played only briefly in that position. The Lions, for their part, made only one change, with Andy Irvine replacing Steele on the wing.

I must confess that this match is my biggest memory of the 1974 tour. I was never more astonished, as the game became the most violent Test match I ever witnessed. Some of the big Springboks forwards actually ran away from the battle, which was why, that night in the Ostrich Hall, Danie Craven said he was ashamed of them.

I sat there in amazement as two massive fist fights broke out, one in each half. The first, just before half-time, occurred when the Springboks ran into a ruck with boots flying and Willie John called a '99'. This meant everybody climbed in; even J.P.R. Williams came rushing in from full-back to join in. Moaner van Heerden became the main target and, in the end, he was forced to retreat. Among many other skirmishes, a further outbreak of all-out war came in the second half, with another huge '99'. These incidents brought much criticism of the '99' philosophy, which was blamed for an increase in dirty play in Britain. It was a ploy, however, to show South Africa that the Lions were not going to be pushed around and bullied as some of their predecessors had been in the past. Whether or not they carried it too far is an argument which is still debated.

Again the Springboks lost the fight and the game. After an eventful first five minutes, when the over-tense Springboks threw all they had at the Lions, they scored first when Snyman kicked a penalty. The Lions pack quickly re-established control over the opposing forwards and began to turn the screw when Andy Irvine kicked a penalty. Late in the half, after the first '99', Gordon Brown came into the shortened lineout near the Springboks line and stole the ball for a try, which made it 7–3 at half-time, with the wind and the sun still to come in their favour for the second half.

Soon after the restart, Irvine showed the strength of the wind by putting over a penalty from about eight yards inside his own half. After the second '99', Bennett dropped a goal and J.P.R. Williams now combined with J.J. Williams in creating a try for the latter, which Irvine converted. With 20 minutes to go, it was already game, set and match, with the Lions leading 19–3. Winning was now a formality, and although Snyman kicked two penalty goals, the Lions made victory secure when J.J. Williams scored a second try, using his favourite party trick of kicking ahead and scooting around the defender to pick up and score. Finally, Bennett dropped a splendid goal, for the Lions to win the third Test by 26–9.

Thus the Lions won the series, having so far scored eight tries to nil (which was as conclusive as you can get), while the Springboks were in the biggest quandary of their history, with the final Test at Ellis Park still to come.

Border, Natal and Eastern Transvaal were then put to the sword. One of the mysteries and extraordinary memories of the tour was the manner in which the Lions played Natal. This, after all, was the most British of all the provinces, a gorgeous place, the 'Côte d'Azur' of South Africa. They had that marvellous man, Tommy Bedford, as captain, and many of the most knowledgeable rugby people in South Africa and the rest of the world knew he should have been the Springboks captain. However, he was too honestly outspoken on both rugby and political issues to be in favour with the Afrikaner-dominated South African Rugby Board, who always described him as 'controversial'. This was a euphemism for his intelligent resistance to racialism and to the structure of South African rugby. Like the Watson brothers in Port Elizabeth, who also suffered grievously for their beliefs, Bedford always championed the cause of the black man in rugby. His sheer force of character, intelligence and personality ensured, in the end, that he captained the Springboks, but he never became one of the inner circle.

In deference to Bedford's influence, the Lions chose a strong side against Natal and all but three of the Test team played. They played an intimidatory sort of game and were leading by a mere 9–6 ten minutes from the end, but won finally by 34–6. Oddly, 21 of those points came in injury time, or perhaps it should have been called 'fighting time', which in itself was a bizarre record. The Lions' behaviour that day was strange and unsmiling and there was nothing stranger than a rush of blood by J.P.R. Williams. He was tackled into touch – quite fairly, I thought – by Bedford, and a boot struck him, apparently accidentally. However, he seemed to go berserk and rained blows on the luckless Bedford, and the crowd and the police had to go to Bedford's aid and restrain Williams. Later in the game, Bedford was flattened again, this time by a forward, and the crowd went berserk and began pelting the Lions with oranges and beer cans. The game was stopped as McBride led his team to the centre of the pitch, while the police restored order. This took a long time, about ten minutes, which was why the referee added 11 minutes of injury time at the end.

Williams, who was actually staying on to work in a hospital in Durban after the tour, was later contrite about the affair and admitted that he had lost his temper. He also said that, during his subsequent stay in Durban, he felt the whole of Natal hated him for a while. His worst punishment was the tremendous dressing-down that his wife gave him in the marquee afterwards; I heard every word of it and she did not spare him.

Another remarkable moment came in Tommy Bedford's post-match speech in the same marquee, when he berated the Springboks selectors and said how delighted he was that they had found their way to Natal at long last, and then put two fingers up to them, which everyone thought was the end of his career. Yes, it was one of the most extraordinary and bizarre afternoons in the Lions' history, and not one of the 1974 Lions' better days.

Although the series was over, more than 80,000 spectators packed Ellis Park for the last Test and saw South Africa rescue a little pride, with a drawn game at 13–13. The Lions were now tour-weary and were wanting to go home, but there was one last controversy, when the referee disallowed a last-minute try which, according to the photographic evidence, was definitely scored by Slattery. The referee, Max Baise, was later to say that Slattery had touched down, but he had already blown the whistle and disallowed the try, a statement which was weak, because surely he had plenty of time even after blowing up to award the try. Slattery, in his account, claims that he scored without doubt, but that the Springboks scrum-half, Paul Bayvel, screamed, 'He hasn't touched it, no try, no try', which influenced the referee. Anyway, that is all water under the bridge and the Lions had almost miraculously gone unbeaten. In the final game of the tour they had scored tries by Uttley and Irvine, with a conversion by Bennett and a penalty goal by

Irvine. For South Africa, Cronje scored the Springboks' only try of the series and Snyman kicked three penalty goals.

The Lions had created the greatest Lions pack ever and did not lose a single match, and you cannot do much better than that. After all, the object of the game is to win, and the Lions had done that and also scored ten tries to one in the Test rubber. I wonder when we will see their like again.

## Results of the 1974 Lions in South Africa

P 22   W 21   D 1   L 0   F 729   A 207

| | | | |
|---|---|---|---|
| Western Transvaal | W | 59 | 13 |
| South West Africa | W | 23 | 16 |
| Boland | W | 33 | 6 |
| Eastern Province | W | 28 | 14 |
| South Western Districts | W | 97 | 0 |
| Western Province | W | 17 | 8 |
| SAR Federation XV | W | 37 | 6 |
| South Africa (Cape Town) | W | 12 | 3 |
| Southern Universities | W | 26 | 4 |
| Transvaal | W | 23 | 15 |
| Rhodesia (Salisbury) | W | 42 | 6 |
| South Africa (Pretoria) | W | 28 | 9 |
| Quaggas | W | 20 | 16 |
| Orange Free State | W | 11 | 9 |
| Griqualand West | W | 69 | 16 |
| Northern Transvaal | W | 16 | 12 |
| Leopards | W | 56 | 10 |
| South Africa (Port Elizabeth) | W | 26 | 9 |
| Border | W | 26 | 6 |
| Natal | W | 34 | 6 |
| Eastern Transvaal | W | 33 | 10 |
| South Africa (Johannesburg) | D | 13 | 13 |

## Willie John McBride's 1974 Lions team

**Full-backs**

| | | |
|---|---|---|
| A.R. Irvine | Heriot's FP | Scotland |
| J.P.R. Williams | London Welsh | Wales |

## Three-quarters

| | | |
|---|---|---|
| R.T.E. Bergiers | Llanelli | Wales |
| G.W. Evans | Coventry | England |
| T.O. Grace | St Mary's College | Ireland |
| I.R. McGeechan | Headingley | Scotland |
| R.A. Milliken | Bangor | Ireland |
| A.J. Morley* | Bristol | England |
| C.F.W. Rees | London Welsh | Wales |
| W.C.C. Steele | Bedford & RAF | Scotland |
| J.J. Williams | Llanelli | Wales |

## Half-backs

| | | |
|---|---|---|
| P. Bennett | Llanelli | Wales |
| G.O. Edwards | Cardiff | Wales |
| C.M.H. Gibson* | North of Ireland | Ireland |
| J.J. Moloney | St Mary's College | Ireland |
| A.G.B. Old | Leicester | England |

## Forwards

| | | |
|---|---|---|
| G.L. Brown | West of Scotland | Scotland |
| M.A. Burton | Gloucester | England |
| A.B. Carmichael | West of Scotland | Scotland |
| F.E. Cotton | Coventry | England |
| T.P. David | Llanelli | Wales |
| T.M. Davies | Swansea | Wales |
| K.W. Kennedy | London Irish | Ireland |
| W.J. McBride (capt.) | Ballymena | Ireland |
| S.A. McKinney | Dungannon | Ireland |
| J. McLauchlan | Jordanhill College | Scotland |
| A. Neary | Broughton Park | England |
| C.W. Ralston | Richmond | England |
| A.G. Ripley | Rosslyn Park | England |
| J.F. Slattery | Blackrock College | Ireland |
| R.M. Uttley | Gosforth | England |
| R.W. Windsor | Pontypool | Wales |

Manager: A.G. Thomas
Assistant Manager and Coach: Syd Millar

*Replacements

## Phil Bennett's 1977 Lions

After those two glorious tours in the early 1970s, 1977 was akin to 'after the Lord Mayor's show', and turned out to be a huge disappointment. They had a hard act to follow and while, before the tour started, it looked quite good on paper, it all went horribly wrong, as many mistakes were made and the pressures on them became absurd. First of all, they struck one of the worst New Zealand winters on record, for it rained and it rained. Once, on the west coast, it did not stop for four days and nights.

They also fell victim to some of the worst and most despicable press coverage I have heard of. I can still see those awful, undeserved headlines in a New Zealand weekly called *Truth*, such as 'Lions are Louts and Animals'. 'Lions are Lousy Lovers' read another paper, followed by a front-page exposé and a so-called sworn affidavit by a young lady called 'Wanda from Wanganui', claiming that she had slept with many of the team, and stating that they were no use in bed. Thirty young men away from home for three to four months are bound to suffer from homesickness or frustration at some point. They therefore behave badly on occasions and there have been many scenes of over-exuberant wrecking on various tours, induced by a few beers too many, but this is why you need good managers and captains, and I have never known a tour when such behaviour got out of hand.

These lurid press reports were another example of the dirty tricks brigade which is occasionally evident in the isolation of New Zealand. It hurt and bit deep into the Lions' morale, as family and girlfriends rang up from home demanding to know what was going on. Consider what these men went through from the moment they surrendered their passports at the start of the tour; they risked serious injury and drew big crowds to their games, without any personal reward apart from the experience, and yet they were often jeered at and treated badly by the public and the media. It makes you wonder if it was worth it!

I am obliged to John Hopkins, who at the time was *The Sunday Times*'s correspondent, for the following statistics. From the time the Lions left London on 10 May until they returned on 19 August, they made 30 different flights, ten major and umpteen minor coach trips and one train journey. They took off and landed 70 times from 20 different airports in three continents; they travelled over 40,000 miles in all, played 26 games of rugby watched by 718,000 spectators and millions more on television, and put $2,025,000 into the coffers of the New Zealand Rugby Union – and all in the name of amateurism. It makes you think!

Against this difficult background, these Lions developed a siege mentality and were led into this by their management. John Dawes later admitted to me that this was his worst mistake and that, if he could have gone back, he would have done things differently. So insular did the management become, that most of the media were at odds with them. A few years later, John Dawes apologised to me for his behaviour towards the press party of which I was a member. I was delighted to accept, for I was always a huge fan of this man who had, and still does have, so much to offer the game. He was, without question, the best tactician and captain of his time, for which he was recognised with the award of an OBE.

George Burrell, the manager, was also a good man, but he, too, succumbed to the pressure of the need for success and to the hateful and unsubstantiated campaign by some elements of the New Zealand press, for he was also imbued with that typical Scottish reserve regarding the press, which is maintained to this day. What a pity that so many tour managements fail in this regard, when all it needs is a little kidology and co-operation, as practised by Carwyn James and Doug Smith.

The management were also a bit paranoid about any references to these predecessors who, on their arrival in New Zealand three weeks before the end of the tour, were hardly embraced. Their sensitivity to criticism was their Achilles' heel, for this caused them to create a protective shield around men quite capable of looking after themselves. This manifested itself in a disapproving look across the room and a shake of the head if they saw a player talking to a pressman.

Phil Bennett was made captain, but, as he wrote so self-effacingly in his book, *Everywhere for Wales*, published after his retirement, 'I should never have accepted the captaincy of the Lions tour in 1977. I have spent many a wistful hour thinking what may have been achieved had the leadership gone to someone far better equipped than I to deal with the all-engulfing pressures of a three-month rugby expedition. By the end of our stay in New Zealand I had no desire to stay in that country since I knew that all my weaknesses as a player and tourist were exposed in that short time. Whilst I admit that I was a bad choice for the captaincy, there were others too who have cause to regret the events of 1977.'

He was not the right choice, particularly as he was having difficulty with his own game at the time, and throughout the tour his backs complained that he was pushing them across the field. Phil is one of the rugby greats in Wales and is one of the nicest, most knowledgeable and most popular of men, but perhaps he did not have that hard edge to his personality which a Lions captain must possess.

The team, when it was announced, contained 16 Welshmen, the largest representation from a single country in recent times. Geoff Wheel of Swansea was to drop out on poor medical advice, as it turned out, and Moss Keane of Ireland replaced him. Charlie Faulkner and Alan Lewis went out as replacements so there were, in the end, 18 Welshmen, six Englishmen including Bill Beaumont, another replacement, five Scots and four Irishmen in the party. This was due to the success of the Welsh team in the 1970s and because Wales finished second to France in the championship that year. On the basis that many of these Welsh players were untried at this level, there were a few too many of them and there were players more worthy of selection from the other countries.

Nevertheless, the record of the 1977 Lions was not at all bad; it merely suffered because of the expectancy after the success of the early 1970s. Remarkably, they out-played the All Blacks forwards in the Tests, but failed miserably behind the scrum to capitalise on this, thus reversing the usual pattern of matches between the All Blacks and the Lions. Considering that the All Blacks pack contained players of the calibre of Lawrie Knight, Tane Norton, Andy Haden, Frank Oliver, Ian Kirkpatrick and Graham Mourie, this was no mean feat. In the 25 games played in New Zealand, they won 21 and lost four, which included three Test defeats. They never lost to a province, which was a fine achievement in itself, and the only other game they lost was when the 'dirt-trackers' lost to New Zealand Universities on the Tuesday before the first Test.

Against this background, it is difficult to understand why this became known as 'the bad news tour' among the Lions themselves. It was all about the pressure induced on them by the fact that they were expected to win the Test matches and live up to the winning tradition of the early 1970s.

As ever, there were some fine players on this tour, including Scotland's flying full-back Andy Irvine, a great player and a charming man. I found him and his fellow Scots, Gordon Brown, Bruce Hay and Ian McGeechan, to be the best-balanced and most delightful of these particular tourists. The front row of Fran Cotton, Peter Wheeler and Graham Price, with Phil Orr in reserve, was a pretty impressive outfit, which had every front row they met in all sorts of trouble. The second row consisted of Gordon Brown and Bill Beaumont, who immediately took his place in the Test team on his arrival as replacement. This speaks for itself and begs the question of why he was not chosen in the first place. I remember how, on Beaumont's arrival at the airport, Willie Duggan sidled up to him and said in his rich Irish brogue, 'If I was you,

Bill, I'd flick off home again on the next plane.' A bemused Beaumont happily decided to stay.

There was also an abundance of cracking back-row forwards in Willie Duggan, Terry Cobner, Derek Quinnell, Tony Neary, Jeff Squire and Trevor Evans, and they all played in a Test match at some time. Terry Cobner was to have a huge influence on affairs; when things began to go wrong, he was the man who chose the forwards and led and motivated them. Gordon Brown tells the tale that, when they were all feeling depressed before the second Test, and very aware of the hostility of New Zealand towards them, Cobner reassured them. Putting it into the context of Pontypool, he turned to them and said, 'You are not alone, because at three in the morning the lights will be going on in the villages and towns of the valleys, and they will be listening on their radios and willing you on, and they will be with you every inch of the way. So remember, when you are out there on that pitch, you are not alone.' This, said Brown, had a profound effect on him and he could relate to such Welsh exhortation.

The tour badly needed a catalyst like Gareth Edwards at scrum-half, and the midfield play deteriorated rather than improved as the tour progressed. As McGeechan said, 'I seemed always to be running towards the touchline.'

The New Zealand view of the tour was that they were a very good team, but behind the scrum they lacked the real class of the 1971 team, who also enjoyed far better public relations.

The Lions had lost only one game, to the Universities, before the first Test, but they went into it without their best locks, as Brown was unfit, Horton had broken his thumb and Beaumont had just arrived. Brynmor Williams, although uncapped by Wales and inexperienced, was picked at scrum-half because of his speed and athleticism, and held the job until his hamstring went in the third Test. He would be the first to admit that he was no Edwards and was on a learning curve at the time, and a very fine player he became.

The All Blacks chose three new caps: Colin Farrell, a young lock called Andy Haden, who had toured Britain in 1972–73 and was to become a legend, and a big loose forward called Lawrie Knight. As usual, the windy city, Wellington, was living up to its name, with the wind blowing directly from Antarctica up the valley that always served as a wind tunnel to Athletic Park, where the *Sunday Telegraph* writer John Reason always reckoned that a jumbo jet could take off without a runway.

The Lions led with a penalty in the second minute, but the lead quickly evaporated when Sid Going bolted through a gap in the forwards for a typical Going try. Bennett, in spite of a shoulder injury inflicted by his own player as he lay on the ground, managed to kick two penalties, one from 50 metres, to give the Lions a lead of 9–4 which lasted until just before half-time. Then Brad Johnstone, following up a Bryan Williams penalty attempt, went over for a try which the Lions disputed, as Bill Osborne seemed to knock the ball over the line. Williams's conversion made it 10–9 to the All Blacks, but another penalty by Bennett restored the lead. Then Grant Batty, that immensely competitive All Blacks wing, intercepted a mistake by Evans (with the Lions on the attack with men to spare and a score seeming inevitable), and ran 60 metres for a try under the posts, converted by Williams to give his side a half-time lead of 16–12. This was effectively a 12-point try, as the score should have been 18–10 to the Lions. On such threads hang much of the history of our game, and there the score stood until the final whistle for, despite the All Blacks having the wind advantage, they failed to harness it and the remainder became a dour, static affair.

For the second Test at Christchurch, the Lions made six changes, all on current form as everyone was available for selection. Brown and Beaumont came in at lock, Quinnell came in to strengthen the back row, and Cotton and Wheeler replaced Orr and Windsor. Surprisingly, Gareth Evans replaced Peter Squires and J.J. Williams was moved from left to right wing. For New Zealand, Batty withdrew with a leg injury and then shocked New Zealand by announcing his retirement. Small, but very strong and combative, he ended a 56-match career for the All Blacks, in which he had scored 45 tries.

It was a poor game with very little flow and it was mean-spirited, resulting in one dreadful all-out brawl after Eveleigh late-tackled Bennett. Nevertheless, it gave the Lions immense pleasure because, after the disappointment of losing that psychologically important first Test, it was a win which would keep the series alive until the last Test and put them in with a chance. It will be remembered as Terry Cobner's Test, for he took command of the forwards. It was even said that he picked them. He made sure that the mistakes of the first Test lineouts would not be repeated, and reorganised them and generally tightened up the forward play. The All Blacks had lost their best tight-head prop, Kent Lambert, with appendicitis, which also played into Cobner's hands.

It was another heavy, muddy pitch, but this test was to show that the Lions forwards were developing into a powerful force, more than capable of beating the All Blacks forwards. It was also evident that the All Blacks were giving Bennett special attention and he was put down fiercely, with one late tackle by Eveleigh producing a huge dust-up. The Lions saw red at this and other incidents and, from time to time, the match generally deteriorated into an unseemly brawl.

Meanwhile, within seven minutes, Phil Bennett had kicked a penalty and soon the Lions were establishing a considerable advantage in the rucks and mauls. J.J. Williams then scored the only try of the game, with a splendid dummy after a kick ahead by Bennett and terrific approach work by Brown, Quinnell and McGeechan. Bennett banged over another penalty and, after a hectic first 20 minutes, they led 10–0. Bryan Williams now kicked a penalty and got his third, and J.J. Williams another, to make it 13–6 at the break. The second half, marred by that tremendous brawl, was a poor affair and the only addition to the score was another penalty by Williams. Although the All Blacks tried desperately to win in the last ten minutes, the Lions held out for a well-deserved win at 13–9.

New Zealand made six changes for the third Test, including dropping Eveleigh for Graham Mourie, but the biggest surprise was that they dropped Syd Going, who had scored three tries against the Lions on tour, for Lyn Davis.

The previous week, the Lions had demolished the powerful Auckland team by 34–15 and were favourites to win at Dunedin. They made only one change, replacing McGeechan with David Burcher.

It was yet another boggy surface, for you could not believe what a wet tour this was, and on the morning of the game they had a helicopter on the pitch trying to dry out the surface.

New Zealand began spectacularly when, from the first lineout, they spun the ball to Bruce Robertson, who kicked ahead; the Lions defence made a hash of gathering and Ian Kirkpatrick scored. Bevan Wilson converted and, within a minute, the All Blacks led 6–0. Five minutes later, a break by Brynmor Williams brought a try by Willie Duggan, and the hectic pace continued as Andy Haden charged over for a try in the 11th minute. The score of 10–4 stood until half-time.

In the second half, the Lions lost Brynmor Williams early on with a hamstring injury and, later in the half, lost J.J. Williams for the same reason. They were replaced by Doug Morgan and Ian McGeechan. Irvine kicked a penalty, but Bevan Wilson, who had an inspired match, kicked two more penalties and Bruce Robertson dropped a goal, to give the All Blacks a well-earned victory by 19–7. The Lions' kicking had been deplorable, the pressure of the captaincy weighing on Bennett's game. Six out of seven attempts at goal had been missed and it was a frustrated and sad Lions team which contemplated the fact that it was now impossible to win the series.

For the fourth Test at Eden Park, Auckland, the Lions had lost four of their best players: Cobner, Quinnell, Brynmor and J.J. Williams, because of injury. Tony Neary and Jeff Squire were brought in. Both of them had been playing superbly, and Neary's game against the Maoris was a *tour de force*. Even with these changes, the Lions pack was still too powerful for the All Blacks. Doug Morgan, a terrier of a scrum-half who was a good kicker, came in for Williams, and Ian McGeechan was restored at centre.

Once more the All Blacks forwards were outclassed, but again the Lions managed to lose a Test that they should have won. Wilson opened the scoring with a penalty and Morgan kicked one for the Lions after 25 minutes, and then scored a tremendous try in which Cotton, Beaumont, Price and Fenwick all played a part. It gave the Lions a half-time lead of 9–3, and with their forward control it was hard to see how they could lose. The All Blacks even tried putting only three men in the scrum, in an attempt to combat the ball-winning of their opponents, but nevertheless the Lions lost. Wilson kicked another penalty and then, in injury time, Osborne gathered a bad clearance kick and put up a speculative high ball. Fenwick and Wheeler were jolted in tackles from Osborne and Mourie. The ball went loose to Lawrie Knight, who ran 15 metres for the corner and the most vital try of the series.

Two more great All Blacks ended their careers with this game, namely Kirkpatrick, a real giant of a flanker in the game and truly one of the finest in the world, and the long-time respected hooker and captain, Tane Norton.

After the game, the Lions' dressing-room was like a morgue, with some of the hardest-bitten forwards in tears. They knew that they had provided the team with every opportunity to win the series, but it had been blown by the profligacy of the back play. It was a sad end to a sad tour, in which the old Lions tradition of having fun had somehow become lost in the unhappy character of the tour. For that, the management was to blame.

On the way home, they licked their wounds in Fiji where, for the first time ever, the Fijian national team played the Lions. However, the jinx followed them and they lost to Fiji 25–21. It was typical that a strike at London Airport of air traffic controllers saw them arriving home 12 hours late, and their planned reception was cancelled. It had been that sort of an experience throughout.

# Results of the 1977 Lions in New Zealand and Fiji

P 26   W 21   D 0   L 5   F 607   A 320

| | | | |
|---|---|---|---|
| Wairarapa–Bush | W | 41 | 13 |
| Hawke's Bay | W | 13 | 11 |
| Poverty Bay–East Coast | W | 25 | 6 |
| Taranaki | W | 21 | 13 |
| King Country–Wanganui | W | 60 | 9 |
| Manawatu–Horowhenua | W | 18 | 12 |
| Otago | W | 12 | 7 |
| Southland | W | 20 | 12 |
| New Zealand Universities | L | 9 | 21 |
| New Zealand (Wellington) | L | 12 | 16 |
| Hanan Shield Districts | W | 45 | 6 |
| Canterbury | W | 14 | 13 |
| West Coast–Buller | W | 45 | 0 |
| Wellington | W | 13 | 6 |
| Marlborough–Nelson | W | 40 | 23 |
| New Zealand (Christchurch) | W | 13 | 9 |
| New Zealand Maoris | W | 22 | 19 |
| Waikato | W | 18 | 13 |
| New Zealand Juniors | W | 19 | 9 |
| Auckland | W | 34 | 15 |
| New Zealand (Dunedin) | L | 7 | 19 |
| Counties–Thames Valley | W | 35 | 10 |
| North Auckland | W | 18 | 7 |
| Bay of Plenty | W | 23 | 16 |
| New Zealand (Auckland) | L | 9 | 10 |
| Fiji | L | 21 | 25 |

## Phil Bennett's 1977 Lions

**Full-backs**

| | | |
|---|---|---|
| B.H. Hay | Boroughmuir | Scotland |
| A.R. Irvine | Heriot's FP | Scotland |

**Three-quarters**

| | | |
|---|---|---|
| D.H. Burcher | Newport | Wales |
| G.L. Evans | Newport | Wales |
| S.P. Fenwick | Bridgend | Wales |

| C.M.H. Gibson | North of Ireland | Ireland |
| I.R. McGeechan | Headingley | Scotland |
| H.E. Rees | Neath | |
| P.J. Squires | Harrogate | England |
| J.J. Williams | Llanelli | Wales |

**Half-backs**

| P. Bennett (capt.) | Llanelli | Wales |
| J.D. Bevan | Aberavon | Wales |
| A.D. Lewis* | Cambridge University & London Welsh | |
| D.W. Morgan | Stewart's Melville FP | Scotland |
| D.B. Williams | Cardiff | |

**Forwards**

| W.B. Beaumont* | Fylde | England |
| G.L. Brown | West of Scotland | Scotland |
| T.J. Cobner | Pontypool | Wales |
| F.E Cotton | Coventry | England |
| W.P. Duggan | Blackrock College | Ireland |
| T.P. Evans | Swansea | Wales |
| A.G. Faulkner* | Pontypool | Wales |
| N.E. Horton | Moseley | England |
| M.I. Keane | Lansdowne | Ireland |
| A.J. Martin | Aberavon | Wales |
| A. Neary | Broughton Park | England |
| P.A. Orr | Old Wesley | Ireland |
| G. Price | Pontypool | Wales |
| D.L. Quinnell | Llanelli | Wales |
| J. Squire | Newport | Wales |
| P.J. Wheeler | Leicester | England |
| C. Williams | Aberavon | Wales |
| R.W. Windsor | Pontypool | Wales |

Manager: G. Burrell
Assistant Manager and Coach: John Dawes

* Replacements

# Changing Times

The 1980s were to see dramatic changes in attitudes concerning overseas tours, due to the economic demands of the age. Amateur players found it harder to get away from work and the sacrifice of a job became too big a price to pay, even for the enormous satisfaction and honour of selection for the Lions. The lure of an all-expenses-paid holiday to one of the more seductively beautiful countries in the world, described so vividly by the title of Alan Paton's famous book *Cry the Beloved Country,* was insufficient recompense for risking a future career, and therefore the short tour became accepted as a necessity, beginning in 1980.

It was, after all, the year when redundancies in Britain began to reach 40,000 a month and unemployment figures topped two million. There was a steel strike against closures, which lasted ten weeks; 100 men died when a North Sea oil rig collapsed; Hitchcock, Sartre, Tito, Henry Miller and Peter Sellers all died; the SAS stormed the Iranian embassy; and Prince Charles had a new girlfriend, Diana Spencer. Borg won Wimbledon for the fifth time, and Ovett and Coe won Olympic gold medals. It was also the year when Rhodesia became Zimbabwe.

Everything was becoming more political in the rugby world. The players were beginning to rethink the old philosophy of amateurism, a process accelerated by the greater exposure to the southern hemisphere, especially in 1987 when, after years of soul-searching debates, the first prototype of the Rugby World Cup was held in Australia and New Zealand. Inevitably, it was the hidebound conservative British establishments which most resisted change and, in the end, England and Scotland in particular were dragged practically kicking and screaming into the World Cup by an ultimatum from the more blithe-spirited New Zealand and Australia.

## BILL BEAUMONT'S 1980 LIONS

The 1980 tour was, therefore, the first of the short tours, condensing 18 matches into ten weeks, which meant greater intensity with fewer easy matches and less time to build Test teams. It was also to be the centre of a bitter controversy in the year preceding the tour, as the anti-apartheid lobby gathered its considerable forces to try and prevent the tour taking place. Remember that resolutions had been passed in the United Nations and in the Gleneagles agreement among Commonwealth leaders, condemning apartheid and discouraging sporting contacts with South Africa. South Africa had not appeared at an Olympic Games since 1960 and were barred from competing internationally at athletics, cricket and soccer. All South African teams were barred from Australia, and a proposed Springboks tour to France was blocked at the last moment when the French government refused to grant them visas.

In the late summer of 1978, the IRFB held a board meeting in South Africa and, while they were there, they investigated apartheid in South African rugby. Consequently, in April 1979, the South African Rugby Board absorbed the Coloured South African Rugby Federation and claimed that they represented all races, that coaching courses were to be arranged along non-racial lines, that equal provision, facilities and opportunities were to be given to players and spectators of all races, and that all national teams would be selected on merit from mixed trials. It all sounded pretty good and it was enough for the Four Home Unions to invite a South African Barbarians side to visit Britain.

The opposition could not believe the naivety of the British rugby authorities in the matter, particularly when it was announced that the team would contain an equal number of black, coloured and white players. This was immediately perceived as being mere cosmetic window-dressing, and it was not surprising that there was immense political hostility to the tour, both externally and internally in South Africa. The forces of HART (Halt All Racist Tours) and SANROC (South African Non-Racial Olympic Committee) mobilised their opposition. The Sports Council, headed by Dickie Jeeps, threatened to remove their annual grant to the RFU and Hector Munro, the Minister of Sport, a rugby man who managed Scotland on their tour to Australia in 1970 and who had been President of the Scottish Rugby Union in 1976, also pleaded with the Tours Committee of the Four Home Unions.

They got short shrift, and the tour went ahead. It was managed by Chick Henderson, an Oxford Blue and Scottish international in the 1950s, and an old friend of mine who is one of the best of men. I played against Chick in the Welsh game in Edinburgh in 1953, and on one occasion we wheeled the first scrum and took the ball away with the feet, as we used to do in those days. However, we pushed the ball a few yards too far and suddenly Chick threw himself on it, just as I took an almighty kick to send it up to the Scottish line. Suffice it to say that the thud was heard all over Murrayfield and Chick was carried off for a few minutes' treatment. Cliff Morgan, in the meantime, was heard to say to Bleddyn Williams, 'We've won this bloody game!' The sequel was that I had not seen Chick for many years until the 1974 tour and, politely, I enquired about the back. Chick ran his hand over it and said, 'It's getting better!' Needless to say, that exchange has become a ritual between us whenever we meet.

The assistant manager was another charming man, Duggie Dyers, from the Coloured community in Cape Town. So good were Henderson's public relations and his relations with the press that the tour got through unscathed, apart from the Irish withdrawing their invitation because of pressure from their government.

All the same, anti-apartheid lobbies applied pressure to the impending Lions tour, as did a few others besides, such as the Supreme Council for Sport in Africa, which threatened to boycott the Olympics in Moscow and to disrupt the Commonwealth Games in 1982 in Brisbane, Australia. Meanwhile, the Four Home Unions continued to keep their cards close to their chest concerning the 1980 Lions to South Africa, and played for time.

Further pleas by Hector Munro on behalf of the government, and by Dickie Jeeps and John Disley on behalf of the Sports Council, were made to the Tours Committee, which was chaired by Micky Steele-Bodger. He was a famous Rugby man steeped in the old traditions, who played for Rugby School, Cambridge and Edinburgh Universities, Harlequins, Moseley, the Co-optimists, the Barbarians and England, and who later was to become President of the RFU and the Barbarians. The pleas were turned down and the Tours Committee decided in January that, as all four home nations were in agreement, the tour would go ahead. The final decision was made in the historic India Sports Club in St James's Square, London, where the news of the winning of the Battle of Waterloo by the Duke of Wellington had been brought to the Prince Regent, as he dined with the Prime Minister, Lord Liverpool, and the Foreign Secretary, Viscount Castlereagh.

They were considered to be supporting the *Verkramptes* (unenlightened) against the *Verligtes* (enlightened) and alienated many people in South Africa. Good men like Donald Woods, the Watson brothers, Peter Hain and Tommy Bedford, among many others, opposed their view, because they understood what was meant by apartheid: a racial ideology which, among many abominations, kept wives, husbands and children apart. The events were overtaken by US President Jimmy Carter's boycott of the Olympic Games in Moscow, which drew most of the media's fire and took the heat off the Lions tour.

The British rugby establishment were seen by these people as giving succour to apartheid: as Bishop Tutu said, 'They made the other chaps (the Government) feel a little better.' The British 'other chaps' believed that, by their going, the South African Government would see the light. I have no doubt that what finally convinced the sports-mad Afrikaners, who had blindly followed the diktats of their government, to see reason was not any economic boycott but the loss of their rugby and cricket, and because world repugnance and the sporting boycott ate so deeply into their psyche.

Mercifully, the bad days are over and the time of reconciliation is upon South Africa and us; the Lions can now go to South Africa in May 1997 with a clear conscience. They will have an experience of a lifetime, and something that money cannot buy: friendship and hospitality the like of which they will never have seen because, thankfully, it is a common ground of both the white and black African.

If 1977 was the unhappy tour, then this was the unlucky tour. They had so many injuries that they required a record number of replacements; thus the party included in all 15 Welshmen, ten English, eight Irish and five Scots. The party had been picked against the background of a disgraceful game at Twickenham, when Paul Ringer was sent off following a series of offences. England had finished top of the Five Nations Championship for the first time in 16 years and, led by their enormously popular captain Bill Beaumont, had won the Triple Crown and pulled off the Grand Slam to end one of their most barren periods without success. France, unusually, had finished bottom. The 41 tries scored in the championship were the most scored for 50 years, and Ollie Campbell with 46 and Andy Irvine with 35 had broken the respective Irish and Scottish points-scoring records. The omens for the tour, therefore, looked bright.

The playing part of the tour was barely a minute old when the first serious injury was sustained, as Stuart Lane tore his ligaments and had to return home. From there on, injuries came thick and fast, with an unprecedented eight replacements having to be sent out. Consequently, we saw three fly-halves employed in the series, in Tony Ward, Gareth Davies and Ollie Campbell. We also saw five centres used and four wings, whereas the front five of the pack played together throughout the series and there were only four back-row men employed. It is evident where the problems were.

It was the first Lions party to take a doctor with them. In Dr Jack Matthews, a Welsh Lion of 1950, they had the right man, and my word, how he was needed! In fact, these Lions could have done with a team of doctors.

Because of the political content of the tour due to the pre-tour controversies, there was the largest-ever contingent of pressmen and photographers from the UK and Ireland covering the tour. By now the tabloids were gaining strength and were looking for off-the-field stories, and they soon became known as 'the rat pack' by the players. So well did these Lions conduct themselves, and so good-natured and comparatively relaxed were they (in contrast with 1977), that these so-called 'colour writers' found little or no dirt to write about.

It was obvious that strong management was needed for such a tour, and the big, bluff and genial Irishman, Syd Millar, with a wealth of experience, was the perfect man. He had forged and coached the glittering 1974 team in the Republic, and, to partner him, they chose an equally genial, gregarious and tough character in Noel Murphy from Cork, who was Ireland's most-capped flanker until Slattery overtook him in 1980. Noel was an unusual animal, for he was a teetotaller, but it never seemed to quash his exuberance. So we had a Northern Irish Protestant and a Southern Irish Catholic in charge, which was a fair balance. They did not have to look far for a captain, and Bill Beaumont was duly rewarded for his success in the Five Nations Championship, and became the first Englishman to captain the Lions since Douglas Prentice 50 years earlier. Bill had the stature, the strength of character, and a deep sense of loyalty to those in his charge, and was one of the most popular choices ever. This triumvirate had no critics whatsoever.

One of the most poignant moments of the tour, which gave me an insight into Beaumont's character, came when a local man in Windhoek, South West Africa, invited the Lions to a shoot on his private game reserve. I happened to be within a couple of yards of Bill when a warden signalled to us to stay still, and suddenly a massive kudu, with huge spiralling horns, appeared out of the bush and Bill was asked to shoot it. I sensed his reluctance to fire but, egged on by his hosts and some of his team, he brought it down. I was studying his face, which suddenly looked distraught, and I knew he was bitterly regretting his action; if you offered him ten thousand pounds to do it again, I am sure he would have refused. He was such a big man, with all the toughness of a world-class rugby player, but underneath he was a sensitive man with deep feelings, and for a while after this incident he was difficult to console.

Because of Beaumont's outstanding captaincy and the guiding hand of the admirable management of Millar and Murphy, the Lions were a well-controlled and disciplined party, but they were not quite good enough. Although they had a powerful pack which could hold its own with anything that the Springboks could throw at them, they again lacked a couple of midfield backs capable of sparking the team in running attack.

In the original squad there were 12 Welshmen, eight English, five Scots and five Irish. They were to meet a Springboks side which, although short of Test experience because of the boycott, were nevertheless able to keep up their standards because of the growing strength of their Currie Cup competition. The Lions won all 14 of their provincial games. Several of these were close encounters, but they beat two of the strongest provinces, Northern Transvaal and Western Province, with some ease, the latter by 37–6, which was their biggest defeat since Hammond's team in 1896.

They also scored one of the finest tries I have ever seen when, against a South African Invitation XV, they scored what must also be the most astonishing and glorious try ever experienced in South Africa, which snatched a 15–6 victory from what looked like certain defeat. It began when David Richards broke from a lineout in his own 22 and darted upfield. What was to happen next beggared belief, for the ball went through a total of four rucks, with Derek Quinnell digging it out three times, and it went through 30 pairs of hands, before Mike Slemen finished it off with a try under the posts. The video tape revealed that the movement lasted one minute and 45 seconds.

The Lions won all six of their provincial games leading to the first Test, but there were signs that the Springboks were stiffening their sinews and it was evident that they had absorbed many of the lessons of 1974. When the Lions were in Bloemfontein to play the Orange Free State, including de Wet Ras who was expected to be in the Springboks team, that archetypal Welshman, the lovable Ray Gravell, destroyed him with a tackle that was almost as high as the altitude at which they were playing, and de Wat Ras was taken off with a broken jaw. I was phoning my copy back to the London paper immediately on the whistle and finding it difficult to describe Ray's indiscretion, so I said, 'Ray Gravell had a pretty woolly game and his high tackle broke Ras's jaw', because everyone who knows Ray believes that he would not have done it on purpose. I did not realise that Carwyn James, his Llanelli coach and mentor, was sitting next to me and heard every word which, gleefully, he related to the always over-anxious Ray, who then made my life a misery for the next couple of days by coming up to me and asking, 'What do you mean by woolly?'

The sequel to this came a few days later, when we were waiting for a plane in Jan Smuts airport, Johannesburg. A voice in a guttural Afrikaans accent came over the tannoy: 'Would Mr Clem Thomas please report to the information desk immediately, because he has left his hotel without paying his bill.' It was Ray Gravell, who was later to become a paid-up member of Equity.

Although the Springboks took their revenge for 1974 and won the series 3–1, things might have been different but for the injuries and illness, including that of Fran Cotton, who developed pericarditis. However, South Africa were a fine side led by one of their greatest leaders, Morne du Plessis, and they contained some tremendous players like Ray Mordt and Rob Louw. It was also to be the Lions' first glimpse of the influential Northern Transvaal fly-half Naas Botha, who became regarded as South Africa's greatest-ever kicker and match-winner. The Springboks perhaps surprised the Lions by their enterprising running, with Gysie Pienaar being especially effective as a running full-back. South Africa also had some typically large locks in 'Moaner' van Heerden (whose real names are Johannes Lodeiwkus), Kevin de Klerk and Louis Moolman.

The Lions already had seven players out of contention for the first Test, but their forwards always had the edge. However, their backs let them down, while the Springboks backs used every opportunity. Rob Louw's pace gave South Africa their first score and it developed into a competition to see whether South Africa could score enough tries to keep up with Tony Ward's exceptional goal kicking. He scored 18 points with five penalties and a drop goal, to break the South African record of 17 points established by Tom Kiernan 12 years earlier. The only Lions try was scored by Graham Price. Meanwhile Willie du Plessis, van Heerden and Gerrie Germishuys all went over for tries and Naas Botha added three conversions, to make it 22–22. It was Rob Louw again who created the winning try for Divan Serfontein, for a narrow 26–22 win by South Africa.

The second Test saw the late arrival, Andy Irvine, at full-back in place of Rodney O'Donnell; Clive Woodward and Ray Gravell came in for Renwick and Richards, and Bruce Hay replaced Mike Slemen, who had to go home due to illness in his family. Gareth Davies replaced Ward at fly-half, but the pack remained in its entirety, so it is obvious where the selectors thought their problems lay. The Springboks team only had one change, with de Klerk coming in for van Heerden.

It was Lions' errors turned to advantage by the Springboks which won the game, and Gysie Pienaar had a marvellous day, punishing many ill-conceived kicks by the Lions. South Africa scored a try almost identical to the one which started their scoring in the first Test, and it was Louw again who scored it. John O'Driscoll replied with one for the Lions from a chip by Patterson, and Davies converted from the touchline.

Botha then kicked a penalty and Stoffberg scored a try, which the neutral referee Francis Palmade (the first, incidentally, in the history of Lions rugby) should have disallowed, for Mordt had got up with the ball after a tackle. However, it stood and Botha converted to make the Lions 13–6 down after a period of sustained attack which ought to have seen them into the lead. It was a mortal blow and there seemed no way back, particularly after Botha had kicked another penalty, but Gareth Davies also scored and it was 16–9 to South Africa at half-time.

The Lions then pulled up to 16–12 with another penalty by Davies, and Irvine kicked a monster to make it 16–15. Davies then became the next casualty with badly injured knee ligaments and Campbell, his replacement, missed a penalty from 30 yards, but wide out. Germishuys scored a try from a cross-kick by Pienaar and the Lions were finally buried by a try by Pienaar, which Botha converted. Gravell had the last word, with a try in the closing minutes to make it 26–19, but by then the Lions had already frittered away the game.

The Lions needed to win the third Test in Port Elizabeth to stay alive in the series. They brought Paul Dodge into the centre for Woodward, who replaced Carleton on the wing, Campbell for Davies at fly-half, and Colm Tucker came in at flanker, as Squire replaced Quinnell at number eight. The Springboks changed only van Heerden for de Klerk. For once, the Lions took the early lead with a penalty by Campbell but, midway through the half, Botha kicked the equaliser. Bruce Hay, a hundred-per-cent player if ever there was one, then went over for a try. Soon after half time, Botha dropped a goal and Campbell landed another penalty; the Lions led by 10–6 and seemed totally in the ascendancy but, as so often happens, South Africa stole another try by Germishuys and Botha converted, to win a game which the Lions should have won comfortably. Morne du Plessis said that the better team lost, but that was no consolation for the Lions forwards, who had won so much ball from rucks, mauls and lineouts, only to see their backs fail to put points on the board.

A midweek frolic against the South African Barbarians, who included the brilliant Argentinian Hugo Porta, followed by a stunning defeat of Western Province, was part of the run-up to the final Test, which showed that the Lions were not giving up and that morale was still high.

In the end, they avoided the ignominy of being the first Lions to be whitewashed by South Africa in the Test matches, and they also became the first Lions to win the fourth Test. After an exchange of penalties by

Campbell and Botha, Clive Williams, the prop, burrowed his way over for a try, for the Lions to lead at half-time. Willie du Plessis then scored a try to level and Pienaar, who replaced Naas Botha as kicker after he was booed by his home crowd in Pretoria, seemed to put the Lions in familiar trouble, but they then scored two tries in as many minutes through Irvine and O'Driscoll, and a final conversion by Campbell saw them secure a narrow victory, which was a meagre return for their forward dominance. It left the South Africans wondering what had happened to British back play as practised, best of all, by the 1955 Lions. We are still pondering that question 16 years later.

As I have said, it was a happy tour for the Lions and their supporters, which was epitomised when my wife, who came out for the last couple of weeks, asked Carwyn James, travelling with myself and John Reason, if he had enjoyed it. His reply to her was, 'I wish it could go on for ever.'

## Results of the 1980 Lions in South Africa

P 18   W 15   D 0   L 3   F 401   A 244

| | | |
|---|---|---|
| Eastern Province | W | 28 | 16 |
| SARA Invitation XV | W | 28 | 6 |
| Natal | W | 21 | 15 |
| SA Invitation XV | W | 22 | 19 |
| Orange Free State | W | 21 | 17 |
| SAR Federation XV | W | 15 | 6 |
| South Africa (Cape Town) | L | 22 | 26 |
| SA Country Districts | W | 27 | 7 |
| Transvaal | W | 32 | 12 |
| Eastern Transvaal | W | 21 | 15 |
| South Africa (Bloemfontein) | L | 19 | 26 |
| Junior Springboks | W | 17 | 6 |
| Northern Transvaal | W | 16 | 9 |
| South Africa (Port Elizabeth) | L | 10 | 12 |
| SA Barbarians | W | 25 | 14 |
| Western Province | W | 37 | 6 |
| Griqualand West | W | 23 | 19 |
| South Africa (Pretoria) | W | 17 | 13 |

# Bill Beaumont's 1980 Lions team

## Full-backs

| | | |
|---|---|---|
| B.H. Hay | Boroughmuir | Scotland |
| A.R. Irvine* | Heriot's FP | Scotland |
| R.C. O'Donnell | St Mary's College | Ireland |

## Three-quarters

| | | |
|---|---|---|
| J. Carleton | Orrell | England |
| P.W. Dodge* | Leicester | England |
| R.W.R. Gravell | Llanelli | Wales |
| P.J. Morgan | Llanelli | Wales |
| H.E. Rees | Neath | Wales |
| J.M. Renwick | Hawick | Scotland |
| D.S. Richards | Swansea | Wales |
| M.A.C. Slemen | Liverpool | England |
| C.R. Woodward | Leicester | England |

## Half-backs

| | | |
|---|---|---|
| S.O. Campbell | Old Belvedere | Ireland |
| W.G. Davies | Cardiff | Wales |
| T.D. Holmes | Cardiff | Wales |
| C.S. Patterson | Instonians | Ireland |
| J.C. Robbie* | Greystones | Ireland |
| S.J. Smith* | Sale | England |
| A.J.P. Ward* | Garryowen | Ireland |

## Forwards

| | | |
|---|---|---|
| J.R. Beattie | Glasgow Academicals | Scotland |
| W.B. Beaumont (capt.) | Fylde | England |
| P.J. Blakeway | Gloucester | England |
| M.J. Colclough | Angoulême | England |
| F.E. Cotton | Sale | England |
| S.M. Lane | Cardiff | Wales |
| A.J. Martin | Aberavon | Wales |
| J.B. O'Driscoll | London Irish | Ireland |
| P.A. Orr* | Old Wesley | Ireland |
| A.J. Phillips | Cardiff | Wales |
| G. Price | Pontypool | Wales |
| D.L. Quinnell | Llanelli | Wales |
| J. Squire | Pontypool | Wales |
| I. Stephens* | Bridgend | Wales |

| A.J. Tomes | Hawick | Scotland |
| C.C. Tucker | Shannon | Ireland |
| P.J. Wheeler | Leicester | England |
| C. Williams | Swansea | Wales |
| G.P. Williams* | Bridgend | Wales |

Manager: Syd Millar
Assistant Manager and Coach: Noel Murphy
Honorary Doctor: Jack Matthews

* Replacements

## CIARAN FITZGERALD'S 1983 LIONS

By now, the principle of the shorter tour was accepted, but not by men like Willie John McBride and Jim Telfer, who were to be manager and coach respectively on the 1983 tour to New Zealand. Both these old warriors understood the necessity of building a team by making these united nations' representatives battle-hardened in the minor skirmishes before going into the real battle. To play a Test match against New Zealand within three weeks of arrival made no sense at all to them. For the first time, this issue of shorter visits made people question the validity of Lions tours, pointing out that perhaps individual countries' teams may be the better option, with their strengths and weaknesses known more instinctively because of familiarity.

Ireland, who were bottom of the Five Nations Championship in 1981 and then, in their irrepressible way, won the Triple Crown in 1982 and the Championship in both 1982 and 1983, were to have a strong influence on the events of this campaign, by virtue of having Ciaran Fitzgerald as captain and McBride as manager. The fact that they had a record only marginally better than the 1966 tour, who held the unenviable record of having the worst results ever by a British Isles team in New Zealand, was not their fault.

At the time, Iranian forces had crossed into Iraq; Breakfast TV commenced; Shergar was kidnapped; Australia won the Ashes; the Greenham Common protest against the siting of missiles in the UK began; President Reagan expounded his Star Wars theory, thus piling the chips so high that Russia eventually abandoned the cold war; the film *Gandhi* won eight Oscars, and Lester Piggott won his ninth Derby.

The Lions were to win little, for the problems which faced the coach Jim Telfer were daunting, due to poor pre-tour selection. Imagine leaving out Paul Dodge, among many other terrible errors of judgement! Why do Lions selectors, time and again, pick captains who are not certain of being the best in their positions on tour? There was also another dreadful injury list, and a failure by many players in key positions to play to their potential and beyond, which is always a basic requirement on such a tour. It was a time, too, when the players of all nations were beginning to question their role as cannon fodder on the world stage, as once again on tour we saw players, in a game which is supposed to be fun and enjoyment, involved in scenes of attrition.

It was no wonder that, at that time, David Lord of Australia was getting players to listen to his wild schemes of a professional circus, and rumours began circulating that some 200 players, including many of the Lions, had signed up. It proved to be pie in the sky, but it was undoubtedly the catalyst which began the rapid advance, over the next 12 years, towards rugby becoming a professional game.

A recurring theme in this Lions story was the scale of injuries sustained on the tours, and I can well remember going to see Terry Holmes, the Welsh scrum-half, in hospital in Christchurch after he received dreadful injuries to his knee. He had torn the anterior cruciate ligament, ruptured the posterior capsule of the knee joint and had also torn his medial ligament. Colin Patterson sustained a serious injury in 1980 when he also tore his knee apart, which was later repaired with carbon fibre. Then there were the events of the game at Manawatu before the first Test, when the Lions' dressing-room was a horrible place to be (and one which the Lions doctor, Donald McLeod, said he viewed with repulsion); and also the injury to Rodney O'Donnell, who broke his neck while making a tackle on Danie Gerber in the Junior Springboks game, necessitating a graft from his hip on the sixth and seventh vertebrae. These finally convinced me, if I needed any convincing after personal experience, that Lions tours were, on occasions, no longer rugby but war, and that, indeed, they were crusades.

Was it any wonder, therefore, that these top players began to look for some reward for such endeavours? The only surprising feature was that the game's administrators took so long to realise that it was they, by piling on the pressure of more and more tours and finally the concept of the World Cup, who guaranteed that professionalism would finally become a reality in 1995.

The results of this tour again mirrored the decline of British rugby in the 1980s and, without any profound analysis, the brutal truth was that the All Blacks were a far better team and the Lions were outplayed in the Test matches. For all that, they were a splendid bunch of men, who accepted their vicissitudes and worked hard for elusive success, and Willie John, who was perhaps too protective of his team at times, kept their morale up and ensured that they soldiered through to the end.

Although the preparation by Telfer was sound, to play seven matches in the first three weeks, including those against Auckland, Wellington and Manawatu and culminating in a Test match, was a suicidal itinerary.

Some critics took a hard line, and one, in the *Irish Tribune*, even went as far as to suggest that 'The nearest some of these Irish Lions should have come to this tour was Dublin Zoo'. It took a long time for the Irish to forgive him, and meanwhile, when covering internationals, he would fly in and out of Dublin on the same day. Much of the criticism revolved around the fact that most thought Colin Deans was the better hooker in the party, this belief also being held by the All Blacks captain, Andy Dalton. The main criticism levelled at Fitzgerald was that his throwing in at the lineout was weak, but otherwise he soldiered like the stalwart he was, for he was a captain in the Irish Army and could always be found in the thick of the fray. He also maintained his dignity as a leader, which was more than you could say of some of his critics. To suggest that the failure was down to him was sheer fantasy.

The zoo story, although it was amusing, was completely over the top, for the Irish were no worse or better than most of the others. Without question, the best forward was Peter Winterbottom, who covered more ground and performed more bravely than anybody. The most indomitable tight forward was Graham Price, who was indestructible; he anchored the scrum from the tight head and was a cornerstone of the scrummaging, and close behind him came Ian Stephens.

Another exceptional forward was Jeff Squire, who was a class player, and when he was injured and flown home with Terry Holmes and Ian Stephens, it was one of the lowest points of the tour morale. You simply could not lose three players of genuine Test class and expect to succeed.

Others forwards to do well were Maurice Colclough, who was now a more mature player, Steve Bainbridge, Bob Norster, John O'Driscoll and the two Scots, Iain Paxton and Jim Calder.

Once more the backs, as a unit, were hardly up to Lions standards. Terry Holmes was irreplaceable. His successor Roy Laidlaw made a fair fist of it, however, and the failure of the attack was not down to him; neither was it down to Ollie Campbell, whose support play, defence and especially his goal kicking, were superlative. Rutherford, too, had moments of inspiration as a runner, and John Carleton on the wing was the most dangerous three-quarter. Roger Baird was another who showed that, with more opportunity, he could be dangerous, but somehow the centre combinations never got going.

The Lions were up against formidable All Blacks forwards – some things never seem to change much, do they? The impressive Andy Dalton, who was picked to captain the All Blacks in the first World Cup but never played due to injury, was chosen as captain and he had some seasoned forwards under his command in Garry Knight, John Ashworth at prop, and Andy Haden and Gary Whetton at lock, and a tremendous back row in 'Cowboy' Shaw, Murray Mexted and Jock Hobbs. Unusually, this pack played the whole series. They had the dynamic scrum-half Dave Loveridge, one of the fastest passers in the game, but the rest of their backs were fairly ordinary, apart from the determined Bernie Frazer, who had Bernie's Corner named after him in Wellington; and, of course, they had Stu Wilson.

The only defeat going into the first Test was against Auckland in the second match of the tour, which, predictably, the Lions lost 13–12. The Lions were badly outplayed in the forwards, and Andy Haden and Gary Whetton, two of the greatest locks in the world at that or any other time, dominated the lineouts.

The first indication of the likely Test team came when they beat Wellington, twice coming from behind and scoring three tries in the last 25 minutes, to win 27–19.

The first Test at Christchurch was seen as the best chance the Lions had of winning a Test before the All Blacks started to gel. It was a fine day at Lancaster Park, but the ground was greasy from rain during the week. Campbell opened the scoring with a penalty after six minutes but, ten minutes later, Hewson replied with one from way out on the touchline and about 50 yards from goal, and then kicked another. Campbell levelled with a drop goal and was successful with another penalty and, at half-time, the Lions led tentatively by 9–6.

Hewson levelled with a penalty for New Zealand and 15 minutes into the half came the only try of the match, when the ball was moved along the All Blacks line and Hewson and Frazer created an opportunity for Shaw to grab the loose ball and power over for an unconverted try. Campbell closed the gap to a single point with another penalty and, with the Lions finishing strongly, it became a desperate battle for victory. With a minute to go, Hewson fielded a clearance kick by Campbell, to drop a superb goal from 45 metres and end what was a close and desperate encounter with a win for New Zealand at 16–12.

The Lions paid a high price when they lost the admirable Holmes midway through the first half, which was all the more upsetting for him as he had gone out of the South African tour three years earlier with a similar injury. He was to be replaced by Nigel Melville, who lasted only one game before being the next victim of the jinx, when he was felled by a rabbit punch in North Auckland in his second game, having scored two tries in his first against Southland. He was to be replaced by the irrepressible Steve Smith.

The Lions knew that they should have won the first Test and this, with three big wins before the second at Wellington, left them full of confidence. The All Blacks made only one change, bringing in Wayne Smith, recovered from injury, for Ian Dunn, while the Lions made five changes. Norster should not have played, due to a back injury. Michael Kiernan, nephew of Tom, replaced Ackerman, John Carleton came in for Trevor Ringland, as did Laidlaw for Holmes, Staff Jones for Stephens, and John O'Driscoll for Squire.

Dalton won the toss and played with the usual strong southerly wind blowing straight down Athletic Park. Its strength could be judged by the fact that Hewson cleared the ball on his own line and it went over the Lions' dead-ball line, a distance of over 100 metres. Loveridge opened the scoring after 15 minutes by darting over from a maul near the line for a try, converted by Hewson, who ten minutes later also kicked a penalty. The Lions attacked strongly for the rest of the half, but the score stood at 9–0 at half-time.

This nine-point deficit seemed far from insurmountable and everybody expected the Lions to win in the second half. Everybody except the All Blacks, that is, who promptly resorted to their old tactic of driving the blind side whenever in trouble. The Lions failed in the first half to convert from a defensive mode to attack and, as the renowned sports writer Hugh McIlvanney (of *The Sunday Times*, then with *The Observer*) observed, 'The final score of 9–0 was a euphemism for disaster.'

Once again the Lions had let two Test matches slip through their fingers and there was now no way back, for two down with two to play was an impossible situation. After a short holiday in the glorious Bay of Islands at Waitangi, they beat North Auckland with an indifferent performance and then lost to Canterbury, and they were not in the best shape for the third Test in Dunedin. They made four changes, with Gwyn Evans replacing Hugo MacNeill at full-back, John Rutherford coming into the centre for Dave Irwin and, in the forwards, Jim Calder replacing John O'Driscoll and Steve Bainbridge substituting for the injured Norster. The All Blacks knew they were on a roll and fielded an unchanged team.

Dunedin, I remember, was gripped by wet and Antarctic weather, and the soggy ground at Carisbrooke did not exactly provide ideal conditions for open play, but the Lions, to their credit, went down with a blazing show of defiance, even though they scored two tries to one.

Frantic early pressure saw the always-alert Roger Baird beat Loveridge for a try in the corner from a kick by Ollie Campbell, but two penalties by Hewson gave the All Blacks a half-time lead of 6–4.

Soon after the restart, Rutherford combined with Baird and Evans to score a fine try. The Lions held this lead until midway through the second half, when Loveridge made an exquisite break for Stu Wilson to score near the posts. Hewson converted, and later kicked a penalty to win the Test 15–8. As usual, the Lions had lost narrowly and the series was over, but nobody could ever say they had not tried. They were simply not as good as the All Blacks.

Their brave efforts in the first three Tests were overshadowed in the end by the superb play of the All Blacks in the final Test at Auckland. Having won the series, they indulged in a breathtaking display of attacking rugby, which left the Lions for dead. The only change in the All Blacks was Ian Dunn for the injured Wayne Smith. The Lions lost Rutherford with an injury and he was replaced by Irwin, and John O'Driscoll was brought back into the forwards.

The All Blacks forwards were at their very best and they totally outplayed the Lions pack, who were left groping at thin air. Behind such a platform, Loveridge had an immense game and New Zealand scored six tries from Stu Wilson (3), who broke the New Zealand record for tries in Test matches, J. Hobbs, A. Hewson and A. Haden. Hewson kicked four conversions and two penalty goals. The only response by the Lions was a penalty apiece by Ollie Campbell and Gwyn Evans. It was New Zealand's largest victory over a British team in a Test match.

It was evident that British rugby had gone backwards since the early 1970s, whereas in New Zealand and Australia it had moved on, due to far better competitive structures. In England, John Burgess had come up with a report and a blueprint for English rugby which made urgent suggestions for more competitive rugby, but typically it was turned down.

Instead, they began questioning the role of the Lions after such a whitewash, but any individual country at the time would have suffered a far greater disaster. Neither was it the fault of the management and leadership, for you would have great difficulty in finding better men than Willie John McBride, Jim Telfer or the much maligned Ciaran Fitzgerald. It was evident that something had to be done about British rugby. This eventually led to the competitive league structures being universally adopted in the British Isles and in Ireland. They failed, however, to close the gap between club and international rugby in the way achieved by the provincial competitions of the southern hemisphere countries.

## Results of the 1983 Lions in New Zealand

P 18   W 12   D 0   L 6   F 478   A 276

| | | | |
|---|---|---|---|
| Wanganui | W | 47 | 15 |
| Auckland | L | 12 | 13 |
| Bay of Plenty | W | 34 | 16 |
| Wellington | W | 27 | 19 |
| Manawatu | W | 25 | 18 |
| Mid Canterbury | W | 26 | 6 |
| New Zealand (Christchurch) | L | 12 | 16 |
| West Coast–Buller | W | 52 | 16 |
| Southland | W | 41 | 3 |
| Wairarapa–Bush | W | 57 | 10 |
| New Zealand (Wellington) | L | 0 | 9 |
| North Auckland | W | 21 | 12 |
| Canterbury | L | 20 | 22 |
| New Zealand (Dunedin) | L | 8 | 15 |
| Hawke's Bay | W | 25 | 19 |
| Counties | W | 25 | 16 |
| Waikato | W | 40 | 13 |
| New Zealand (Auckland) | L | 6 | 38 |

## Ciaran Fitzgerald's 1983 Lions team in New Zealand

**Full-backs**

| | | |
|---|---|---|
| G. Evans | Maesteg | Wales |
| W.H. Hare | Leicester | England |
| H.P. MacNeill | Oxford University | Ireland |

**Three-quarters**

| | | |
|---|---|---|
| R.A. Ackerman | London Welsh | Wales |
| G.R.T. Baird | Kelso | Scotland |
| J. Carleton | Orrell | England |
| D.G. Irwin | Instonians | Ireland |
| M.J. Kiernan | Dolphin | Ireland |
| T.M. Ringland | Ballymena | Ireland |
| C.R. Woodward | Leicester | England |

**Half-backs**

| | | |
|---|---|---|
| S.O. Campbell | Old Belvedere | Ireland |
| T.D. Holmes | Cardiff | Wales |

| | | |
|---|---|---|
| R.J. Laidlaw | Jedforest | Scotland |
| N.D. Melville* | Wasps | |
| J.Y. Rutherford | Selkirk | Scotland |
| S.J. Smith* | Sale | England |

**Forwards**

| | | |
|---|---|---|
| S.J. Bainbridge | Gosforth | England |
| J.R. Beattie | Glasgow Academicals | Scotland |
| S.B. Boyle | Gloucester | England |
| E.T. Butler* | Pontypool | Wales |
| J.H. Calder | Stewart's Melville FP | Scotland |
| M.J. Colclough | Angoulême | England |
| C.T. Deans | Hawick | Scotland |
| C.F. Fitzgerald (capt.) | St Mary's College | Ireland |
| N.C. Jeavons* | Moseley | England |
| S.T. Jones | Pontypool | Wales |
| D.G. Lenihan* | Cork Constitution | Ireland |
| G.A.J. McLoughlin* | Shannon | Ireland |
| I.G. Milne | Heriot's FP | Scotland |
| R.L. Norster | Cardiff | Wales |
| J.B. O'Driscoll | London Irish | Ireland |
| I.A.M. Paxton | Selkirk | Scotland |
| G. Price | Pontypool | Wales |
| J. Squire | Pontypool | Wales |
| I. Stephens | Bridgend | Wales |
| P.J. Winterbottom | Headingley | England |

Manager: W.J. McBride
Assistant Manager and Coach: J.W. Telfer
Honorary Medical Officer: Donald McLeod FRCS

* Replacements

In April 1986, the Four Home Unions, beset by the world lobby against apartheid, broke the Lions tour schedule by calling off their projected tour to South Africa, but a Lions team was selected to help celebrate the centenary of the International Board, the principal governing body. It was only the second time for a Lions team to appear on British soil, and a squad of 21 players was assembled to play a team drawn from the rest of the International Board countries, at Cardiff Arms Park, under the management of Clive Rowlands and coached by Mick Doyle.

The Lions team was A.G. Hastings (Scotland); T.M. Ringland

(Ireland), B.J. Mullin (Ireland), J. Devereux (Wales), R. Underwood (England), J.T. Rutherford (Scotland); R. Jones (Wales); J. Whitefoot (Wales), C.T. Deans (Scotland), D.C. Fitzgerald (Ireland), W.A. Dooley (England), D.G. Lenihan (Ireland), J. Jeffrey (Scotland), J.R. Beattie (Scotland), N.J. Carr (Ireland). Rutherford was replaced by M. Dacey (Wales) and Dooley was replaced by I.A.M. Paxton (Scotland). The other four replacements on the bench were M.J. Kiernan (Ireland), R.J. Hill (England), I.G. Milne (Scotland) and S.E. Brain (England). The Overseas Unions won 15–7.

This was the only time that blazers and ties were issued to the players, and they were considered official British Lions. On another occasion, a British Lions team played in Paris after the 1989 tour to celebrate the forming of the French Republic. It was not a full British Lions team, as late replacements were made and Finlay Calder refused to have anything to do with it, because wives and girlfriends were not invited.

Now came the first World Cup in 1987 in Australia and New Zealand which, together with the gathering strength of the Hong Kong Sevens as a world rugby event, was to provide a forum which would have a profound effect on the attitudes and aspirations of the players, and which helped to accelerate the process of ultimate change to professionalism. The strict interpretation of the amateur laws was already being heavily breached by the southern hemisphere and European countries such as France and Italy and, indeed, by Wales. Many of them had been driving a double-decker bus through the regulations for some years, and people were beginning to be fed up with the dreadful hypocrisy of it all.

## FINLAY CALDER'S 1989 LIONS

The Lions, because of the South African boycott, now had a gap of six years since their last tour. They were to become the first team to visit Australia on a full-blown Lions tour since the Rev. Mullineux's side in 1899. It was also the only sizeable British tour to Australia since 1959, when the Lions played six matches there.

Fittingly, it was the Australians Kylie Minogue and Jason Donovan who topped the British charts in 1989. It was the hottest summer in England since 1976; the Bradford Moslems burnt Salman Rushdie's *Satanic Verses*; Tyson stopped Bruno and the Hillsborough disaster claimed 94 lives. The Queen was the first British monarch to visit Russia since 1917; Margaret Thatcher completed ten years in power;

Bush took over from Reagan in America; and Boris Yeltsin won the Soviet poll. Solidarity triumphed in Poland, but Chinese troops massacred demonstrating students and others in Tiananmen Square. Sir Laurence Olivier died and Sky Television was launched, and was to have a huge influence on the development of rugby in the southern hemisphere.

The size of the new-style Lions tour was cut back even further and the fixtures were reduced to 12 matches. Whether Australia had the strength and the facilities to sustain even a 12-match tour was a major talking-point before the tour began. During recent years, Australian rugby, which had been in a parlous situation throughout the 1970s, had really put its house in order, and they gave a clear warning of this when Andrew Slack's team, coached by the maverick Alan Jones, whitewashed the Four Home Unions on their tour of Britain and Ireland in 1984.

It was also true that the Australians had become some of the most innovative thinkers on the game world wide. They have, in the last 15 years, introduced such ideas as the 'up your jumper' move, which amused the Fijians so much that, when they saw it performed by the New South Wales Country team in Nandi in 1977, those who had climbed trees for a better view simply fell out of them in their mirth. They were also to preach the gospel of the quick-quick pass and the swarm defence.

The 'up your jumper' plan was to have a huddle from a penalty, where somebody concealed the ball under his jersey as they exploded to all parts of the field. By the time the opposition worked out where the ball was, the runner with the ball had either scored the try or done considerable damage by piercing the defence. Under the existing laws, it was entirely legal, but the IRB quickly moved to outlaw it under the law 26 (2) concerning unfair play.

Following the England tour there in 1988, when they were beaten in both Tests and by New South Wales, the Lions knew what to expect, and five of their forwards, Brian Moore, Wade Dooley, Gareth Chilcott, Andy Robinson and Dean Richards, together with Rob Andrew and Rory Underwood, were looking for revenge. After losing the first Test, they became the first Lions to come from behind to win the series 2–1.

The tour was managed by Clive Rowlands, or 'Top Cat', as they called him in Wales, due to the fact that he captained Wales on his first and every appearance in the red jersey. He also created a world record 112 lineouts in an international at Murrayfield, by kicking mercilessly from scrum-half to win the game. He was later to coach the Wales team and become President of the Welsh Rugby Union. A notable character in his own right and a jovial man, he did a marvellous job as manager. He had excellent lieutenants in his coaches, Ian McGeechan, who was by far the most intellectual and dedicated coach of the Lions since Carwyn James, and his assistant, Roger Uttley, who did such a great job with the England pack which was to dominate Europe for the next seven years. The Lions had now moved to taking two coaches on tour.

The team was captained by the Scot Finlay Calder, who demanded and gave everything. His manager was to say of him in his report, 'His pride and leadership were always in evidence and these qualities, coupled with his strong views on the conduct of players both on and off the field, add up to a very successful captain of a BIRUT team. One should not omit two more qualities necessary for success: honesty and modesty, both of which belong to Finlay Calder.'

When you look back, you can see how many good and hard players they had on that tour. You start with Gavin Hastings, and you can't do better than that, for he was the finest player in his position since J.P.R Williams, with the same, if not better, physical attributes. His place-kicking was to be a vital winning ingredient. Ieuan Evans on the wing was to haunt David Campese, who was one of Australia's most exciting players of all time. The try he scored in the final Test from a poor pass by Campese was his deserved dividend for being unimpressed and undaunted in marking such a fine and established player, and it launched Evans on a great career of his own.

Scott Hastings, another delightful member of the Watsonians Club and the Hastings family, a powerful runner and intimidating tackler, together with that silky and deceptive runner Jeremy Guscott, were to become the preferred centres for the last two Tests, after the battling Mike Hall and the elegant Brendan Mullin had played in the first. As ever, his roaring pace and elusive running saw Rory Underwood having the freehold on the left-wing position. There was more than ample reserve cover with the powerful Welsh centre or wing John Devereux, who was to make a name for himself in rugby league, and Chris Oti, who was unfortunate to have his try-scoring talent curtailed by injury. Ian McGeechan said at the end of the tour that he regretted that he never had time to develop the British back play to its full potential.

At half-back, the loss of Paul Dean in the opening game in Perth, although a personal tragedy for the Irishman, was perhaps a blessing in disguise for the Lions, as it allowed Rob Andrew to fly out and claim the fly-half berth from Craig Chalmers for the second and third Tests. Andrew brought steadiness and a new tactical dimension to the side which, for all the quality of its backs, was struggling to find itself in attack, because of Bob Dwyer's tactic of swarm defence. Andrew also found a soul mate in the superb Welsh scrum-half Robert Jones, who on this tour was at the top of his considerable game, behind a dominant pack of forwards.

The forwards, under the uncompromising command of Finlay Calder, who had some of the characteristics of a modern-day Wallace, were at times magnificent, once they absorbed the lessons of the first Test, when they crumbled under the force of the Australian forward effort which gave their halves, Nick Farr-Jones and Michael Lynagh, control of the game. They played only ten forwards in the three Tests, Rob Norster being replaced by Dooley after the first, and Mike Teague, who was injured, missing the first Test, with that hundred-per-cent Scottish flanker Derek White taking his place.

The forwards of the tour were Dean Richards, Mike Teague and Paul Ackford, but the whole Test pack was magnificent. One other forward must be mentioned for his invaluable contribution to the success of the tour, even though he never made the Test team; he was Donal Lenihan, who virtually took command of the 'dirt-trackers'. 'Donal's Donuts', as they were known, became a force to be reckoned with and an essential back-up for the Test team, as well as being essential for the morale of the tour. Every tour should have a Donal Lenihan or a Bob Hiller, if it is to be successful.

It was a well-selected side which brought home the bacon, just as they did in 1971 and 1974. Those who might say that Australia were of lesser strength than New Zealand or South Africa would be wrong, for it was Australia who were to win the World Cup two years later in 1991, and this was part of the learning curve for that great side. Furthermore, this tour clearly illustrated the new and growing strength of Australian rugby and they easily sustained a 12-match tour. Today, with the vast improvement in the Australian Capital Territories team (known as ACT), they have developed even further and, whereas a decade ago they had only about 30 players of Test calibre to call upon, they now have 50 or 60.

It was as physically demanding a Test series as any I have witnessed or heard about, and the second Test in particular provided scenes of violence of which neither side could feel proud. This created a great deal of acrimony between the two teams; some of the Australian press went right over the top with their one-eyed allegations against the Lions and you have never heard such whingeing about the Poms. Farr-Jones, their captain, was quoted as saying, 'I think that the third Test could develop into open warfare. As far as I am concerned the Lions have set the rules and set the standards and, if the officials are going to do nothing about it, then we are going to have to do it ourselves. We won't sit back and cop it again.'

The Australian Rugby Union also issued an intimidatory press release on the eve of the final Test which read:

> At a Council meeting held today at the Union Headquarters at Kingford, the Australian Rugby Football Union (ARFU) resolved the following: 1) to condemn the violence in the game; 2) that the Executive Director prepare a video depicting certain incidents which occurred during the second Test at Ballimore, which were believed to be prejudicial to the best interests of the game. The video, when prepared, will be sent to the Committee of the Four Home Unions for their information and for any action which they may deem appropriate; 3) the ARFU delegates to the International Rugby Football Board (IRFB) have been requested to raise the matter of video evidence as part of the game's judicial system.
> Signed: R.J. Fordham, Executive Director.

Ian McGeechan and the delightful Australian assistant coach, Bob Templeman, who is one of the elders of Australian rugby and highly respected wherever rugby is played, had got together and decided that it was impossible to wage war and play good rugby. They both believed that the team playing the better rugby would win the series. They were adamant that there would be no trouble in the final Test, and condemned the hysteria of the media in whipping up bad feeling.

In his captain's report on the tour, Finlay Calder was to say:

> The large part of Australian life is sport; winning is everything. However, when it comes to playing anything against the 'Poms', we should never underestimate the undercurrent of their hatred towards their ancestry and, having played against them on several occasions, the explosive situations that occurred only highlighted that feeling. To the credit of the Lions, despite provocation both physical and verbal, the series was settled by tremendous commitment and team spirit. As we approach the 1990s, it is a marvellous tribute to rugby and all it stands for that players from the Home Unions can still come together, enjoy each other's company, play for each other and defeat Australia.

The tour did much to restore the status of the Lions down under, after the previous dud tours of 1977 and 1983. It could be bracketed with the success of the 1974 team in South Africa, for its undoubted strength was in the forwards, who carried all before them apart from in the first Test.

The Lions won their six games before the first Test, including the two mini-Tests against Queensland and New South Wales. Every game counted, for three weeks is no time at all to prepare and select a team which has to start from scratch, and which is drawn from the cosmopolitan talent of four different countries. They were consoled by the fact that Australia, too, would be playing their first Test for seven months. They were in good heart and perhaps in too confident a mood for the first Test in Sydney, and their only worry was the extent of their injuries. When they named the team, five players were not considered for that reason, including Mike Teague, Chris Oti and John Devereux.

On a sunny day and before a capacity crowd at the Sydney Football Stadium, they were to be deeply disappointing as, having carried all before them in the previous matches, the forwards failed and were well beaten everywhere by a very good Aussie performance. Australia won the set pieces and were quicker to the breakdown, which saw Farr-Jones and Lynagh, in particular, having a field day. Australia scored four tries to none, through Walker, Gourlay, Maguire and Martin, and Lynagh devastatingly converted all four and kicked a penalty and a drop goal. For the Lions, Gavin Hastings kicked two penalties and Craig Chalmers a penalty and a drop goal.

After such an emphatic defeat, it was a sadder and wiser Lions team which took stock of itself for the second Test at Brisbane, after an interim game against ACT, a provincial side which was beginning to realise its potential. They gave the Lions a hard time in the first half, leading by 21–11 at the interval, before succumbing to a battering by the Lions forwards in the second half. Although this brought the Lions a win by 41–25, there was much criticism concerning their approach, for they scarcely used their backs, even when the game was won.

The Test team showed five changes from the previous Saturday; Wade Dooley and Mike Teague came in for Bob Norster and Derek White, while in the backs the Lions changed their whole midfield, with Rob Andrew for Craig Chalmers, and Scott Hastings and Jerry Guscott for Mike Hall and Brendan Mullin. Taunted about their toothless performance in the first Test, you could sense that they were up for this game and they gave Australia a shock by the ferocity of their approach. The philosophy should have been to let sleeping Lions lie, not to madden them by poking them with jibes.

To say the least, the game was ill tempered and violence was sparked off by the tiniest incident. On one occasion, Robert Jones appeared to tread on Farr-Jones's foot and, when the Australian captain had a go at him, the usually calm and collected Robert Jones astonished everybody by flying at him. While they were rolling on the ground like two ferrets in a sack, with the hapless French referee René Horquet trying to pull them apart, the forwards were slamming at each other. Although nobody was sent off, the teams remained on a short fuse and there were innumerable punch-ups, including one when David Young seemed to stand on Steve Cutler's head. He was lucky to go unpunished by the French referee, but Tom Lawton was to lead the Wallabies forwards into another huge fracas over the incident.

The Australian media were later to have a ball, highlighting every transgression by the Lions, but conveniently forgetting about a terrible raking of Mike Hall in an earlier game, or the bruising treatment handed out to Mike Teague and Gavin Hastings. In the match, however, the ruthless driving forward play of the Lions pack saw Australia outplayed, as Robert Jones and Rob Andrew, with some tremendous tactical kicking, dominated as effectively as their counterparts had done in the first Test. The Lions had rediscovered their forward authority, and their surging commitment to the ruck and maul situations entirely knocked the Wallabies out of the game in the later stages. However, for all their forward dominance, the Lions had trailed until close to the final whistle.

Lynagh kicked two penalties and converted an early try by Greg Martin, while Hastings kicked a penalty and Andrew dropped a goal. This gave Australia a 12–6 lead at the interval, which they held until midway through the second half. Andrew landed another penalty, but it was still 12–9 to Australia until the last five minutes, when the dominance of the Lions forwards, supported by the brilliant box-kicking of Robert Jones, brought two decisive tries, the first by Gavin Hastings from a splendid movement and the second by Jerry Guscott from his own deft kick ahead. A conversion by Andrew made it 19–12 and the Lions had won a Test which had been bitterly fought out with great passion by both teams.

The Lions went off for a short holiday to Surfers Paradise on the Gold Coast, to lick a few wounds and to reflect that they were going to have to do it all again on the following Saturday. They were now confident that they could handle anything the Wallabies could throw at them, and the harshness of the criticism by the media only served to increase their motivation to win the rubber. However, the Australian competitive spirit is one of the best developed in the sporting world, and it would not be easy. The final Test in Sydney, happily, did not become the blood-bath that Nick Farr-Jones and the media implied it might be. Good sense prevailed and the game's ethics were restored.

Both teams were unchanged and once more the Lions forwards took control, but they still struggled against these competitive Australians to win what was an exciting match. The winning of it hinged on one piece of mental aberration by David Campese, who is nothing if not a rugby genius and a huge competitor. Part of his charm is that he tries to do the impossible at times and, when he tried to run a ball out from behind his own line and threw a calamitous pass to Greig Martin, Ieuan Evans, who had kept Campo in check throughout the series (which, in itself, reflected great credit on him), pounced to score a try which virtually won the series.

The Australian media pilloried Campese without giving any regard to the years of artistry, skill and match-winning with which he had blessed them. Mark Ella put it best of all when, in typical amusing Australian fashion, he coined the phrase 'One day "Wonderman", next day "Blunderman"'.

It was absurd to blame Campese for a defeat, when their pack was destroyed. At half-time it was 9–9, with three penalties from Gavin Hastings to an Ian Williams try, a conversion and a penalty from Lynagh. Three minutes into the second period, Australia took the lead with another Lynagh penalty, only for Evans to score the try, and Gavin Hastings kicked two more penalties to bring his haul to five, opening up a seven-point lead. The Wallabies competed to the death and two more penalties by Lynagh had the Lions desperately hanging on, as the Australians threw everything into all-out attack in the closing minutes. They failed heroically, and the Lions won 19–18, having recovered for the first time ever from losing the first Test to win a series.

The Lions still had two games to go, a romp against New South Wales Country and an unusual fixture against an ANZAC side. It was supposed to be a Test strength team drawn from New Zealand and Australia, but unfortunately the All Blacks failed to support and embrace the concept, and 12 of them dropped out of the squad. Of the three who turned up, Fran Botica, Kieron Crowley and Steve McDowell, only the last was a current All Black. The Lions won this final match and became one of the three most successful sides in Lions history. They could look back on their tour with great pride.

The Lions had again discovered that the best way to win Test matches was through the forwards, and were prepared to drop their old tradition of attacking back play. As five of the Lions pack in the last two Tests were English, it was not surprising that this became a successful obsession with England for the next few years. They were to use big, tight forwards, especially the marvellous Ackford and Dooley, at the lineouts to gain possession, and were to employ big back rows as a battering ram to subdue and penetrate. It was effective but not pretty to watch and, because of this static approach, they became bogged down when they attempted to play the open attacking game. In the World Cup final in 1991, they were unable to do so and lost to Australia.

Australia had given the answer to those who said that they were not strong enough for a Lions tour. On the contrary, the Lions were relieved to go home having won the series, and they had a marvellous time in a lovely country, where the pressures of touring are not as intense as they are in New Zealand and South Africa.

## Results of the 1989 Lions in Australia

P 12   W 11   D 0   L 1   F 360   A 182

| | | | |
|---|---|---|---|
| Western Australia | W | 44 | 0 |
| Australia B | W | 23 | 8 |
| Queensland | W | 19 | 15 |
| Queensland B | W | 30 | 6 |
| New South Wales | W | 23 | 21 |
| New South Wales B | W | 39 | 19 |
| Australia (Sydney) | L | 12 | 30 |
| ACT | W | 41 | 25 |
| Australia (Brisbane) | W | 19 | 12 |
| Australia (Sydney) | W | 19 | 18 |
| NSW Country | W | 72 | 13 |
| ANZAC XV | W | 19 | 15 |

## Finlay Calder's 1989 Lions team

**Full-backs**

| | | |
|---|---|---|
| P.W. Dods | Gala | Scotland |
| A.G. Hastings | London Scottish | Scotland |

**Three-quarters**

| | | |
|---|---|---|
| J.A. Devereux | Bridgend | Wales |
| I.C. Evans | Llanelli | Wales |
| J.C. Guscott | Bath | England |
| M.R. Hall | Bridgend | Wales |
| S. Hastings | Watsonians | Scotland |
| B.J. Mullin | London Irish | Ireland |
| C. Oti | Wasps | England |
| R. Underwood | Leicester & RAF | England |

## Half-backs

| | | |
|---|---|---|
| C.R. Andrew* | Wasps | England |
| G. Armstrong | Jedforest | Scotland |
| C.M. Chalmers | Melrose | Scotland |
| A. Clement* | Swansea | Wales |
| P.M. Dean | St Mary's College | Ireland |
| R.N. Jones | Swansea | Wales |

## Forwards

| | | |
|---|---|---|
| P.J. Ackford | Harlequins | England |
| F. Calder (capt.) | Stewart's Melville FP | Scotland |
| G.J. Chilcott | Bath | England |
| W.A. Dooley | Preston Grasshoppers | England |
| M. Griffiths | Bridgend | Wales |
| J. Jeffrey | Kelso | Scotland |
| D.G. Lenihan | Cork Constitution | Ireland |
| B.C. Moore | Nottingham | England |
| R.L. Norster | Cardiff | Wales |
| D. Richards | Leicester | England |
| R.A. Robinson | Bath | England |
| S.J. Smith | Ballymena | Ireland |
| D.M.B. Sole | Edinburgh Academicals | Scotland |
| M.C. Teague | Gloucester | England |
| D.B. White | London Scottish | Scotland |
| D. Young | Cardiff | Wales |

Manager: D.C.T. Rowlands
Coaches: I.R. McGeechan and R.M. Uttley
Tour Doctor: B. Gilfeather
Physiotherapist: K. Murphy

* Replacements

# The Last Amateurs

*So Close to Glory* was the title of the paperback which Ian McGeechan produced after the last Lions tour in 1993. For all the tenuous truth of that statement, he might just as easily have called it 'Same Old Story', for this is the tale of another Lions team which came so near to, and yet was so far from, winning a series against the All Blacks, who euphemistically have been called 'The Unsmiling Giants' and 'The Winter Men'. In their previous ten tours of New Zealand since 1888, the Lions had won only one series in 1971, and they had won only five of the 32 Test matches played.

Selection procedures, which had improved immensely in recent years with the adoption of the principle that coaches should have a say, meant that it was a well-selected team and management which set out on what is one of the toughest missions that any team in any sport can conceivably undertake. If you do not believe me, then look at the photo of Scott Hastings taken by the team doctor, James Robson of Dundee, which so graphically illustrates the ferocity of such a tour of New Zealand. They confirm my recurring theme, that a Lions tour to New Zealand, Australia or South Africa is more of a crusade than a pleasure trip.

## GAVIN HASTINGS'S 1993 LIONS

The manager was Geoff Cooke, the man who brought efficiency and realism into the England squad, building them into the most successful England team since 1980, and making them the major European power during the first half of the 1990s. He was not a popular man with the Twickenham establishment, for he tended to be a players' man. He understood and identified more easily with their aspirations concerning reward for the shameless exploitation of their talents than did most of his masters at HQ.

Ian McGeechan was Lions coach for the second time. It was the first time that anybody has coached the Lions on two occasions, which was testament to his rugby intellectualism and the high esteem in which he is held by all the Four Home Unions. His assistant coach, Dick Best, was rewarded for his hard work with Harlequins and England. It was a popular triumvirate with the players and they all had the necessary qualifications.

The issue of the captaincy exercised everybody's minds throughout the season prior to the tour and it was probably true that Will Carling must have been in poll position until England's defeat by Ireland at Twickenham. The other outstanding candidate was Gavin Hastings, but he must have felt his chance had gone with the Calcutta Cup defeat at Twickenham. In the end, Hastings was chosen for his greater experience of New Zealand conditions, for already having toured with the successful Lions to Australia, and for his personal charisma and popularity with the players from all the Four Home Unions. Even so, Geoff Cooke, as Chairman of Selectors, had him rung twice to ensure that he wanted it. There had been some needle between the England and Scotland captains since the World Cup, when the Scottish players had turned up at the final wearing Australian colours.

Geoff Cooke assured me that there was no problem whatsoever on tour between the two, that Carling was dropped from the Test side purely on a loss of form, and that Gavin Hastings had no say in Carling's omission from the Test team. He was to emphasise that they were both men of extremely high calibre in both rugby and personal terms. These Lions were lucky that they had three very experienced international captains who were all strong personalities, in Gavin Hastings, Will Carling and Ieuan Evans.

There was universal approval of Gavin Hastings as the Lions captain, for there is no man more respected for his abilities both on and off the field than this delightful Scot, who is the epitome of the rugby man; brave, resolute, adventurous and one who enjoys a party. He was to break many Lions records during the tour, including the most points by a player in a series; most penalty goals in a series (12); most penalty goals in a match (six); most points in a Lions Test career (66) and equalled Tony Ward's record of most points in a match (18). His achievements speak for themselves.

England's continuing success in the Five Nations saw them having their biggest representation ever on a Lions tour, with the manager, the assistant coach and 17 players. Perhaps the most intriguing debate was whether Rob Andrew or Stuart Barnes would win the fly-half berth. It was settled emphatically when Rob Andrew proved himself as the ultimate competitor with his superb performance in the second Test, and he played in all the Test matches. Dewi Morris also excelled and his gutsy competitive play was splendid. The pick of the three-quarters was Ieuan Evans, but Scott Gibbs, who displaced Carling in the last two Tests, was also one of the most aggressive and exciting players of the tour, and he would have played in all the Tests but for an early injury.

The outstanding Lions forward was Ben Clarke, who played in three different back-row positions, and close behind were Dean Richards and Peter Winterbottom. Martin Bayfield, who had a marvellous second Test, and Martin Johnson became the Test locks and Brian Moore, having lost his place for the first Test, showed his character by getting back for the last two.

During that year of 1993, two young boys were charged with the murder of James Bulger; there was the *Braer* ship disaster in the Shetlands; the siege in Waco ended in tragedy; Norman Lamont was fired by John Major and Michael Mates resigned, after allegations of links with Asil Nadir; Lord Owen admitted the failure of his peace plan in Bosnia, and US troops attacked a Somali warlord. It was announced that the Queen would be taxed on her income and that part of Buckingham Palace was to be opened to tourists.

The Lions were to discover that the New Zealand team were as tough a nut to crack as ever. They lost six of their 13 matches, but they gave a tremendous account of themselves in the first two Tests and actually won the second which, as the statistics show, was a considerable achievement.

There was one huge controversy during the tour, which again illustrated the growing gulf between players and administration, and which became known as the 'Wade Dooley affair'. It was born from the sad, sudden death of Wade Dooley's father; the extremely popular Wade was immediately flown home and arrangements were made to fly out Martin Johnson as the replacement.

The Lions had suffered a spate of injuries in the Otago match, which included bad shoulder and neck injuries to Martin Bayfield, after he was upended in a lineout. Will Carling strained a muscle at the top of his leg and was replaced by Scott Hastings, who early in the second half suffered a badly depressed fracture of his cheekbone. In addition, the Lions lost substantially by 37–24 in this, the fifth match of the tour, and spirits were fairly low. Consequently, when it was discovered that Wade would not be rejoining them, even though the New Zealand Rugby

Union had specifically said that he could come back after his father's funeral, the Lions became angry and immediately took it out on the Secretary of the Four Home Unions, Bob Weighill. He was 'sent to Coventry' by the players, who did not fully understand the background of it all, including the implications of the Tour agreement.

When Wade arrived home, Weighill had arranged for him to be met at Manchester airport, and sent a special floral tribute to his father's funeral. On the following Wednesday, Wade mentioned to him that he had been invited to return to New Zealand by the NZ RFU, but that he was unlikely to do so. Weighill was surprised when, about a week later, Wade rang him and said he would like to return to the team. At the same time he had received a request from the manager, Geoff Cooke, for Wade to rejoin the party and to fly out with Weighill, who was joining the team on 17 June. Weighill, therefore, with some difficulty booked him a ticket.

As Secretary, he now had to inform the Chairman of the Tours Committee and there were discussions with the Secretary of the RFU, the Secretary of the IRFB, and the Chairman of the NZ RFU, who was also Chairman of the IRFB at the time. There was considerable sympathy with the unfortunate circumstances, but there was also a perception that the IRB regulations and the Tour Agrement must be complied with. It was decided that Wade should accept the invitation to return, but could not rejoin the party as a player. The Chairman of New Zealand RFU admitted that it had been a mistake to issue the invitation in the first place without consulting the Four Home Unions, when it was possible that another solution could have been arrived at.

Wade was informed of the decision, but declined to rejoin the tour on those terms. Consequently Bob Weighill, who had only followed the book as he was bound to, arrived in New Zealand and ran into a wall of hostility from the Lions who, foolishly in retrospect, decided to shoot the messenger. There is no doubt that Bob was hard done by, but this illustrates that there is no flexibility in aspects of the administration, when there ought to be. As Gavin Hastings pointed out in his autobiography, 'It gave us something to bitch about during a low point of the tour.'

The first Test defeat at Christchurch by 20–18 was a bitter disappointment, and a bitter blow because of the highly controversial awarding of the first try in the opening two minutes. A high kick by Grant Fox was caught by Ieuan Evans, who fell over the line still holding the ball, with Frank Bunce also clutching at it. As television audiences world wide were able to see, Evans never let go of the ball, yet the referee, from a long way off, awarded the try to New Zealand. The Lions recovered and took the lead with two penalties by Hastings and, before half-time, Fox kicked two more and Hastings another, to leave the All Blacks leading by 11–9. There was also much controversy concerning the Lions' first penalty, for Michael Jones held Carling without the ball when he would have been in support of Guscott for a try under the posts.

In the second half, the Lions played some of their best rugby of the series and Dean Richards, Peter Winterbottom and Ben Clarke were immense, while Martin Bayfield had a tremendous game in the lineouts. Fox, that remarkable winner of Test matches for New Zealand, kicked another two penalties early in the second half, but so did Hastings and then, with only ten minutes to go, Hastings put the Lions ahead at 18–17 with a terrific penalty into the wind from a difficult angle, and the game was there to win. With only a minute to go, the Australian referee, Brian Kinsey, awarded an outrageous penalty to New Zealand. The disbelief on Dewi Morris's face was there for all to see on television, but Fox kicked the goal to win the game.

Losing to Auckland and Hawke's Bay in the two matches before the second Test in Wellington was hardly confidence-boosting preparation! If there was a criticism of this tour it was the fact that in percentage terms they lost too many provincial matches, losing to Otago, Auckland, Hawke's Bay and Waikato. The 'dirt-trackers' let them down badly against Hawke's Bay and Waikato.

In the second Test, McGeechan and Hastings decided on the dangerous ploy of playing into the wind and sun in the first half, as they believed this would force them to keep the ball in play and concentrate. Hastings wanted to withdraw because he had a hamstring strain, but McGeechan insisted that he played and he lasted the game. The biggest problem came when, after 30 minutes, Fox hoisted a ball and Hastings lost it in the sun, for Eroni Clarke to get the bounce and score and Fox to convert. It was to be the only score by the All Blacks, as the Lions never gave away another penalty for Fox to convert into points. He had not failed to kick a penalty in a Test for five years, so this was some achievement. Gavin Hastings then kicked two penalties and Andrew dropped a goal, for a half-time lead of 9–7.

Early in the second half, Gavin kicked another penalty before the Lions scored a glorious try from a counter-attack. The irrepressible Dewi Morris started it by picking up a loose pass inside his own half, and made the break before giving to Jeremy Guscott, who has great ability to inject pace. He did so to beat Frank Bunce and check John Kirwan, before giving to Rory Underwood, who made a 50-metre sprint up the touchline for a try. Gavin Hastings kicked another penalty, to give the All Blacks as big a beating as they have ever had at home.

It was the most points the Lions had ever scored against New Zealand in a Test match. The hero of the game was Rob Andrew, who never put a foot wrong, and close behind him was the combative Dewi Morris. The forwards, for their part, could say for the rest of their lives that they saw off the All Blacks forwards in a Test match in New Zealand, and not many people can make a claim like that.

The 'dirt-trackers' were to lose heavily in the penultimate game at Hamilton against Waikato, who were the reigning provincial champions, before the final Test, with a dreary performance similar to the one against Hawke's Bay the week before. This is always a difficult time as, at this stage of a tour, those who have not made the final Test team have nothing left to play for and they are thinking about going home. This is why a leader of the second team is of such great value on tour, but this side had no Donal Lenihan or Bob Hiller to jolly them along, and they crashed to their biggest defeat of the tour, Waikato playing splendid rugby to win by 38–10.

The All Blacks had called in Andy Haden as their lineout consultant for the final Test, and they solved the problem by compressing the lineout and crowding Bayfield. They also decided not to kick for touch, thus considerably reducing the number of lineouts with the Lions throw. They continued to play for their lives and produced all that old All Blacks imperative commitment to winning and, completely changing their tactics, outplayed the Lions as decisively as they themselves had been beaten the week before. The Lions were unchanged, but New Zealand made three changes. Eroni Clarke was replaced by Lee Stensness, and they also dropped Zinzan Brooke for the hard-driving Otago number eight, Arran Pene, and reinstated Ian Jones in place of Mark Cooksley at lock.

The Lions snatched an early lead of ten points with a Gavin Hastings penalty and a try, when Andrew played inside to Rory Underwood on the burst and the ball bounced off Bunce and into the hands of Scott Gibbs who scored, for Hastings to convert. It was, however, no contest, as the All Blacks climbed into the driving seat and stayed there for the rest of the game. A try by Bunce, converted by Fox, and another try by the All Blacks skipper Sean Fitzpatrick, again converted by Fox, made it 14–10 at the interval. There was no let-up by the All Blacks and Fox kicked a penalty. It was followed by one from Hastings, but then Fox kicked another, and although the Lions were attempting to run the ball, it was with increasing desperation. Preston finished them off when he dummied his way over for a try, converted by Fox, who then kicked another penalty to give the All Blacks their second highest score against the Lions.

It was, in the end, the same old story. The All Blacks wanted to retain their reputation more than the Lions wanted immortality, but then that was always the difference between British teams and those in the southern hemisphere. Perhaps winning in the new frontier countries is a necessity more ingrained into the psyche than it is in the more relaxed comfort of the old world, where the prospect of losing is never quite as alarming.

There now follows a selection of extracts from Ian McGeechan's coaching report on the tour to the Four Home Unions.

New Zealand remains the ultimate challenge for a tourist and I felt it important that we had as much time as possible to prepare players to cope with the unique environment which New Zealand provides. I was also aware that a number of players, particularly the English players who made up the majority of the party, had not experienced New Zealand at first hand. As with all tours to the southern hemisphere, it is the physical intensity which has to be successfully mastered.

Before the tour my early objectives revolved around producing consistent, dynamic rucking and mauling drives and providing quick ball, from which the backs could move at pace. An awareness of this requirement allowed the forwards to realise what was vital, to enable the backs to have enough space to show what they were capable of. Our aim was to be successful in New Zealand and to adapt to their referees, their climate, their rugby, their people and their attitude. Not least, we had to adapt to the implication of the new laws.

I made it clear to the players that fitness must not be an issue; they had to be responsible for their own fitness levels, and consequently, after discussions with Rex Hazeldene, we supplied each player with a fitness programme.

In our first week in New Zealand, our team session priorities were:

• To build up a rhythm in our play, both in the forward drives and back movements, but more importantly, in the continuity of reaction between backs and forwards, to allow for consistent recycling of the ball.

• To provide quick driving and players available to the half-back for second drives at pace.

• The transfer of attacks to outside centre and wing, once space was available and the defence had been committed.

• It was also vital that we realised the importance of the gain line in New

Zealand both in attack and defence, and once it was crossed, that pace and momentum were maintained. The watchwards were 'stay on your feet' and 'body contact at hip height'.

By the first game on 22 May, codes, short penalties and free kicks had been added and all we had to do now was to make it work where it mattered.

Our aim was to win the first two Test matches, but two crucial decisions, one in the first 60 seconds and the other in the last minute of the first Test, meant that we lost the match I felt we should have won comfortably. We were desperately disappointed at the end of the game, not only because we felt it should have been ours, but because we knew we had to produce an outstanding performance in the second Test and again in the very last match of the tour. It was all going down to the wire.

The big problem in the second Test was whether Gavin Hastings played. He did not feel he could, but I felt it was imperative that he did, even if it was for only one minute, because it was difficult to overestimate his influence as a captain during the build-up and on the attitude of the other players. With the help of Jeremy Guscott and Rob Andrew, he was convinced that he would not be letting the side down if he had to leave the field in the first minute, and that it was more important that in the next 24 hours he played a significant role in preparing the team. Having agreed, he was a changed man and took everything in his positive style. As a result, we had a side which was very focused for that 80 minutes at Wellington.

It was an outstanding team performance and this will remain one of the most satisfying performances I have seen from a Lions team. We now had everything to play for, but it meant another week of concentration and commitment.

In the final Test, the All Blacks were almost over-psyched and we simply could not match their onslaughts, and we spent the game playing catch-up rugby. It was a very disappointing result, for over the series we probably had the better of them.

The New Zealand environment is intimidating simply because, from waking up in the morning and talking to waiters and waitresses, the key note is rugby. Outside the hotel, people talk in the shops about the rugby, and at the receptions the talk was also obviously about rugby. Some players found this almost too intrusive and did not feel totally comfortable with the atmosphere; others, and in particular Ben Clarke, Martin Bayfield and Scott Gibbs, found it challenging and their progress throughout the tour was dramatic.

## GENERAL REVIEW

Like all Lions tours I have been associated with, the players produced many positive reactions to the challenge they were given. I think, with careful development, it should show again in our domestic rugby how much we have on board. The players should return with more confidence in their abilities rather than less, and I would venture to say that all of the 1993 Lions will be looking forward to the next occasion when they can play the All Blacks. There is nothing to fear, only an approach which requires total commitment, error-free rugby under pressure, and a positive attitude to think the game on their feet and react flexibly to the developing situations.

## THE MANAGEMENT TEAM

Once again I felt fortunate to be amongst experienced personnel and we did constantly swap ideas, comments and thoughts about rugby, the game in general, New Zealand, food, wine, and aspirations. In fact, our regular Friday evening dinners together were very happy, and an essential element in drawing together our ideas, as well as reviewing the week's activities.

This was a very happy tour, and all the players had a very positive attitude and commitment. I feel there were only a couple who let themselves down on occasions, and that I am sure was due to the positive directions and input given by Geoff Cooke, and the obvious enthusiasm and interest in their wellbeing from Kevin Murphy and James Robson.

### Geoff Cooke

Geoff is a very professional and modern manager, and extremely well organised, which meant that the tour ran very smoothly. The fact that we had no significant problems shows how detailed his organisation and planning had been. His use of the video camera, and subsequently our video analysis of the teams and the swapping of ideas, helped us to continually adapt and respond to each challenge.

### Dick Best

Dick had probably got the most difficult job on the tour, because, as assistant coach, more than anyone else he had to remain flexible and adaptable in his role, and this I thought he did very well. We had interesting conversations and were able to share ideas to develop our coaching sessions, and his onfield quips were invaluable in keeping the players on their toes. He was very supportive and we were able through our conversations to share the development and progress, not only with the team and his tactics, but of the individual players as well.

## James Robson

James, I feel, was an inspired choice as doctor, simply because he is sportsminded, and is a physiotherapist as well. He and Kevin Murphy worked wonders in the medical room and did it so professionally that the players had total confidence in their ability to make them right. James is very aware of the sports needs in the players, and his medical knowledge in that field helped, with the use of the correct drugs and treatment, to dramatically shorten the injury period of a number of players. In fact, only one player, Richard Webster, was injured for longer than one week, and potentially a number of injuries could have taken two to three weeks for recovery. I would also suggest that, if the Four Home Unions consider the development of a medical group in sports injuries, James Robson should be part of it, as he is the best doctor I have ever worked with in the sports injury field.

## Kevin Murphy

Kevin is quite outstanding at his job; he never stops and his room is always available for players. He, along with James, had a very approachable attitude and, even when his room was littered with bodies, he never failed to keep a sense of humour. This is very important in the depths of New Zealand in the middle of a tour, when it is easy for players to become negative or depressed because they are injured.

All in all, I feel again a great privilege to be part of a Lions tour and to be a part of a management team that did get on very well together, making a very intense eight weeks so enjoyable. The management of the tour was easy and professional.

## THE CAPTAIN: GAVIN HASTINGS

Gavin was quite outstanding as a captain. He has the respect of all the players, but, more importantly, he had already had the respect of New

Zealanders from his previous visit, and his performances during this tour only strengthened their views about him, both as a player and as a character.

He was not only professional, but friendly and positive in his dealings with the press, and he defused many potentially difficult questions from what is, at times, a very rugby-illiterate press corps. The fact that his presence in the second Test was viewed with such seriousness by all the Test players shows the influence and input he gave in the preparation. The 1993 Lions were seen in New Zealand as one of the best touring teams ever to visit as a group, and this was the result of the attitude, presence and approach that Gavin gave to the public of New Zealand.

He is a competitor and on the field, when it mattered, he led by example; and, in the end, when you are looking at a very professional approach from your top players, this, more than anything else, significantly makes credible leadership.

### COMMENTS AND RECOMMENDATIONS

1 As a tour, the 1993 tour was a successful rugby experience both for those in the Lions party and for New Zealanders in general. I had never come across so many positive comments about our presence and displays. However, in pure results terms, we would have to say that, at the final whistle, we failed.

2 The 13-match tour is a very difficult proposition, particularly in New Zealand or South Africa, and it requires a balanced itinerary and the facility to prepare correctly before departure. As far as the itinerary was concerned, only the Waikato game was completely wrong.

3 The manager, but more particularly, the coach, must have significant, even final, decision on the composition of the tour party, as it is the rugby and the results which are ultimately the most important part of the tour. It would be beneficial for the manager and the coach to have no national involvement during the season prior to the tour.

4 Once again, I felt it was important that we had an additional weekend together, but this was very difficult to organise because of club commitments. If we are to prepare properly and have the players in the correct mental and physical state for such an intense tour, then consideration has to be given to presenting the Lions preparation programme at least 18 months before the tour and asking each of the Home Unions to organise, for that season only, a change to some domestic fixtures. It seems ridiculous to me that we were finally at the mercy of the clubs as to how we could organise our preparation.

Realistically, the players should also have at least two or three weeks' break before having to attempt a tour of this intensity.

5 Travel in all respects was excellent, apart from some occasional early morning starts. It is definitely an advantage to be able to train first and travel internally immediately after lunch. One further recommendation I could make is that, on some occasions, it would have been better not to travel at all on the Sunday, particularly after a big game in the major centres. This would allow a complete day off for organisation of free time and, on the Monday, training could then take place, followed by travel.

6 The equipment available for training, i.e. balls, tackle pads and scrummaging machine, were all excellent and, along with small cones, they all travelled with us, which meant we were completely self-reliant.

7 The major weakness in our squad was the absence of a strong character who could captain the midweek side and give it purpose and focus. I would recommend future selection actually selects a player with this responsibility.

8 There were significant differences in law interpretations, but we did expect this. The only point I would make is that, in New Zealand, the referees are told the type of game that they have to referee towards, and this allows players to develop continuity. They view very harshly the following:

- the player on the ground should be penalised at all times if he either does not release the ball or move away and that he is rucked dynamically if he is directly in the way of the ball. This undoubtedly helps continuity.
- the lineout throwing is geared to give the side throwing in possession.
- scrums hit and continue driving so again the ball is put in quickly and favours the side in possession; squint put-in was almost never penalised.
- I know we have a meeting between coaches and referees; the significant difference between the two hemispheres is that referees are dictated to more in the southern hemisphere to produce a certain type of game and, under the new laws, contact, continuity and the availability of the ball are seen as a priority. This is allowing Australia and New Zealand to develop faster, more continuous rugby, and our own players did benefit from this approach. If a Home Unions team is ever to win the World Cup, then we have to look carefully at the way we want our game to develop, and we must interpret the laws positively towards that end. It might not be the purest approach, but it is the practical approach, and it is the only way in which we will be able to compete in the world environment and competitions.

Whilst in New Zealand, both Geoff and I heavily criticised their interpretation of the third man 'who can be off his feet and scooping back'. This, more than anything else, took us time to adapt to, particularly as we had emphasised that we wanted our players on their feet.

9 The role of assistant coach could be extended, possibly to take official responsibility for the midweek team, and this would help to give a focus to the duties of the assistant coach.

10 It would have been very useful to have the squad's photograph with signatures on a card (Christmas card format), to distribute during the tour.

11 A selection of headed notepaper (standard and airmail) would also be very useful for communication purposes.

12 The final selection meeting should not take place immediately after the last international weekend. It would be more beneficial for seven to ten days to elapse before this final meeting.

13 The Lions must continue – the Test matches provide an arena which is completely different from any other experience the players get and the response in New Zealand is completely different from any national tour. As they kept reminding us, the Lions are the biggest thing which ever happens to New Zealand, and South Africa for that matter. We must not underestimate the Lions' role and their significance in the world rugby stage. Whatever we think nationally, we cannot provide what the Lions provide and, although there will be inherent difficulties of bringing four countries together, the advantages far outweigh any problems, and British rugby will always benefit from the existence of the Lions.

Finally, I would like to thank Bob Weighill for the time and effort in the preparation and organisation of the party at Oatlands Park, as well as the distribution of the tremendous amount of kit received. Once again, Bob provided a very effective base from which Geoff and I could work, to develop a closely knit touring party.

My thanks also go to John Lawrence, Treasurer, whose swift reimbursal of expenses and clear directions are appreciated by both management and players, as travelling can be an expensive business.

Ian R. McGeechan
Honorary Coach and Assistant Manager

# Results of the 1993 Lions in New Zealand

P 13   W 7   D 0   L 6   F 314   A 285

| | | | |
|---|---|---|---|
| North Auckland | W | 30 | 17 |
| North Harbour | W | 29 | 13 |
| New Zealand Maoris | W | 24 | 20 |
| Canterbury | W | 28 | 10 |
| Otago | L | 24 | 37 |
| Southland | W | 34 | 16 |
| New Zealand (Christchurch) | L | 18 | 20 |
| Taranaki | W | 49 | 25 |
| Auckland | L | 18 | 23 |
| Hawke's Bay | L | 17 | 29 |
| New Zealand (Wellington) | W | 20 | 7 |
| Waikato | L | 10 | 38 |
| New Zealand (Auckland) | L | 13 | 30 |

## Gavin Hastings's 1993 Lions team

**Full-backs**

| | | |
|---|---|---|
| A. Clement | Swansea | Wales |
| A.G. Hastings (capt.) | Watsonians | Scotland |

**Three-quarters**

| | | |
|---|---|---|
| W.D.C. Carling | Harlequins | England |
| V.J.G. Cunningham* | St Mary's College | Ireland |
| I.C. Evans | Llanelli | Wales |
| I.S. Gibbs | Swansea | Wales |
| J.C. Guscott | Bath | England |
| S. Hastings | Watsonians | Scotland |
| I. Hunter | Northampton | England |
| R. Underwood | Leicester & RAF | England |
| T. Underwood | Leicester | England |
| R.M. Wallace* | Garryowen | Ireland |

**Half-backs**

| | | |
|---|---|---|
| C.R. Andrew | Wasps | England |
| S. Barnes | Bath | England |
| R.N. Jones | Swansea | Wales |
| C.D. Morris | Orrell | England |
| A.D. Nicol* | Dundee HS FP | Scotland |

**Forwards**

| | | |
|---|---|---|
| M.C. Bayfield | Northampton | England |
| A.P. Burnell | London Scottish | Scotland |
| B.B. Clarke | Bath | England |
| D.F. Cronin | London Scottish | Scotland |
| W.A. Dooley | Preston Grasshoppers | England |
| M.J. Galwey | Shannon | Ireland |
| M.O. Johnson* | Leicester | England |
| J. Leonard | Harlequins | England |
| K.S. Milne | Heriot's FP | Scotland |
| B.C. Moore | Harlequins | England |
| N.J. Popplewell | Greystones | Ireland |
| A.I. Reed | Bath | England |
| D. Richards | Leicester | England |
| M.C. Teague | Moseley | England |
| R.E. Webster | Swansea | Wales |
| P.J. Winterbottom | Harlequins | England |
| P.H. Wright | Boroughmuir | Scotland |

Manager: Geoff Cooke
Coach: Ian McGeechan
Assistant Coach: Dick Best
Tour Doctor: James Robson

* Replacements

# The Future

The habitual problem which has beset Lions tours throughout the decades has been the availability of players for long tours, because of disruption of family life, studies, training or career. Nevertheless, the incredible adventure of such an odyssey has seen players placing everything at risk to take part, even though there has always been that other recurring theme of remarkable and unacceptably high levels of violence and injury. Almost every tour has been affected from time to time, for there can be no doubt that the southern hemisphere countries, by their very nature, produce and accept far higher levels of ferocity in what, after all, is only a game. Furthermore, one has the feeling that the old colonies enjoy putting the representatives of their 'mother countries' to the test.

This is what caused people like Carwyn James and Willie John McBride to coin such phrases as 'Get your retaliation in first' and 'Take no prisoners'. Willie John will tell you that the media misinterpreted his motives and that it was designed purely as a retaliatory measure, to prevent any bullying of his team, and that the call was invoked only about three times throughout the 1974 tour. It also had the added value of preventing individual players from having to fight solitary battles and run the risk of being sent off.

There has never been anything amateur about the length and commitment of Lions tours, but too often other factors, such as selection, have been in the hands of the dabbler, and there have been difficulties in satisfying the national aspirations of our separate countries.

It all changed dramatically over the years, as the pace of the tours quickened, helped by the change in modes of travel from boat and train to propeller aircraft, followed by fast jets, with travel time reduced from months to hours. The length of tours and number of matches also changed to suit the times, as did the role of the captain, when coaches were introduced. We have now come to the most critical change of all, which has thrown the whole matter of Lions tours into jeopardy: the change from the amateur to professional age.

What have remained unchanged, and what may save the whole, marvellous concept of Lions tours, are such matters as pride in representing the best of British; the sense of adventure that such an experience brings; the camaraderie from soldiering together; the boundless hospitality of the host countries for, fierce though they are on the field, they are kindness itself off it; and, finally, the lifelong friendships formed with team members and with opponents.

As far back as the early 1980s, memoranda were being prepared and considered by the Four Home Unions concerning the suggestion that Lions tours should be discontinued, and that single-country tours should be arranged on a more frequent and rotational basis.

The advent of the World Cup was the catalyst for this idea, as New Zealand pointed out that a World Cup scenario would require teams to have a single national identity. The historical non-availability of some players was another factor in this new equation, together with the nationalistic problems of fair Lions selection, and the difficulties of staging long tours, with short, single-nation tours from Britain and Ireland being far easier and cheaper to organise.

Subsequently, there was a proliferation of such tours, which continue to this day, but with disappointing results, for none of the individual countries has succeeded, as yet, in being as competitive as a Lions team. This even includes England with their powerhouse pack in the early 1990s.

In the 1980s, when these matters were examined, it was, in the end, agreed by the International Board that Lions tours should continue, and that the pattern of the tours should be an out-going Home Union tour and an incoming Overseas Union tour every six years in rotation; with an Overseas Union to house a Lions tour every nine years, and two Home Union tours in the intervening period.

Recent results of the short tours undertaken by individual countries to Australia, New Zealand and South Africa have seen many of them back-track on the idea that they are strong enough to take on the southern hemisphere, and they have reverted to thinking that the Lions should be the preferred option.

The current pattern is a World Cup every four years, a Lions tour every four years, and individual countries touring in the two years in between the World Cup and a Lions tour. Thus the four-year programme reads: World Cup – Country – Lions – Country. It was recommended and accepted that long Lions tours should be discontinued and replaced by medium tours of 12 or 13 matches.

Short tours, however, have great difficulty in finding a rhythm, while the longer tour gives time to develop a style of play. The coaches say repeatedly that they do not have the time to build a team from the separate countries or to develop their team as they would like. At the end of both short tours to Australia in 1989 and New Zealand in 1993, Ian McGeechan said he needed more time to develop the potential of both teams, especially in the backs.

The public simply would not understand such an issue, for their only perception of the tours abroad is usually derived from viewing one-off Test matches on television. There is no understanding of the problems posed by jet-lag, building a side and team spirit, new diets, homesickness, different beds twice a week, and local conditions such as altitude, warm weather and so on.

The arrival of professional rugby has given the question of whether Lions tours should continue an entirely new twist. For the first time, the southern hemisphere countries are no longer dependent on the Lions for improving their cash-flow every nine years or so. They have become financially more secure, due to the television deal with Rupert Murdoch and the great success of their Super-12 Competition and the Tri-Nations Championship, which is beginning to look as big a golden goose as the Five Nations Tournament has been for the British Isles.

At home old alliances are being damaged, as England have decided to go it alone over the negotiation of the Five Nations television contract. Their argument is that, as they had 38 million of the population of the British Isles, they are the major market with the largest parish to administer. Certainly they have a point, but does that mean that in future years if, say, China, America or Russia, with their huge populations, become involved in rugby union, England will be prepared to concede the major share of the television contracts to them? This is a shining example of the new philosophies which, it seems, are going to prevail in rugby's future. The Celtic countries are claiming that England, by dealing behind their back, have been guilty of duplicity and that they are guilty of wrecking old friendships and alliances. Such wounds will take a long time to heal.

Further questions are raised by the various contracts signed by the players with club and country. Are they going to have a clause allowing them to play for the Lions? Then what about the players who have signed contracts with both codes, for it is now possible to play rugby union for Bath or Leicester in the winter and Northern League rugby with Wigan or Leeds in the summer? They, surely, will not be able to go on tour if they are selected by the Lions.

For these and other reasons, the future for Lions tours may look bleak at the moment. However, it is my view that the southern hemisphere will want them to continue not only for traditional reasons, but also to provide a change of diet for their rugby public. I also believe that, in the end, it will be the players who will have the last say in the matter. They will surely want the Lions to continue, for becoming a Lion is a last act of fulfilment in any person's rugby career, and those rugby citadels in the other half of the world will still represent the ultimate challenge. Financial viability is surely no problem, and money guarantees to the players and insurance for both the club and the individual can be worked out.

I gather that the new professional 1997 Lions will receive around £15,000 per man, or about £2,000 a week, for touring South Africa, which is an extraordinary change from the relative poverty of the past. It was going to be £12,000 a man plus £2,000 for playing in a Test match, but this was thought to be too divisive and Fran Cotton, when he was made manager in June 1996, suggested that the idea be scrapped. When you consider that the players will provide million-pound gates at Test matches and take huge risks of serious injury, it is no more than they deserve and they will be worthy of their hire.

Everything presupposes that the same level of support from the television companies will continue. It should, for the undoubted success of the Super-12 and Tri-Nations southern hemisphere competitions, and the growing interest in the Five Nations or an equivalent championship, plus the embryonic European Competition in Europe and the continuing movement towards Pay-TV for sport, should keep the money flowing in. As that is going to be the name of the game, we had better get used to it.

Many, however, are questioning the changes and the build-up of power in the game, and are asking themselves whether they like what they see, with the demise of club loyalties and the replacement of playing for money instead of love.

The age of rugby's amateurism and innocence may be dead, but if we lose a great institution like the British Lions, with their remarkable crusades to the southern hemisphere, then the world of rugby will be a far poorer place.

# The First Professionals

*Sadly, Clem Thomas's death in September 1996 meant that he did not experience the joy of the 1997 British Lions' series win against South Africa. The following chapter was written by Greg Thomas, Clem's son, formerly the media and public relations manager for the Australian Rugby Union and now working as a sports journalist.*

When rugby became 'open' in 1995, casting off the shackles of amateurism, much was said and written about how the game's administrators had to preserve the ethos and character of the game in the new era of professionalism. Many critics went as far as to herald the end of traditional values that made rugby such a popular international sport. Rugby would never be the same again.

The game undoubtedly struggled in the northern hemisphere in the early days of this new era, while the southern hemisphere surged forward positively towards the new millennium. After all, the southern powers of New Zealand, South Africa and Australia had virtually dragged the rest of the rugby world kicking and screaming into the environment of professional sport.

Rugby was the last major sport to shed its amateurism tag, but at the end of the day everyone involved – administrators, players and the like – must be congratulated for the relatively smooth transition. The early problems in the north were merely regarded as hiccups, and while many more speed bumps may lie ahead, it is fair to say that rugby will never be the same again. It will be bigger, better and more exciting.

The pessimists back in 1995 predicted the demise of one of rugby's best traditions, the British Lions. It was argued that with professional club competitions, expanded Test schedules and convoluted player contracts there was simply no room for the British Lions in the new order. History will record that such thinking was unfounded and wide of the mark. A Lions tour to South Africa in 1997 had been pencilled into the Test schedules many years previously and the South African Rugby Football Union (SARFU), which had lost several million rand in the transition to professionalism, desperately wanted the tour to proceed. It was to be the first such tour since 1980 and predicted ticket-sale revenue would dramatically boost the coffers of the Union. As it panned out, the tour was such a windfall in terms of crowds, excitement and revenue that SARFU Chairman Dr Louis Luyt called for Lions tours to become more frequent. While rugby fans in the south appreciate and enjoy individual countries from the north touring, nothing whets their appetite as much as the four-nation conglomeration that is the British Lions. It simply shows that money cannot buy tradition and history. While it is unlikely that the Lions will tour more frequently than every four years, their future – and one of rugby's greatest traditions – seems assured.

## MARTIN JOHNSON'S 1997 LIONS

When the British Lions boarded their Virgin Atlantic jumbo jet for South Africa with 2.5 tonnes of baggage, no one gave them a cat in hell's chance of winning the three-Test series. Confident bookmakers were posting odds of 5–1 on them losing every Test.

The southern hemisphere 'super powers' were simply light years ahead. The Super-12 and Tri-Nations tournaments had given them a huge edge. They played the game at breathtaking pace, tackles and hits were ferocious and their management and administration were far superior. South Africa were confident of a victorious series, one that would be the perfect warm-up for their 1997 Tri-Nations campaign. They even had a cup made, aptly named the Lion Trophy (after its major sponsor).

The Lions management had anticipated such attitudes and, under-standing the task ahead of them, had plotted long and hard in the months preceding the tour, leaving no stone unturned to ensure the first tour to South Africa for 17 years would be a winning one. The player-selection process involved comprehensive analysis of ability, attitude and fortitude. Fact-finding trips were made to South Africa, including visits to 1996 Tri-Nations Tests, and advice was sought from such rugby luminaries as All Blacks coach John Hart.

The outcome was a tour party of 35 players (which became 40 after injuries struck) and a huge management contingent that included the usual medical personnel plus a dedicated kicking coach, Dave Alred, and a tactician-cum-technical-guru, Andy Keast, the Harlequins coach. Manager Fran Cotton and coach Ian McGeechan, supported by assistant coach Jim Telfer, were meticulous in their preparation. Both had been Lions on the famous 1974 tour to South Africa and had first-hand experience of the psyche of their opponents and the climatic conditions they would encounter.

McGeechan, on his unprecedented third consecutive Lions tour as coach, knew ·the type of player he wanted for the tour. 'I wanted decision-makers, players who would not be afraid to play as they saw it. This meant strong individuals, ones who would be tough and uncompromising and never troubled by thoughts of failure. We had to have people who had no fear of trying things, because if you never try you will never succeed.'

Leicester and England lock Martin Johnson fitted this mould and was chosen as captain on the basis that he would be an automatic choice in the Test team. McGeechan and Cotton were not prepared to carry a player in the team just because he was captain. Debate on the selection of the captain raged for many months prior to Johnson's appointment. When it was announced, his lack of experience as a captain was regarded as a gamble by several critics, but generally the decision was accepted. A Lion in New Zealand in 1993, he became the first English-man since Bill Beaumont to lead a tour party and would be instrumental in the success of the tour.

His leadership, along with the management of Cotton and McGeechan, established within the touring party a spirit and camaraderie not seen since the 1974 tour. The players became a tight unit and their loyalty and trust in each other became an important factor in repelling the Springbok onslaught in the Test series.

The tour party comprised 18 Englishmen, eight Welshmen, five Scots and four Irishmen. The oldest player was Welsh wing Ieuan Evans, on his third Lions tour, and the youngest was Irish back-row forward Eric Miller, at just 21. Reflecting rugby's new professionalism, the squad included six players who had returned from rugby league: three-quarters Allan Bateman, Scott Gibbs, Alan Tait and John Bentley, prop David Young, and back-row forward Scott Quinnell. All of the backs went on to win Test honours and distinguish themselves through their tour performances. Young failed to win a Test spot and Quinnell's tour finished abruptly after sustaining a groin injury against Northern Transvaal.

Centre Gibbs was a revelation, and probably the player of the tour. Likened to a pocket battleship by the media, his fearless and bone-jarring defence rattled the Springboks, and when he wasn't knocking green shirts over, his physical and committed running caused consternation in the locals' defensive lines. His stature, barrel-chested and five foot ten inches tall, caused co-centre Jeremy Guscott to describe Gibbs during the tour as 'the fastest prop I have ever seen'!

It would be hard not to mention all of the tour party, as everyone contributed immensely to the success, but Irish lock Jeremy Davidson was extremely impressive, improving as the tour wore on, and his fellow countryman, hooker Keith Wood, free of injury after a string of bad luck in previous years, proved a human dynamo with his work rate around the field.

Jeremy Guscott provided the class behind the scrum, full-back Neil Jenkins laid claim to being the best goal kicker in world rugby and props Smith and Wallace showed a maturity and skill level that surprised their critics and enabled them to confront the much larger 'Bok front row. After a slow start the tour party gelled into a formidable unit, and the tour record of 11 wins from 13 matches, including a 2-1 Test series triumph, was a testament to the resolve of the squad. The pressure to perform in the shadow of the 1974 side was immense, especially as the tour progressed, but the stunning triumph was a shot in the arm for northern hemisphere rugby after several years in the doldrums. What is more, it cast doubt over the Springboks' ambitions of success in the Tri-Nations series against New Zealand and Australia later that year.

For a nation that adores its rugby and treats its Springboks as national heroes, the loss of the Test series, following the loss to New Zealand in 1996, was hard to stomach. Arrogant in their belief that South Africa is the leading rugby nation, the media in particular turned on the Springboks and novice coach Carel du Plessis. The Springboks' final Test victory did little to quell the national disappointment.

It was an abrasive tour, but not unique in that respect. Lions teams of years gone by can testify to the physical and mental stress that goes with touring South Africa. Six players were ruled out of the tour as the physical nature of the campaign took its toll. By the kick-off in the last Test, nearly half of the original Test team had been ruled out through injury.

A notable aim of McGeechan throughout the tour was to avoid the situation where two separate teams within the squad were developed: the Test team and the midweek team. He stated at the outset that there would be no such policy, and this proved true. This had the effect of giving all players ample opportunity to push for Test places and contributed greatly to player morale.

The tour kicked off in positive fashion in Port Elizabeth against Eastern Province. A 39–11 victory over the 'Elephants', while satisfying, was not overly impressive, but it did not merit an attack by opposition coach Johan Kluyts, who declared that the 'Boks would win the Test series 3–0. He also proclaimed that full-back Neil Jenkins was a poor player and that the 'Boks would kill him. Such rantings would come back to haunt him.

Next up the Lions headed further east along the Cape to East London, where they disposed of a plucky Border in the mud. The 18–14 victory, however, highlighted several shortcomings in the forward play and only a late try by Rob Wainwright saved the day. Centre Gibbs caused a scare by damaging his ankle, an injury which necessitated X–rays and kept him out of several matches. It was a similar story in Cape Town against Western Province, where frailties in the pack again surfaced, but the play of the three-quarters indicated that an expansive game plan was part of the tour tactics. Captain Johnson took the field for his first appearance of the tour, but it was obvious that after a gruelling domestic season for the powerful lock McGeechan was going to use him sparingly outside of the Tests. Such tactics reaped dividends later in the tour when Johnson's form peaked for the Test matches.

A plus from the match was the form of scrum-half Howley, but this was tempered by the loss of fly-half Paul Grayson who, after completing the match, was told his tour was over due to a thigh injury. His replacement was Englishman Mike Catt who, much to the displeasure of England coach Jack Rowell, left the English tour of Argentina to go to South Africa.

After a week of intense training under the guidance of 'scrum doctor' Jim Telfer which the Lions forwards will find hard to erase from the memory, the Lions took the field against Mpumalanga in Witbank with Jenkins at fly-half due to the late arrival of Catt. The 64–14, ten-tries-to-two victory was reward for an expansive philosophy, but the match will always be remembered for the vicious and cowardly thuggery of Mpumalanga lock Marius Bosman. An out-and-out thug, he was guilty of several indiscretions before callously stamping on the knee of lock Doddie Weir. The injury ruled Weir out of the tour and threatened his career. To the disgust of the Lions management he stayed on the field and was only reprimanded by the national union and fined a paltry sum. The postscript to this episode was the call-up of veteran English lock Nigel Redman from Argentina.

With four victories behind them the Lions were slowly coming to terms with the local conditions, but ahead lay matches against three

Super-12 provinces, Northern Transvaal, Gauteng and Natal. The first real examination for the Lions came in Pretoria against the Blue Bulls, and the 30–35 loss was the first against a province in the Republic since 1968. It was a match the Lions could and should have won, but poor ball retention and costly errors were the order of the day, along with another patchy performance up front. The experiment of moving Miller from number eight to open side was a fizzer, as McGeechan continued his search for answers to his Test pack make-up. What is more, Scott Gibbs, who took the field as a replacement, was later suspended for one match for punching, and the day after the match number eight Scott Quinnell was ruled out of the tour because of a groin injury. Centre Bateman, who was pushing for his first Test spot, also aggravated a hamstring injury, putting his tour participation in doubt.

English back-row forward Tony Diprose joined the tour as Quinnell's replacement, just as wing Tony Underwood injured his shoulder against Gauteng. The Lions won the match 20–14 but it took two second-half tries to seal the win. One was a spectacular effort by winger John Bentley, who raced 70 metres to score. Jenkins, who took the field as a replacement, converted both tries after fly-half Catt had missed five penalty attempts.

Leaving the high altitude of Pretoria and Johannesburg, the Lions headed to Durban at sea level to face Currie Cup holders Natal at King's Park. This was considered to be the 'fourth Test' of the tour, but the Lions showed sublime form to comprehensively thrash the Sharks 42–12. It was an outstanding win, and for the first time the South African media and public sat up and took notice of a team that was now clearly capable of winning the first Test. Tries by Townsend, Catt and Dallaglio were complemented by more superlative kicking by Jenkins, who kicked 24 points including six penalties to secure his spot at full-back for the first Test, ahead of pre-tour favourite Tim Stimpson.

However, the horror injury stretch continued. Scrum-half Howley, a vital cog in the Test team, left the field with a severe shoulder injury in the first half and he became the fourth player to return home. Another Englishman, Kyran Bracken, who was at the time on holiday in Tobago, was brought in as his replacement.

The last match before the first Test saw the Lions dispose of the Emerging Springboks. They cut loose in the second half with the fast, attacking rugby that had become their trademark, and young wing Beal crossed for a hat-trick. The team was captained by veteran English prop Jason Leonard, which indicated he would miss out on a Test berth.

For the first Test in Cape Town McGeechan opted for an all-Celtic front row, consisting of two Irishmen and a Scot. Props Tom Smith and

Paul Wallace (who had only joined the tour three days before departure when Peter Clohessy withdrew) got the nod ahead of the more experienced Young and Leonard. Hooker Wood was following in the footsteps of his father, who had propped the Lions scrum in 1959. The number eight spot went to Tim Rodber, with Eric Miller being ruled out with the flu. Scrum-half Matt Dawson, out of favour with England months earlier, took Howley's position, Guscott and Gibbs continued their centre partnership from 1993 and Alan Tait, selected as a centre for the tour, won a spot on the wing ahead of Bentley.

Novice Springbok coach du Plessis, with little senior coaching experience and a single Test against Tonga under his belt, stuck with the tried and tested, although he had no room in his side for lock Kobus Wiese and centre Hennie le Roux, much to the angst of the public. Winger James Small became the most-capped Springbok of all time with 38 caps.

On the shortest day of the year the Lions stunned the Newlands crowd and delighted their legions of supporters by finishing the stronger team to win 25–16. It was a hard-earned victory, as they had only gone to the break leading 9–8 thanks once again to Jenkins, after the 'Boks had scored the first try of the match through gargantuan prop Os du Randt.

South Africa clearly had the upper hand with regard to territory and possession, and the match looked beyond the reach of the Lions when replacement Springbok wing Bennett crossed for the second try of the match after 43 minutes. The turning point occurred with 12 minutes to go. Bennett appeared to have scored his second try, only to be called back for a forward pass, and the Lions entered the last ten minutes only 16–15 down.

The boot of Jenkins and never-say-die defence had kept them in the match. The front row had met the challenge of the enormous 'Bok scrum, and a moment of individual brilliance broke the hearts of the South Africans. From a scrum on the right of the Springbok twenty-two, scrum-half Dawson broke right down the blind side and outsped flanker Kruger into a gap. With number eight Teichmann about to smash him, he feigned an overhead pass back inside. Teichmann took the dummy and Dawson scampered over unopposed to put the Lions ahead with minutes remaining. Then, in the final minute, Tait sealed victory in the left-hand corner with a try after most of the Lions had been involved in the lead-up. The Lions reserves took to the field in celebration and McGeechan's bear hug of Dawson in the tunnel after the match summed up his emotions at his team scoring a record number of Test points at Newlands.

All those months of plotting and scheming by Cotton and McGeechan had paid off. Their mission to put the Springboks on the back foot from the outset had proved successful. The trick now was to maintain the momentum and prevent the wheels falling off the bandwagon.

Wing John Bentley further pressed his claims for a Test spot with a well-taken hat-trick of tries in the tenth match of the tour against Free State. The Lions had chosen to fly to the high altitude of Bloemfontein on the same day as the match, and Fran Cotton declared after the 52–30 victory, 'One of the all-time great Lions performances, when you consider we travelled up on the day and were playing a Super-12 province at altitude.'

With preparations in hand for the second Test and the victory that would secure the series, the Lions lost another two members of the tour party. Uncapped English centre Will Greenwood was knocked unconscious during the Free State match and Test winger Ieuan Evans damaged his groin in training. Such disruptions became a weekly occurrence for tour doctor James Robson and physio Mark Davies, but, undeterred, the touring party's resolve grew stronger as the tour progressed and the competition for Test spots became intense. Scottish three-quarter Tony Stanger, in South Africa with the Scottish Development team, was called into the squad as cover for Evans and Greenwood.

Evans's misfortune opened the door for Bentley and he was the only change in the Lions team for the second Test at King's Park, Durban. Du Plessis, however, was forced into making several changes behind the scrum. Injured centres Lubbe and Mulder were replaced by the recalled Danie Schalkwyk and new cap Percy Montgomery, while the injured James Small was replaced by new cap Pieter Rossouw on the wing.

What eventuated at King's Park was the greatest rearguard action since O'Rourke's Drift. The vastly underrated Lions heroically withstood wave after wave of Springbok pressure and despite conceding three tries triumphed 18–15, thanks to the golden boot of Jenkins and a match-winning drop goal from Jeremy Guscott.

Prepared for an onslaught after the first Test, the Lions could not have imagined how ferociously the massive South African pack would attack them second time round. Yet, led from midfield by Gibbs, who tackled his heart out and whose aggression in defence rubbed off on the likes of Tom Smith, Tim Rodber and Keith Wood, they constantly repelled the opposition.

The 'Boks simply dominated territory for 70 minutes but paid the ultimate price for not having in their midst a goal kicker of Test standard. Fly-half Honiball missed two kicks, Montgomery three and full-back Joubert one. Delighted former Lions flanker John Taylor wrote in his newspaper column, 'The Lions committed grand larceny.'

The Lions refused to give in and managed to stay in touch until the last few minutes, thanks to Jenkins's five penalty goals. When it appeared they were out on their feet they found a second, even third, wind and made ground towards the 'Bok twenty-two. Dawson, unable to find his fly-half Townsend, fed Guscott, who went for broke and the drop goal. It sailed high and true to put the Lions in front at 18–15. The final whistle, minutes later, signalled an historic series victory for the Lions and the opportunity to whitewash the Springboks in the final Test.

The local media called for the head of the coach and lambasted the players. One journalist from *The Cape Times* declared, 'The most positive aspect of Saturday's result was that the powers that be now know that their decision to appoint du Plessis was not a moment of inspiration but one of madness.'

The British press lauded the Lions and dismissed claims that they had been lucky. Had the Springboks not beaten New Zealand in the World Cup final in similar circumstances in 1995? Headlines proclaimed "Bokbusters!', 'Lions Break 'Bok Hearts', 'Truly the Stuff of Legends' and 'Lionhearts Steal Glory at the Last'.

The Lions left Durban buoyed by their success and once again headed for the high veldt and the final Test at Ellis Park, Johannesburg. On the way they stopped at Welkom to play Northern Free State in the penultimate match of the tour. The Lions ran riot, scoring ten tries in the last midweek match to record the highest score of the tour and pass the 50-point mark for the fourth time.

Poised to make history by attempting to win the Test series 3–0, the Lions were a sore and bruised bunch. Spirits were high but there was no denying that several of the Test team could not muster the energy for a third encounter with the Springboks. Ellis Park is the fortress of South African rugby and the scene of its greatest triumph in 1995. Entering the third Test against the All Blacks in 1996, also 2–0 down, the 'Boks had defended their temple to win the Test and salvage some pride. The Lions took the field with five changes from the second Test. Tony Underwood replaced Tait on the wing, Mike Catt took over the fly-half role from Townsend, Mark Regan replaced Wood at hooker, Neil Back, rejected by England for being too small, replaced Hill and, on the morning of the Test, Scottish captain Rob Wainwright was drafted into the back row when Rodber was hit by a gastro bug.

Carel du Plessis, fighting for his coaching future, was also forced into changes due to injury and poor form. Bennett took over at full-back for

Joubert, fly-half Honiball was relegated to the bench in favour of out-and-out goal kicker Jannie de Beer, James Dalton was recalled at hooker for Naka Drotské, Dawie Theron replaced prop Garvey, Johan Erasmus replaced flanker Kruger and Krynauw Otto replaced the injured Andrews at lock.

It proved to be a game too far for the Lions. They were battered and bruised, and it was beyond them to compete for the full 80 minutes. To the very end they fought like champions, though, and although two late Springbok tries distorted the final scoreline, the Lions were in the match until the last ten minutes. With Jeremy Guscott equalling Mike Gibson's record of eight Tests at centre, there was a certain irony to the encounter: the Lions' performance was in many ways a more authoritative one than that of the second Test. Dallaglio had a huge match, as did Tom Smith, in a game that was once again overly physical at times. Indeed, on four occasions various Springbok forwards were warned for foul play.

The South Africans scored two tries to one in the first three-quarters of the match, but with the score at 23–16 to the home side they went on to score two further tries in the last 12 minutes. Full-back Jenkins kicked three penalties to create a new Lions record for points scored in a Test series, his 41 points surpassing Gavin Hastings's 38 points in New Zealand in 1993.

At the end of the day it came down to one thing: who wanted to win more. The Lions were chasing history, but with the series already secured – and although they would not admit it – the hunger for success so evident in the earlier matches was definitely not so fierce. The 'Boks, on the other hand, were desperate for victory. Castigated by their supporters and the media, it was do-or-die time for most of the players. Their hunger proved greater in the final battle.

## Results of the 1997 Lions in South Africa

P 13  W 11  D 0  L 2  F 480  A 278

| | | | |
|---|---|---|---|
| Eastern Province | W | 39 | 11 |
| Border | W | 18 | 14 |
| Western Province | W | 38 | 21 |
| Mpumalanga | W | 64 | 14 |
| Northern Transvaal | L | 30 | 35 |
| Gauteng | W | 20 | 14 |
| Natal | W | 42 | 12 |
| Emerging Springboks | W | 51 | 22 |

| South Africa (Cape Town) | W | 25 | 16 |
|---|---|---|---|
| Free State | W | 52 | 30 |
| South Africa (Durban) | W | 18 | 15 |
| Northern Free State | W | 67 | 39 |
| South Africa (Johannesburg) | L | 16 | 35 |

## Martin Johnson's 1997 Lions team

### Full-backs

| Neil Jenkins | Pontypridd | Wales |
|---|---|---|
| Tim Stimpson | Newcastle | England |

### Three-quarters

| Allan Bateman | Richmond | Wales |
|---|---|---|
| Nick Beal | Northampton | England |
| John Bentley | Newcastle | England |
| Ieuan Evans | Llanelli | Wales |
| Scott Gibbs | Swansea | Wales |
| Will Greenwood | Leicester | England |
| Jeremy Guscott | Bath | England |
| Tony Stanger* | Hawick | Scotland |
| Alan Tait | Newcastle | Scotland |
| Tony Underwood | Newcastle | England |

### Half-backs

| Kyran Bracken* | Saracens | England |
|---|---|---|
| Mike Catt* | Bath | England |
| Matt Dawson | Northampton | England |
| Paul Grayson | Northampton | England |
| Austin Healey | Leicester | England |
| Robert Howley | Cardiff | Wales |
| Gregor Townsend | Northampton | Scotland |

### Forwards

| Neil Back | Leicester | England |
|---|---|---|
| Lawrence Dallaglio | Wasps | England |
| Jeremy Davidson | London Irish | Ireland |
| Tony Diprose* | Saracens | England |
| Richard Hill | Saracens | England |
| Martin Johnson (capt.) | Leicester | England |
| Jason Leonard | Harlequins | England |
| Eric Miller | Leicester | Ireland |

| | | |
|---|---|---|
| Scott Quinnell | Richmond | Wales |
| Nigel Redman* | Bath | England |
| Mark Regan | Bristol | England |
| Tim Rodber | Northampton | England |
| Graham Rowntree | Leicester | England |
| Simon Shaw | Bristol | England |
| Tom Smith | Watsonians | Scotland |
| Rob Wainwright | Watsonians | Scotland |
| Paul Wallace | Saracens | Ireland |
| Doddie Weir | Newcastle | Scotland |
| Barry Williams | Neath | Wales |
| Keith Wood | Harlequins | Ireland |
| David Young | Cardiff | Wales |

Manager: Fran Cotton
Coach: Ian McGeechan
Assistant Coach: Jim Telfer

*Replacements

# Missed Opportunities

Barely two years after rugby entered a new professional era the triumphant tour to South Africa in 1997 rekindled the ethos and spirit of Lions tours. Strictly speaking it was the first tour to take place within the new era and the unfancied Lions beat the Springboks, winners of the 1995 World Cup, to bring much needed balance into the international game.

However, it is fair to say that the 2001 Lions were the first touring party to experience the full implications of professionalism, an arena in which the rugby tour as we knew it has all but disappeared from the cluttered international rugby calendar. The tour to Australia, then, was an important litmus test for the future direction of Lions tours.

Unfortunately, the management's interpretation of professionalism meant an environment where it focused entirely on a winning outcome at the expense of balancing athletic pursuits with the life education experiences usually gathered on Lions tours. Many of the traditional touring ideals were disregarded in the quest for outright success.

So intense was the regime that apart from closed training sessions, team meetings and matches, the players were lucky to see anything of the country they were visiting other than the four walls of their hotel room. This is not what Lions tours are about.

This siege mentality, manufactured by the senior management, Graham Henry and manager Donal Lenihan, was always going to be a double-edged sword with regards to the judgement of their – and indeed the tour's – success. With a winning campaign, though, such methods would perhaps be vindicated.

Of course, the series was ultimately lost and the 2001 Lions became the first tourists to lose a series in Australia. In the final analysis it would be fair to say that the squad was one of the unhappiest Lions touring parties ever to leave Britain and Ireland.

Strong ambition and a desire to be successful are admirable qualities but, for players at the pinnacle of their careers, Lions tours should comprise a balance of elite competition and personal adventure.

It had all started out so promisingly. In this fully-fledged professional climate Henry was appointed as the first overseas coach to take the helm of the Lions, and the brooding English bulldog Martin Johnson once again assumed the captaincy. What is more, the Lions arrived in Australia as favourites for the first time in a series in the southern hemisphere, due to the core of the squad comprising the resurgent English team that had beaten Australia and South Africa at the end of 2000 – albeit at home.

However, the all-important mind games that are part and parcel of professional sport were clearly won by the Australians. That the Wallabies successfully labelled themselves underdogs for the series highlights the psychological advantage coach Rod Macqueen established over the Lions. For this was a Wallaby team that were the reigning World Champions and holders of the Bledisloe Cup and Tri-Nations Trophy. No British team had won in Australia since the 1989 Lions series and the Wallabies, the best side in the world, were enjoying the most successful era in their history under Macqueen.

The series was the most anticipated clash for many years of two of rugby's superpowers and the Lions were accompanied by probably the biggest contingent of British and Irish supporters ever. It didn't disappoint. The series went down to the wire, both teams scored seven tries apiece, and it hinged on a couple of key moments in the second and third Tests. Ultimately the series was lost in the last few minutes of the third Test and represents a major missed opportunity in the eventful history of the British and Irish Lions. They simply dominated their opposition for the majority of the series.

Off the field it was also a missed opportunity as the Lions remained largely unknown to the Aussie public, as the players became increasingly sceptical of the management regime. In stark contrast, the tens of thousands of marvellous travelling Lions supporters endeared themselves to Australia with their passionate support, and good-natured revelry.

The 'Red Barmy Army' provided the human face of the tour as the Lions management failed to embrace this important side of touring with their reluctance to allow media access to the players and the players themselves to enjoy the hospitality of their hosts.

This may seem a critical summary of the events surrounding the tour but it is one largely echoed by the players themselves. The Lions sought success but the management's attempt to achieve it at all costs was hugely disappointing. The financial success of the tour is unquestionable, as is the immense interest it created around the world. In Australia, where rugby continues to surge in popularity, the Lions tour injected around AUS $100 million into the economy and ticket and merchandise sales reached new heights.

The Lions are one of rugby's most potent and emotionally charged brands and hopefully lessons learned in Australia will ensure that future tours recreate the right balance on and off the field. The Lions must be restored to their rightful ambassadorial role for northern hemisphere rugby, and they must be allowed, even in the new professional era, to enjoy the delights of host countries.

## MARTIN JOHNSON'S 2001 LIONS

The biggest ever squad to represent the British and Irish Lions was announced in mid-April at the Crown Plaza Hotel, Heathrow Airport, to unprecedented media coverage. The media and the public's interest in the tour to Australia was immense and coach Graham Henry was left in little doubt as to the pressure he was under from day one.

Early tension started with valid criticism of the need for a 37-man squad (which became 44 after injuries struck) for the relatively short 10-match tour. Six lead-up matches to the first Test, including two first-up matches against sub-standard opposition, left little time for experimentation, development of combinations, or a valid assessment of all 37 players. The pressure intensified when it was revealed that several players, including Englishmen Lawrence Dallaglio, Phil Greening and Mike Catt, would travel with significant injuries.

The spotlight of pressure made Henry look uncomfortable and it was the last thing he needed, considering the chronic foot-and-mouth epidemic in Britain and Ireland had already hampered the Lions pre-tour preparations. The Six Nations had been severely disrupted with Tests being cancelled due to travel restrictions put in place by the British and Irish Governments. This left the selectors short of matches to assess tour candidates – and the players short of crucial Test match preparation.

Nevertheless, the omens appeared positive for the Lions who were earning a guaranteed £15,000 – and up to £22,000 if they remained unbeaten and won the series. Their record in Australia was excellent with a record of 14 Test wins from 17. The Lions had never lost a series in Australia and the successful 1997 series win in South Africa was a not too distant memory for 16 of the players heading for Australia. On paper the squad looked impressive with the necessary depth to cover all positions and a confidence stemming from England's recent success over southern hemisphere teams. If the squad played to its full potential there was every chance that the Lions' third century of rugby would start on a winning note.

Interestingly, the selection of the eighteen English, ten Welsh, six Irish and three Scots raised only limited debate. The omission of the robust Welsh centre Scott Gibbs, the player of the tour in South Africa four years earlier, did appear to be one glaring error, along with the versatile English backrow forward Martin Corry.

The selection of former rugby league wing Jason Robinson, who had not played a full Test prior to the tour, was greeted favourably. It was to prove an inspired selection as Robinson was one of the best-performing Lions on the tour, bamboozling and confusing defenders with his blistering pace and effective side-step. Martin Johnson, the rugged pillar of English rugby, on his third tour, made history by being the first player to captain two Lions tours. With a seemingly permanent furrowed brow, he led from the front as usual and carried the Lions' frustrations and aspirations on his considerable shoulders. The only real 'surprise' in the squad was the promising 21-year-old Scottish number 8 Simon Taylor, with only three caps to his name. Unfortunately after a bright start on his debut in the opening game, he badly damaged his knee and was ruled out of the rest of the tour.

The main reason for the muted debate on selection was that there appeared to be an identifiable Test line-up within the squad, leaving the areas of keenest debate around those players likely to figure in the mid-week fixtures. This single fact – while it appeared to be a positive at the outset – turned into one of the key reasons why the tour hit the rails in terms of player morale once the players reached Australia. For clearly certain players believed there was one tour for the perceived Test squad and another for the 'dirt trackers' – those who had to make do with appearances in the mid-week fixtures. The preferential treatment given to Dallaglio and Catt was unpopular with a large part of the squad, especially the Celts, even as early as at the training camp prior to departure.

Keeping the balance between such groups of players, managing the four-country chemistry, and the maintenance of morale and competition for Test places has been a dilemma for every Lions management. The importance of these aspects of a tour cannot be overstated and they need shrewd and diplomatic treatment in order for the management to harness the full potential of the squad. Sadly, evidence of such thinking was missing within the new professional framework.

Henry acknowledged at the Lions pre-tour camp in Hampshire that the task ahead was an onerous one and that perhaps the lack of match fitness was a concern:

> Playing against Australia will be a different game to the one being played in the Six Nations. It will be a huge step up for all concerned. We are in for a huge challenge and our playing levels have to go up if we are to beat the number-one nation. But there are one or two guys that we're keen not to play in the early part of the tour, simply because they've had so much rugby recently. Others are a little under-done: the Irish, for instance, have played very little because of the foot-and-mouth outbreak. It's a question of finding the right balance.

Henry's response to his concerns over the mixed preparation and fitness levels within the squad manifested itself in a severe early training regime that pushed the players to their limits. He appeared to settle on the lowest common denominator in terms of fitness and was keen to taper off the training as the Tests approached. The large English contingent, the fittest and more hardened professionals within the squad, took exception to this approach, believing such fitness and routine skill work was unnecessary and wasteful. This created another despondent faction within the squad. Indeed, several English players, through hard-hitting syndicated newspaper columns, vented their frustration at the Lions management and caused conflict within the camp, despite Lenihan's attempts to paper it over. One article, written by wing Austin Healey before the final Test in Sydney, undermined Henry's management and ridiculed Wallaby lock Justin Harrison, providing so much psychological ammunition to the Wallabies that it could be argued that it was almost treasonable.

Nonetheless, the Lions came within minutes of securing a second successive series victory over a reigning world champion side. For the large part of the series they were the better team, playing a wonderful brand of expansive rugby, comprising a vigour and urgency up front that was never matched by the Wallabies.

The demolition of the Wallabies in the first Test was remarkable for its ruthlessness, as the Lions took every opportunity that came their way. With total dominance up front, the Test put the Lions on the front foot and put the pressure firmly on the Wallabies to win both remaining Tests. The first 40 minutes of the second Test provided more of the same – except crucially the Lions failed to convert their superiority into points. At half-time the Wallabies appeared ready for the taking, barely resembling the team that had won the 1999 World Cup.

Remarkably, however, they turned the 11–6 deficit into a record-winning margin to run out victors 35–14, turning the series around. The renowned mental fortitude of this generation of Wallabies came to the fore once again and it was the home team that snapped up the half-chances to score three second-half tries.

The Olympic Stadium in Sydney, fresh from hosting the most successful Games in history, provided the backdrop for the deciding rubber. Indeed, tickets were harder to find than for the Games opening ceremony a year earlier, and for sheer tension and drama it is hard to remember a more intense match.

The Lions, showing signs of fatigue (and suffering a lengthy touring injury list), trailed 29–23 with minutes to go. Searching for a last elusive score they failed to capitalise on late territorial advantage and when they lost their own throw at a line within the Wallaby twenty-two, the match and the series were blown.

It was a devastating blow for the estimated 15–20,000 Lions supporters who had provided such ardent support for the tourists. At the end of the day the Lions, so ruthless in the early stages of the tour, failed to inflict a killer punch against a side struggling for form and they paid the price. The Wallabies, with fewer opportunities and a more conservative, structured game plan prevailed – finding their form late in the series.

The tour had kicked off in sunny Perth on Australia's west coast against Western Australia. The match was played at the famous WACA cricket stadium and the Lions fans were treated to a real cricket score with the visitors winning 116–10. The locals were clearly not up to the challenge despite their invitations to New South Wales players Duncan McRae and Patricio Noriega to bolster their amateur ranks.

Henry surprised everyone by selecting Irish centre O'Driscoll at full-back, in an experiment that failed to provide any clear solutions. Lock Grewcock and scrum-half Howley were two of the best on the field, while wing Luger and number 8 Quinnell helped themselves to three tries each.

It was a ruthless win, but costly however, as the fresh-faced Scottish back-row forward Simon Taylor smashed his knee to end his tour. English back-row forward Martin Corry, who missed initial selection, was called from England's tour of North America to replace Taylor, while Scottish hooker Gordon Bulloch was summoned as a cover for hooker Phil Greening who had failed to shrug off a pre-tour injury. He never made it onto the field and was later sent home.

The standard of competition increased slightly for the second match but the Lions disposed of a Queensland President's XV 83–6 in Townsville, North Queensland. After a sluggish start against a spirited opposition that included ten Super Twelve players, the Lions scored a record 73 points in the second half.

With seven run-on debutants, the Lions scored thirteen tries – with Robinson scoring five and centre Henderson three. Man of the match was flanker Charvis who was the catalyst for the second-half points avalanche. In the first half they were stopped on the gain line far too often as too much of their play was lateral, with the ball shuffling across the field with little subtlety.

Lions manager, Lenihan declared after the match: 'There are always three or four moments that define a Lions tour and I think we saw one there tonight. They didn't panic. The team got rid of their first-half anxiousness and their character showed through.'

With 31 tries scored in just two matches, the Lions faced their first real test of the tour against Queensland at Ballymore in Brisbane. In a sometimes spiteful match the Lions thrashed an injury depleted Reds side 42–8. With Wilkinson kicking beautifully and controlling the match tempo and tactics, Hill, Henderson, O'Driscoll, Luger, and James all scored tries. The only concern for the Lions was adjusting to the southern hemisphere refereeing interpretations at the breakdown. The Lions gave away several penalties for slowing the ball down at the ruck and for not releasing the ball in the tackle; areas that were to prove troublesome for the rest of the tour.

The fourth match of the tour against Australia A at Gosford, north of Sydney, was basically the 'fourth Test' of the tour, and a major hurdle for the Lions' midweek XV. Indeed, Eddie Jones' shadow Wallaby Test side held off a late charge from the Lions to claim a deserved 28–25 win, destroying the Lions' perfect record. A try-less first half saw Australia A 15–6 up at the break as Manny Edmonds exchanged penalties with Neil Jenkins. There were four tries in the second half, with Scott Staniforth scoring Australia's only touchdown, and the Lions grabbing their three late scores from Mark Taylor, Matt Perry and Jason Robinson on the final whistle.

But the constant infringement of the Lions team at the ruck cost them dearly, and reinforced Eddie Jones' claims prior to the game of cynical play from the tourists in slowing the ball down. Lawrence Dallaglio, playing his first match of the tour, spent ten minutes in the sin-bin for repeated transgressions.

After the match Henry declared, 'Our lineout was not acceptable. We lacked basic sharpness, and a lot of negatives came out of this game. We need to put some more time into our lineout work, which needs to be quality time. But this could be the baseline we require. Reality has really set in.'

Worrying for the Lions was Mike Catt's departure from the field in his first match. He aggravated the calf injury he had been nursing from the outset and played no further part in the tour. Welshman Scott Gibbs was flown out to replace him for the remaining matches. Hooker Robin McBryde also joined the casualty list during the match and Englishman Dorian West joined Gibbs on the plane to Australia as his replacement. But there was worse to come a day later when likely Test winger Dan Luger fractured his cheekbone in training when he clashed heads with Neil Back. Luger had been looking impressive until that point but the injury put him on the plane home and he was replaced by Irishman Tyrone Howe. Without doubt several players keen to break into Test reckoning ruled themselves out of contention in Gosford. Cohen, Jenkins, O'Kelly, Young, Murray and McBryde saw their Test aspirations disappear. The pack was outplayed for most of the game with the Australia A second-row of Justin Harrison and Tom Bowman dominating the lineout.

The match against New South Wales, who were devoid of their test squad players, will be remembered for one moment of madness by full-back Duncan McRae. Inexplicably, he launched a savage punching attack on replacement fly-half Ronan O'Gara as both players lay on the ground. O'Gara left the field and needed 11 stitches in two deep cuts around his left eye. McRae was sent from the field by referee Scott Young and the incident caused deep friction between the Lions and Bob Dwyer's Waratah team.

Five other players were sent to the sin-bin in what was a stormy match – Bowman, Blades and Cannon from the home side and Grewcock and Vickery of the Lions. At one point in the second-half, 12 Waratahs played 13 Lions.

Until the distractions of these sending-offs and the sin-binnings, the Lions looked generally impressive during victory in their last major outing before the first Test. Of some concern was a dip in performance in the second half but they scored five tries to their opponents' four. Robinson helped himself to two more, Wilkinson ensured victory with his goal kicking, while a rejuvenated O'Driscoll in the centre, and outstanding performances from forwards Quinnell and Grewcock, indicated that the Lions were developing into a series-winning team. Following the match, tempers were frayed over the O'Gara incident and the Lions' management also accused home coaches of orchestrating a media campaign that attacked the Lions' methods, in order to influence referees during the tour. The Test matches were looming and the attendant psychological war of words had clearly started.

There was yet more bad news on the injury front when potential Test centre Will Greenwood suffered an ankle ligament injury that was to prevent him from playing any further part in the tour. Then, a week later, flanker Neil Back suffered a rib injury that put him out of the first Test.

Furthermore, Lawrence Dallaglio aggravated the knee ligament problem he came to Australia with, and was sent home for surgery. He should never have toured. Interestingly, his replacement – Irishman David Wallace – created a unique piece of Lions history. He became the third Wallace brother to become a Lion, following winger Richard in 1993 and prop Paul in 1997. (All three were replacement players.)

The New South Wales town of Coffs Harbour – the Wallabies training headquarters – hosted the last match before the first Test. A mediocre mid-week Lions team stuttered their way to an unconvincing 46–3 victory over the part-time NSW Country Cockatoos.

Captained by Tamworth poultry farmer Bernie Klasen, the Cockatoos put up a spirited performance. Prior to the match they sang the national anthem in the dressing-room and their pride in Country rugby could be measured by the tears shed.

The Lions' lacklustre performance could be attributed in part to the lengthening injury list and the shock of the death of their gear steward, Anton Toia, who died of a heart attack while swimming in the sea off Coffs Harbour. A popular Australian rugby official with many touring teams, his death was marked by the wearing of black arm bands in the match.

The selection of the first Test team produced little surprise. It had, in fact, largely picked itself following the six lead-up matches and with the major injuries to eight of the squad. The dependable Matt Perry was preferred at full-back to the below-par Balshaw, while Robinson picked himself on the wing where Dafydd James joined him in place of Luger.

The Irish centre pairing of O'Driscoll and Henderson showed outstanding form, with halves Wilkinson and Howley clearly head-and-shoulders ahead of their nearest rivals. Tom Smith, Keith Wood and Phil Vickery won the front-row spots, with skipper Martin Johnson and fellow countryman Danny Grewcock packing down in the second row. Neil Back's injury left the door open for Martin Corry to claim the number 6 jersey, following impressive form after joining the tour as a replacement. Richard Hill moved to open side with Scott Quinnell locking the scrum at number 8.

With Ballymore deemed too small and the larger SunCorp Stadium under redevelopment, the first Test was played at the 38,000-capacity Wollongabba cricket ground in Brisbane. The scene of many an Australian cricket test victory, the ground was filled to the rafters and the Red Army, with its singing and boisterous support, virtually turned the arena into a mini Twickenham or Murrayfield.

The Wallabies, with only a single match against the New Zealand Maoris as their preparation, started the match with Chris Latham at full-back in preference to Matthew Burke. Flanker Owen Finegan came back into the side after suspension in the Super Twelve, and Nathan Grey was given the inside-centre shirt ahead of Elton Flatley. The biggest talking point was the relatively inexperienced front-row combination of debut prop Stiles, hooker Paul and tight-head Panoho.

The rest of the side comprised the tried and tested, including halves Gregan and Larkham, and locks Eales and Giffin. The talented 20-year-old open-side George Smith made up the back-row contingent along with number 8 Toutai Kefu.

The Lions' optimism was high, especially as they had played fast, expansive and effective rugby, had been able to unlock decent defences and up front had scrummaged better and more aggressively than any of their opposition. This optimism was not out of place, as the Lions scored four tries to two in a convincing 29–13 victory that sent shock waves through Australian rugby. The margin could have been even greater, as the Wallabies only scored their tries in a late flourish when the Lions had been reduced to 14 men on two occasions, when referee Watson sin-binned Vickery and then Corry.

Man of the match O'Driscoll and his partner in crime Henderson cut the Wallaby defence to shreds and tackled like demons. Robinson, scoring the first try after just two minutes with a classic in-and-out swerve and step, proved electric in everything he did; Wilkinson was the rock and locks Johnson and Grewcock proved unstoppable. Hooker Wood and flanker Hill were simply everywhere, causing havoc around the ruck.

The Lions dominated the lineout and out-scrummaged a docile Wallaby eight that was clearly short of match practice and stunned by the ferocity of the Lions' onslaught. The pace at which the Lions played was impressive and authoritarian, and James' late first-half try after a sortie by Robinson made the Lions advantage 12–3 at the break – a scoreline that flattered Australia.

The game was all but sealed two minutes into the second half when O'Driscoll waltzed his way through weak Wallaby tackling to score a superlative solo try under the posts. A Wilkinson penalty and a converted try to the ever-rampaging Quinnell after 51 minutes extended the lead to 29–3. The Wallabies replied with two consolation tries from Walker and Grey after Flatley had replaced an out-of-sorts Larkham, but they were well beaten. To make matters worse, hooker Jeremy Paul suffered a season-ending knee injury.

With the Red Army in raptures at the final whistle, the Lions strode elated but purposefully off the field. They were perhaps tempted to indulge in a lap of honour, but they resisted, knowing the series had not been decided and that victory in the second Test, as in South Africa four years earlier, would clinch the Series.

The Lions' tour moved on to the Australian capital Canberra for the last mid-week match against the Super Twelve champions. The Brumbies, devoid of their nine Test players, fielded a mix of Super Twelve squad players and young development players, and were incredibly unlucky not to inflict the tourists' second defeat of the tour. Marshalled by former Wallaby number 8 Jim Williams, and Pat Howard, recently returned from several years in England, the Brumbies stunned the tourists in the first half with coach Eddie Jones opting to take the Lions' defence on out wide. The Lions played as poorly as any time on tour and in midfield they were carved open by Howard's passing and the angled running of centres Bond and Holbeck. Three tries to the home side to a late intercept by Healey saw the Brumbies lead 22–10 at half-time.

The second half proved to be a complete reversal, with the Lions enjoying far greater possession. Wallace reduced the lead with a 44th-minute try. Dawson (awarded the goal-kicking duties ahead of O'Gara) and Hall then swapped penalties through this half of the game as the Lions slowly ground down their opponents.

With the score 28–23 in the locals' favour as the clock ticked over into injury time, the Lions launched one last offensive and after numerous phases Healey side-stepped his way across the line. It left Dawson (who had been pilloried mid-week for writing a derogatory newspaper column) to kick the winning conversion. He duly did so and the villain become a hero. The Lions had staged a remarkable comeback.

History was made in Melbourne for the second Test when the match was played under a closed roof at Colonial Stadium. The atmosphere was electric and the ARU's attempt to coerce greater vocal and visual support to offset the Red Army's included giving away tens of thousands of gold-coloured scarves and broadcasting good-luck messages from the tennis player Pat Rafter and runner Cathy Freeman.

However, the combined British and Irish choir – led as always by the Welsh – easily won the singing and they took their seats expectantly as the Lions took the field with only one change. Neil Back replaced a very unlucky Martin Corry in the back-row. The in-form Corry moved to the bench to replace Charvis who had been suspended for two matches having been found guilty of kneeing an opponent late in the first Test. Hooker West came onto the bench too for Bulloch.

Wily veteran Michael Foley replaced the injured Jeremy Paul at hooker for the Wallabies, with Brendan Cannon moving onto the bench. Prop Panoho was declared unfit and Rod Moore took his spot. Matthew Burke was preferred at fullback to Latham who moved to the bench.

The first 40 minutes of the match resembled the 'Gabba Test with the Lions dominating most facets of the game and breaking the first line of defence to cross the gain line on numerous occasions. But for all their superiority the Lions only led 11–6 at half-time, following a tremendous try from a lineout set piece and two penalties each to Wilkinson and Burke. Grewcock secured possession at a lineout deep in the Wallaby twenty-two and the Lions pack ferociously drove the maul across the line for Back to touch down.

How very different it was in the second 40 minutes. The Lions lost Howley, Hill and Wilkinson (rib, head and leg injuries respectively), conceded three tries and proceeded to lose their discipline, resulting in Burke kicking four penalties. The Wallabies won the match 35–14 by scoring 29 points in the second half.

The loss of Richard Hill at half time after an errant elbow to the head by Nathan Grey infuriated the Lions' management but the pivotal point of the match –and perhaps the series – was Roff's first try. Wilkinson, running right, noticed he had an overlap and opted for a long, looping ball to his outside runners. Unfortunately the ever-alert Roff intercepted and galloped 30 metres to score in the left corner.

The score revived the Wallabies who were floundering badly and, shortly after this, Roff scored a second with a delightful change of pace and a left step. Surprisingly the possession had been secured when the Wallaby eight disrupted a Lions scrum, Eales secured the ball and Larkham released Roff down the left touchline.

Worrying signs started to appear in the Lions ranks. The inclusion of flanker Neil Back had seriously diminished the lineout options and he started to struggle against Wallaby open-side, Smith. The dominant scrum lost its cohesiveness and the Wallabies were not being stopped at the gain line.

When Burke crossed for his try mid-way through the half, the Lions lost their pattern and the match. The Wallabies had reasserted their dominance of world rugby following the humiliation of the first Test. It was a significant achievement and one that swung the series in their favour. Eales, playing his 50th match as captain, returned to his best form, Moore shored up the scrum, Gregan was dominant around the fringes while Finegan provided the hard yards up the middle. Macqueen declared after the match, 'Whenever this side has been asked questions, they have reached and found the answers.' He also announced that he would step down as coach following the third Test, adding a huge emotional edge to the match in Sydney.

The Wallabies lost Larkham for the decider (two big hits late in the second Test damaged his already suspect shoulder) along with second-row Giffin. Flatley was given the number 10 shirt while Brumby lock Harrison made his Wallaby debut.

Miraculously Wilkinson, after having his bruised leg cast in plaster for two days, was passed fit but Healey, preferred to James on the wing, withdrew with a back problem. James consequently assumed the wing position while injuries meant that Dawson replaced Howley at scrum-half and Corry replaced Hill on the side of the scrum. Such was the extent of injuries and non-availability of players that the side failed to have a complete run together in the week before the Test. Scottish scrum-half Andy Nicol, a replacement on the 1993 tour to New Zealand, was summoned from a supporters' tour to sit on the bench as reserve scrum-half after wing Healey, the scrum-half cover, dropped out.

It was a tumultuous, rollercoaster of a game that saw the lead chop and change several times as the match drew towards its conclusion. In front of a record crowd for a Lions Test (84,188), the teams slogged it out until the Lions simply ran out of energy for the fight.

Burke gave Australia a 9–3 lead at the quarter-hour mark, with three penalties to one from Wilkinson, before the irrepressible Robinson crossed for a try in the left corner.

The Lions had looked set to score a pushover try, only for referee Paddy O'Brien to reset the scrum because of the front rows popping. From the next scrum the ball went right before Dawson switched left, and excellent handling from Wilkinson and front-rowers Wood and Smith created the score. Wilkinson's conversion gave the Lions a 10–9 lead but he then missed a penalty letting the Wallabies off the hook after a period of pressure.

The Wallabies regained the lead with a try created by some deft handling by Roff, Herbert and Walker down the right-hand blindside. A last inside pass saw Herbert cross for a try, which Burke converted. The Lions responded immediately but territorial dominance at the end of the half only led to a Wilkinson penalty which meant the Lions trailed 13–16 at the break.

Revitalised after the break, the Lions drove deep into the Wallaby quarter with Wood, Grewcock and O'Driscoll all prominent. Finally, when the ball went right near the posts, Wilkinson scuttled past Toutai Kefu to score. He converted and the Lions' hopes soared as they once again resumed the lead.

The Lions' dreams of defending and extending their lead evaporated when some excellent driving play and recycling led to Kefu and Foley putting Herbert across for his second try. Burke's conversion was followed by a Wilkinson penalty to tie the scores at 23–all. Significantly, the penalty was for a dangerous tackle on O'Driscoll by Herbert who was sin-binned for ten minutes; unfortunately the tiring Lions failed to score any points with Herbert off the field, and as the final whistle approached the dishevelled Lions conceded two penalties which Burke kicked for a 29–23 lead.

A converted try could still have won the game, though, and in the last two minutes the Lions somehow rallied to secure a lineout well inside the Wallaby twenty-two. Fearing a driving maul, an effective weapon in the Lions' armoury all tour, the Wallabies appeared ready to counter the tactic which meant not contesting the throw. However, debutant Harrison decided he would contest and grabbed the ball in front of Johnson – it was cleared by the Wallabies and the Lions' opportunity was lost, along with the Test and the Series. For the Lions it was despair; for the Wallabies, and the retiring Macqueen it was jubilation.

As in previous tours, injuries once again proved insurmountable for the Lions even though it was a short ten-match tour. Losing key players at crucial times cost the Lions dearly and by the end of the tour the Test players were literally out on their feet. Dallaglio, Catt, Greening, Greenwood, Luger, Quinnell, Back, Jenkins, Taylor, Healey and Howley were either injured or carrying injuries at some point in the tour.

When asked to assess the tour and to say what future recommendations he would make, manager Donal Lenihan announced, 'In the professional era the whole tour structure needs to be looked at. If you are going to play a tour of this intensity at the end of the domestic season you will have to look at more time between matches. Players need more time to recover. It is a question of whether you can afford so many mid-week matches.'

Graham Henry added: 'We thought that maybe – and there needs to be some discussion on this – that there should be a reduced number of players: 28 or something like that, and [we should] just concentrate on having one game a week, building correctly for those games and going on from there. You are probably talking about Saturday games only, with a smaller squad.'

The post-tour analysis clearly shows that the top British and Irish players are simply playing too much rugby compared to their southern hemisphere counterparts. Therein lies the problem and it is perhaps the greatest concern for future tours.

Scaling back mid-week matches and further reducing the number of other matches would be calamitous for the future of Lions tours. Besides it is highly unlikely to gain approval from South Africa, Australia or New Zealand. For the future success of tours, the players' domestic on-field workload in the year of Lions tours must be reduced to prevent burnout and to minimise the injury toll.

## Results of the 2001 Lions in Australia

P 10  W 7  D 0  L 3  F 449  A 184

| | | | |
|---|---|---|---|
| Western Australia | W | 116 | 10 |
| Queensland Presidents XV | W | 83 | 6 |
| Queensland | W | 42 | 8 |
| Australia A | L | 25 | 28 |
| New South Wales | W | 41 | 24 |
| NSW County | W | 46 | 3 |
| Australia (Brisbane) | W | 29 | 13 |
| ACT | W | 30 | 28 |
| Australia (Melbourne) | L | 14 | 35 |
| Australia (Sydney) | L | 23 | 29 |

## Martin Johnson's 2001 Lions Team

**Full-backs**

| | | |
|---|---|---|
| I. Balshaw | Bath | England |
| M. Perry | Bath | England |

**Three-quarters**

| | | |
|---|---|---|
| M. Catt | Bath | England |
| B. Cohen | Northampton | England |
| S. Gibbs* | Swansea | Wales |
| W. Greenwood | Harlequins | England |
| R. Henderson | Wasps | Ireland |
| T. Howe* | Dungannon | Ireland |
| D. James | Llanelli | Wales |
| D. Luger | Saracens | England |
| B. O'Driscoll | Blackrock College | Ireland |
| J. Robinson | Sale | England |
| M. Taylor | Swansea | Wales |

**Half-backs**

| | | |
|---|---|---|
| M. Dawson | Northampton | England |
| A. Healey | Leicester | England |
| R. Howley | Cardiff | Wales |
| N. Jenkins | Cardiff | Wales |

| R. O'Gara | Cork Constitution | Ireland |
| J. Wilkinson | Newcastle | England |
| A. Nicol* | Glasgow Caledonians | Scotland |

**Forwards**

| N. Back | Leicester | England |
| G. Bulloch* | Glasgow Caledonians | Scotland |
| C. Charvis | Swansea | Wales |
| M. Corry* | Leicester | England |
| L. Dallaglio | Wasps | England |
| J. Davidson | Castres | Ireland |
| P.Greening | Wasps | England |
| D. Grewcock | Saracens | England |
| R. Hill | Saracens | England |
| M. Johnson (capt.) | Leicester | England |
| J.Leonard | Harlequins | England |
| R. McBryde | Llanelli | Wales |
| D. Morris | Swansea | Wales |
| S. Murray | Saracens | Scotland |
| M. O'Kelly | St Mary's College | Ireland |
| S. Quinnell | Llanelli | Wales |
| T. Smith | Brive | Scotland |
| S. Taylor | Edinburgh | Scotland |
| P. Vickery | Gloucester | England |
| D. Wallace* | Garryowen | Ireland |
| D. West* | Leicester | England |
| M. Williams | Cardiff | Wales |
| K. Wood | Harlequins | Ircland |
| D. Young | Cardiff | Wales |

Manager: Donal Lenihan
Coach: Graham Henry
Assistant Coach: Andy Robinson

* Replacements

# APPENDICES

# Appendix I

During the period of Lions tours there have been changes in the points values for tries, converted tries, drop goals and penalty goals.

Prior to 1891 there was no uniformity of scoring values adopted by the countries who were members of the International Board. Usually it was one point for a try and three points for a goaled try, which made a conversion worth two points. England refused to take part in the deliberations of the Board on the matter. In 1891 peace prevailed and for the first time there were uniformity of scoring values, which over the years changed as follows:

1891    The IB and the Four Home Unions adopted that:
A match shall be decided by a majority of points. A try shall equal two points, a penalty goal three points, a goal from a try (the try not also to count) five points. Any other goal shall equal four points. If the number of points is equal the match shall be drawn.

1894    The try was changed to three points; the penalty goal remained at three points and the goal from the try was five points (the try not also to count), with any other goal four points. Thus the conversion was now worth two points instead of three.

1905    Try remained at three points; the goal for a try five points (the try not also to count). A dropped goal except from a mark or penalty kick four points. Goal from a mark or penalty kick three points.

1948   Try three points, a goaled try five points, a goal from a free kick or a penalty kick three points. A dropped kick otherwise obtained three points.

1972   Try altered to four points; other values remained the same.

1992   Try altered to five points; other values remained the same.

Surprisingly, there have been few changes in over a hundred years.

# Appendix II

**30 July 1891 in Port Elizabeth**
**British Isles 4  South Africa 0**

W.G. Mitchell
P.R. Clauss
R.L. Aston 1T
W.E. Maclagen
A.Rotherham 1C
W.Wotherspoon
W.E. Bromet
J.H. Gould
J.Hammond
P.F. Hancock
R.G. MacMillan
C.P. Simpson
A.A. Surtees
R.Thompson
T.Whittaker 1T

**29 August 1891 in Kimberley**
**British Isles 3  South Africa 0**

W.G. Mitchell 1GM
P.R. Clauss
R.L. Aston
W.E. Maclagen
E. Bromet
H. Marshall
W.E. Bromet
J.H. Gould
J. Hammond
P.F. Hancock
R.G. MacMillan
W.E. Mayfield
A.A. Surtees
R. Thompson
T. Whittaker

## 5 September 1891 in Cape Town
## British Isles 4  South Africa 0

W.G. Mitchell
P.R. Clauss
R.L. Aston 1T
W.E. Maclagen 1T
A. Rotherham 1C
H. Marshall
E. Bromet
W.E. Bromet
J. Hammond
P.F. Hancock
R.G. MacMillan
W.E. Mayfield
A.A. Surtees
R. Thompson
T. Whittaker

## 30 July 1896 in Port Elizabeth
## British Isles 8  South Africa 0

C.A. Boyd
L.Q. Bulger 1T
J.F. Byrne 1C
O.G. Mackie
R. Johnston
M.M. Mullineux
L.M. Magee
T.J. Crean
A.D. Clinch
J.Sealey
W.J. Carey 1T
P.F. Hancock
W. Mortimer
A.F. Todd
R.C. Mullins

## 22 August 1896 in Johannesburg
## British Isles 17  South Africa 8

J.T. Magee
L.Q. Bulger
J.F. Byrne 2C
O.G. Mackie 1DG
R. Johnston
S.P. Bell
L.M. Magee
T.J. Crean 1T
A.D. Clinch
J. Sealey
W.J. Carey
P.F. Hancock 1T
W. Mortimer
A.F. Todd 1T
J. Hammond

## 29 August 1896 in Kimberley
## British Isles 9  South Africa 3

A.W.D. Meares
L.Q. Bulger
J.F. Byrne 1DG, 1C
O.G. Mackie 1T
R. Johnston
S.P. Bell
L.M. Magee
T.J. Crean
A.D. Clinch
J. Sealey
W.J. Carey
P.F. Hancock
W. Mortimer
A.F. Todd
R.C. Mullins

**5 September 1896 in Newland**
**British Isles 0  South Africa 5**

A.W.D. Meares
J.T. Magee
J.F. Byrne
O.G. Mackie
L.Q. Bulger
S.P. Bell
L.M. Magee
T.J. Crean
A.D. Clinch
J. Sealey
W.J. Carey
P.F. Hancock
W. Mortimer
A.F. Todd
J. Hammond

**26 August 1903 in Johannesburg**
**British Isles 10  South Africa 10**

E.M. Harrison
I.G. Davidson
R.T. Skrimshire 1T
L.L. Greig
G.F. Collett
J.I. Gillespie 2C
P.S. Hancock
M.C. Morrison
W.P. Scott
W.T. Cave 1T
A. Tedford
R.S. Smyth
F.M. Stout
Joseph Wallace
T.A. Gibson

**5 September 1903 in Kimberley**
**British Isles 0  South Africa 0**

R.M. Neill
E.F. Walker
R.T. Skrimshire
L.L. Greig
G.F. Collett
J.I. Gillespie
P.S. Hancock
M.C. Morrison
W.P. Scott
W.T. Cave
A. Tedford
R.S. Smyth
F.M. Stout
Joseph Wallace
T.A. Gibson

**12 September 1903 in Cape Town**
**British Isles 0  South Africa 8**

R.M. Neill
E.F. Walker
R.T. Skrimshire
L.L. Greig
G.F. Collett
J.I. Gillespie
P.S. Hancock
M.C. Morrison
W.P. Scott
W.T. Cave
A. Tedford
R.S. Smyth
Joseph Wallace
F.M. Stout
T.A. Gibson

### 6 August 1910 in Kimberley
### British Isles 10  South Africa 14

S.H. Williams
A.R. Foster 1T
J.P. Jones 1DG
K.B. Wood
M.E. Neale
J.A. Spoors 1T
G.A.M. Isherwood
D.F. Smith
P.D. Waller
R. Stevenson
H. Jarman
O.J.S. Piper
F.G. Handford
T.J. Richards
J. Webb

### 27 August 1910 in Port Elizabeth
### British Isles 8  South Africa 3

S.H. Williams
A.R. Foster
J.A. Spoors 1T
J.P. Jones
M.E. Neale 1T
C.H. Pillman 1C
G.A.M. Isherwood
T. Smyth
D.F. Smith
P.D. Waller
R. Stevenson
H. Jarman
F.G. Handford
T.J. Richards
J. Webb

### 3 September 1910 in Cape Town
### British Isles 5  South Africa 21

S.H. Williams
A.M. Baker
J.P. Jones
K.B. Wood
M.E. Neale
J.A. Spoors 1T
G.A.M. Isherwood
D.F. Smith
R. Stevenson
T. Smythe
F.G. Handford
H. Jarman
J. Webb
C.H. Pillman 1C
P.D. Waller

### 16 August 1924 in Durban
### British Isles 3  South Africa 7

D. Drysdale
I.S. Smith
R.M. Kinnear
R.B. Maxwell
W. Wallace
H. Waddell
H. Whitley 1T
R. Cove-Smith
A.F. Blakiston
N. Macpherson
D.S. Davies
R.A. Howie
D. Marsden-Jones
T.N. Brand
J. McVicker

**23 August 1924 in Johannesburg**
**British Isles 0  South Africa 17**

D. Drysdale
W. Rowe Harding
R.M. Kinnear
H.J. Davies
I.S. Smith
H. Waddell
A.T. Young
R. Cove-Smith
A.F. Blakiston
N. Macpherson
D.S. Davies
R.A. Howie
D. Marsden-Jones
T.N. Brand
K.G.P. Hendrie

**13 September 1924 in Port Elizabeth**
**British Isles 3  South Africa 3**

D. Drysdale
S. W. Harris
R.M. Kinnear
V.M. Griffiths
W. Rowe Harding
W. Cunningham 1T
H. Whitley
R. Cove-Smith
A.F. Blakiston
R.A. Howie
D.S. Davies
R.G. Henderson
N. Macpherson
J. McVicker
A.T. Voyce

**20 September 1924 in Cape Town**
**British Isles 9  South Africa 16**

D. Drysdale
S.W. Harris 1T
R.M. Kinnear
V.M. Griffiths
W. Rowe Harding
H. Waddell
H. Whitley
R. Cove-Smith
A.F. Blakiston
A.T Voyce 1T, 1PG
N. Macpherson
R.G. Henderson
D.S. Davies
R.A. Howie
J. McVicker

**6 August 1938 in Johannesburg**
**British Isles 12  South Africa 26**

V.G.J. Jenkins 3PG
E.J. Unwin
D.J. Macrae
H.R. McKibbin
E.L. Jones
F.J. Reynolds
J.L. Giles
S. Walker
M.E. Morgan
W.G. Howard
C.R.A. Graves
R.B. Mayne
G.T. Dancer
A.R. Taylor 1PG
R. Alexander

**3 September 1938 in Port Elizabeth**
**British Isles 3  South Africa 19**

C.F. Grieve
E.J. Unwin
H.R. Mc Kibbin
B.E. Nicholson
C.V. Boyle
F.J. Reynolds
H. Tanner
S. Walker
M.E. Morgan
W.H. Travers
R.B. Mayne
G.T. Dancer
P.L. Duff 1T
A.R. Taylor
R. Alexander

**10 September 1938 in Cape Town**
**British Isles 21  South Africa 16**

C.F. Grieve 1DG
E.L. Jones 1T
H.R. McKibbin 1C, 1PG
J.L. Giles
C.V. Boyle
G.E. Cromey
G.J. Morgan
S. Walker
W.H. Travers
C.R. A. Graves
R.B. Mayne
G.T. Dancer 1T
J.A. Waters
P.L. Duff 1T
R. Alexander

**6 August 1955 in Johannesburg**
**British Isles 23  South Africa 22**

A. Cameron 4C
A.J.F. O'Reilly 1T
J. Butterfield 1T
W.P.C. Davies
A.C. Pedlow 1T
C.I. Morgan 1T
R.E.G. Jeeps
W.O.G. Williams
B.V. Meredith
C.C. Meredith
R.H. Williams
R.H. Thompson
R. Higgins
R.J. Robins
J.T. Greenwood 1T

**20 August 1955 in Cape Town**
**British Isles 9  South Africa 25**

A.Cameron 1PG
A.J.F. O'Reilly
J.Butterfield 1T
W.P.C. Davies
G.M. Griffiths
C.I. Morgan
R.E.G. Jeeps
W.O.G. Williams
B.V. Meredith 1T
C.C. Meredith
R.H. Williams
R.H. Thompson
R.J. Robins
T.E. Reid
J.T. Greenwood

**3 September 1955 in Pretoria**
**British Isles 9  South Africa**

D.G.S. Baker
G.M. Griffiths
J. Butterfield 1T, 1DG
W.P.C. Davies
A.J.F. O'Reilly
C.I. Morgan
R.E.G. Jeeps
W.O.G. Williams
B.V. Meredith
C.C. Meredith
R.H. Williams
T.E. Reid
R.C.C. Thomas
R.J. Robins
J.T. Greenwood

**24 September 1955 in Port Elizabeth**
**British Isles 8  South Africa 22**

D.G.S. Baker
G.M. Griffiths
J.Butterfield
A.J.F. O'Reilly 1T
A.C. Pedlow 1C
C.I. Morgan
R.E.G. Jeeps
W.O.G. Williams
B.V. Meredith
C.C. Meredith
R.H. Williams
R.H. Thompson
R.C.C. Thomas
R.J. Robins
J.T. Greenwood 1T

**23 June 1962 in Johannesburg**
**British Isles 3  South Africa 3**

J.G. Wilcox
A.R. Smith
D.K. Jones 1T
M.P. Weston
N.H. Brophy
G.H. Waddell
R.E.G. Jeeps
S.Millar
B.V. Meredith
K.D. Jones
W.A. Mulcahy
K.A. Rowlands
D.P. Rogers
M.J. Campbell-Lamerton
A.E.I. Pask

**21 July 1962 in Durban**
**British Isles 0  South Africa 3**

J.G. Wilcox
A.R. Smith
D.K. Jones
M.P. Weston
D.I.E. Bebb
G.H. Waddell
R.E.G. Jeeps
S. Millar
B.V. Meredith
K.D. Jones
W.A. Mulcahy
K.A. Rowlands
A.I.E. Pask
M.J. Campbell-Lamerton
H.J. Morgan

**4 August 1962 in Cape Town**
**British Isles 3   South Africa 8**

T.J. Kiernan
A.R. Smith
D.K. Jones
M.P. Weston
D.I.E. Bebb
R.A.W. Sharp 1DG
R.E.G. Jeeps
S. Millar
B.V. Meredith
K.D. Jones
W.A. Mulcahy
W.J. McBride
A.E. I. Pask
M.J. Campbell-Lamerton
H.J. Morgan

**25 August 1962 in Bloemfontein**
**British Isles 14   South Africa 34**

J.G. Wilcox 1C, 1PG
R.C. Cowan 1T
D. Hewitt
M.P. Weston
N.H. Brophy
R.A.W. Sharp
R.E.G. Jeeps
S. Millar
B.V. Meredith
K.D. Jones
K.A. Rowlands 1T
W.J. McBride
W.A. Mulcahy
M.J. Campbell-Lamerton 1T
D.P. Rogers

**8 June 1968 in Pretoria**
**British Isles 20   South Africa 25**

T.J. Kiernan 5PG, 1C
K.F. Savage
F.P.K. Bresnihan
J.W.C. Turner
M.C.R. Richards
B. John*
G.O. Edwards
S. Millar
J. Young
J.P. O'Shea
P.K. Stagg
W.J. McBride 1T
R.J. Arneil
R.B. Taylor
M.G. Doyle

**22 June 1968 in Port Elizabeth**
**British Isles 6   South Africa 6**

T.J. Kiernan 2PG
K.F. Savage
F.P.K. Bresnihan
J.W.C. Turner
A.J.W. Hinshelwood
C.M.H. Gibson
G.O. Edwards
S. Millar
J.V. Pullin
A.L. Horton
P.J. Larter
W.J. McBride
R.J. Arneil
J.W. Telfer
R.B. Taylor

* Replaced by C.M.H. Gibson

**13 July 1968 in Cape Town**
**British Isles 6  South Africa 11**

T.J. Kiernan 2PG
K.F. Savage
T.G.R. Davies
J.W.C. Turner
M.C.R. Richards
C.M.H. Gibson
R.M. Young
M.J. Coulman*
J.V. Pullin
A.L. Horton
P.K. Stagg
W.J. Mc Bride
R.J. Arneil
J.W. Telfer
R.B. Taylor

* Replaced by W.D. Thomas

**8 June 1974 in Cape Town**
**British Isles 12  South Africa 3**

J.P.R. Williams
W.C.C. Steele
I.R. McGeechan
R.A. Milliken
J.J. Williams
P. Bennett 3PG
G.O. Edwards 1DG
J. McLauchlan
R.W. Windsor
F.E. Cotton
G.L. Brown
W.J. McBride
J.F. Slattery
T.M. Davies
R.M. Uttley

**27 July 1968 in Johannesburg**
**British Isles 6  South Africa 19**

T.J. Kiernan 2PG
K.F. Savage
J.W.C. Turner
F.P.K. Bresnihan
M.C.R. Richards
C.M.H. Gibson
G.C. Connell
W.D. Thomas
J.V. Pullin
A.L. Horton
P.K. Stagg
W.J. McBride
R.J. Arneil
J.W. Telfer
R.B. Taylor

**22 June 1974 in Pretoria**
**British Isles 28  South Africa 9**

J.P.R. Williams
W.C.C. Steele
I.R. McGeechan 1DG
R.A. Milliken 1T
J.J. Williams 2T
P. Bennett 1PG, 1T, 1C
G.O. Edwards
J. McLauchlan
R.W. Windsor
F.E. Cotton
G.L. Brown 1T
W.J. McBride
J.F. Slattery
T.M. Davies
R.M. Uttley

**13 July 1974 in Port Elizabeth**
**British Isles 26  South Africa 9**

J.P.R. Williams
A.R. Irvine 2 PG, 1C
I.R. McGeechan
R.A. Milliken
J.J. Williams 2T
P. Bennett 2PG
G.O. Edwards
J. McLauchlan
R.W. Windsor
F.E. Cotton
G.L. Brown 1T
W.J. McBride
J.F. Slattery
T.M. Davies
R.M. Uttley

**27 July 1974 in Johannesburg**
**British Isles 13  South Africa 13**

J.P.R. Williams
A.R. Irvine 1PG, 1T
I.R. McGeechan
R.A. Milliken
J.J. Williams
P. Bennett 1C
G.O. Edwards
J. McLauchlan
R.W. Windsor
F.E. Cotton
C.W. Ralston
W.J. McBride
J.F. Slattery
T.M. Davies
R.M. Uttley 1T

**31 May 1980 in Cape Town**
**British Isles 22  South Africa 26**

R.C. O'Donnell
J. Carleton*
J.M. Renwick
D.S. Richards
M.A.C. Slemen
A.J.P. Ward 5PG, 1DG
C.S. Patterson
C. Williams
P.J. Wheeler
G. Price 1T
W.B. Beaumont
M.J. Colclough
J.B. O'Driscoll
D.L. Quinnell
J. Squire

* Replaced by R.W.R. Gravell

**14 June 1980 in Bloemfontein**
**British Isles 19  South Africa 26**

A.R. Irvine 1PG
J. Carleton
C.R. Woodward
R.W.R. Gravell 1T
B.H. Hay
W.G.Davies* 2PG, 1C
C.S. Patterson
C. Williams
P.J. Wheeler
G. Price
W.B. Beaumont
M.J. Colclough
J.B. O'Driscoll 1T
D.L. Quinnell
J. Suire

* Replaced by S.O. Campbell

## 28 June 1980 in Port Elizabeth
## British Isles 10  South Africa 12

A.R. Irvine
C.R. Woodward
P.W. Dodge
R.W.R. Gravell
B.H. Hay 1T
S.O. Campbell 2PG
C.S. Patterson
C. Williams
P.J. Wheeler
G. Price
W.B. Beaumont
M.J. Colclough
J.B. O'Driscoll
J. Squire
C.C. Tucker

## 12 July 1980 in Pretoria
## British Isles 17  South Africa 13

A.R. Irvine 1T
J. Carleton
P.W. Dodge
R.W.R. Gravell
B.H.Hay
S.O. Campbell 1PG, 1C
J.C. Robbie
C. Williams 1T
P.J. Wheeler
G. Price
W.B. Beaumont
M.J. Colclough
J.B. Driscoll 1T
J. Squire
C.C. Tucker

## 21 June 1997 in Cape Town
## British Isles 25  South Africa 16

N. Jenkins 5PG
I. Evans
J. Guscott
S. Gibbs
A. Tait 1T
G. Townsend
M. Dawson 1T
P. Wallace
K. Wood
T. Smith *
M. Johnson
J. Davidson
L. Dallaglio
T. Rodber
R. Hill

* Replaced by J. Leonard

## 5 July 1997 in Johannesburg
## British Isles 16  South Africa 35

N. Jenkins 1C, 3PG
J. Bentley
J. Guscott*
S. Gibbs
T. Underwood**
M. Catt
M. Dawson*** 1T
P. Wallace
M. Regan
T. Smith
M. Johnson
J. Davidson
L. Dallaglio
R. Wainwright
N. Back

* Replaced by A. Bateman
** Replaced by T. Stimpson
*** Replaced by A. Healey

**28 July 1997 in Durban**
**British Isles 18   South Africa 15**

N. Jenkins 5PG
J. Bentley
J. Guscott 1DG
S. Gibbs
A. Tait*
G. Townsend
M. Dawson
P. Wallace
K. Wood
T. Smith
M. Johnson
J. Davidson
L. Dallaglio
T. Rodber
R. Hill**

*Replaced by A. Healey
** Replaced by N. Back

# Appendix III

**13 August 1904 in Wellington**
**British Isles 3  New Zealand 9**

A.B. O'Brien
P.F. McEvedy
W.M. Llewellyn
R.T. Gabe
E.T. Morgan
P.F. Bush
T.H. Vile
R.J. Rogers
D.H. Trail
D.D. Dobson
T.S. Bevan
R.W. Edwards
S.N. Crowther
B.I. Swannell
A.F. Harding 1PG

**6 June 1908 in Dunedin**
**British Isles 5  New Zealand 32**

E.J. Jackett
J.L. Williams
J.O. ('Ponty') Jones
H.H. Vassall
R.A. Gibbs 1T
J. Davey
H. Laxon
W.L. Oldham
R. Dibble
F.S. Jackson 1C
P.J. Down
H.A. Archer
J.A.S. Ritson
G.V. Kryke
A.F. Harding

**27 June 1908 in Wellington**
**British Isles 3  New Zealand 3**

E.J. Jackett
J.L. Williams
J.O. ('Ponty') Jones 1T
H.H. Vassall
P.F. McEvedy
J.P. ('Tuan') Jones
W.L. Morgan
R.A. Gibbs
T.W. Smith
R. Dibble
P.J. Down
H.A. Archer
E. Morgan
G.R. Hind
A.F. Harding

**25 July 1908 in Auckland**
**British Isles 0  New Zealand 29**

E.J. Jackett
F.E. Chapman
J.O. ('Ponty') Jones
H.H. Vassall
P.F. McEvedy
J.P. ('Tuan') Jones
W.L. Morgan
E. Morgan
R. Dibble
J.F. Williams
P.J. Down
T.W. Smith
H.A. Archer
G.R. Hind
A.F. Harding

**21 June 1930 in Dunedin**
**British Isles 6  New Zealand 3**

J.A. Bassett
J.C. Morley 1T
H.M. Bowcott
C.D. Aarvold
J.S.R. Reeve
R.S. Spong
P.F. Murray
H. Rew
D. Parker
H.O'H. O'Neill
J.L. Farrell
B.H. Black
J.McD. Hodgson
G.R. Beamish
I.E. Jones

**5 July 1930 in Christchurch**
**British Isles 10  New Zealand 13**

J.A. Bassett
J.C. Morley
H.M. Bowcott
C.D. Aarvold 2T
A.L. Novis
R.S. Spong
P.F. Murray
H. Rew
D. Parker
H.O'H. O'Neill
J.L. Farrell
F.D. Prentice 2C
B.H. Black
G.R. Beamish
I.E. Jones

**26 July 1930 in Auckland**
**British Isles 10  New Zealand 15**

J.A. Bassett
J.C. Morley
H.M. Bowcott 1T
C.D. Aarvold 1T
J.S.R. Reeve
R.S. Spong
H.Poole
H.Rew
D.Parker
H.O'H. O'Neill
J.L. Farrell
J.McD. Hodgson
B.H. Black 1C
G.R. Beamish
I.E. Jones 1C

**9 August 1930 in Wellington**
**British Isles 8  New Zealand 22**

J.A. Bassett
A.L. Novis 1T
H.M. Bowcott
C.D. Aarvold
J.S.R. Reeve
R.S. Spong
P.F. Murray
H. Rew
D. Parker 1PG
H.O'H. O'Neill
J.L. Farrell
W.B. Welsh
B.H. Black 1C
G.R. Beamish
I.E. Jones

**27 May 1950 in Dunedin**
**British Isles 9  New Zealand 9**

W.B. Cleaver
K.J. Jones 1T
J. Matthews
I. Preece
R. Macdonald
J.W. Kyle 1T
A.W. Black
J.D. Robins 1PG
K.D. Mullen
T. Clifford
D.J. Hayward
E.R. John
R.T. Evans
P.W. Kininmonth
J.W. McKay

**10 June 1950 in Christchurch**
**British Isles 0  New Zealand 8**

W.B. Cleaver
K.J. Jones
J. Matthews
B.L. Williams
M.C. Thomas
J.W. Kyle
A.W. Black
J.D. Robins
K.D. Mullen
T. Clifford
D.J. Hayward
E.R. John
R.T. Evans
P.W. Kinimonth
J.W. McKay

279

**1 July 1950 in Wellington**
**British Isles 3  New Zeland 6**

W.B. Cleaver
N.J. Henderson
J. Matthews
B.L. Williams
M.C. Thomas
J.W. Kyle
G. Rimmer
J.D. Robins 1PG
D.M. Davies
T. Clifford
D.J. Hayward
J.E. Nelson
R.T. Evans
E.R. John
J.W. McKay

**29 July 1950 in Auckalnd**
**British Isles 8  New Zealand 11**

B.L. Jones 1PG, 1C
K.J. Jones 1T
J. Matthews
B.L. Williams
M.F. Lane
J.W. Kyle
W.R. Willis
G.M. Budge
D.M. Davies
C. Davies
J.E. Nelson
E.R. John
R.T. Evans
P.W. Kinimonth
J.W. McKay

**18 July 1959 in Dunedin**
**British Isles 17  New Zealand 18**

K.J.F. Scotland
P.B. Jackson 1T
M.J. Price 2T
D. Hewitt 1PG
A.J.F. O'Reilly
A.B.W. Risman 1C
R.E.G. Jeeps
H.F. McLeod
A.R.Dawson
B.G.M. Wood
R.H. Williams
W.R. Evans
N.A.A. Murphy
J. Faull
G.K. Smith

**15 August 1959 in Wellington**
**British Isles 8  New Zealand 11**

T.J.Davies 1PG, 1C
J.R.C. Young 1T
M.C. Thomas
W.M. Patterson
A.J.F. O'Reilly
M.J. Price
R.E.G. Jeeps
H.F. McLeod
A.R. Dawson
S. Millar
R.H. Williams
W.R. Evans
A. Ashcroft
R.W.D. Marques
N.A.A. Murphy

**29 August 1959 in Christchurch**
**British Isles 8  New Zealand 22**

K.J.F. Scotland
P.B. Jackson
M.J. Price
D. Hewitt 1T
A.J.F. O'Reilly
J.P. Horrocks-Taylor
R.E.G. Jeeps
H.F. McLeod
A.R. Dawson
B.G.M. Wood
R.H. Williams
W.R. Evans
G.K. Smith
J. Faull 1PG, 1C
H.J. Morgan

**19 September 1959 in Auckland**
**British Isles 9  New Zealand 6**

T.J. Davies
P.B. Jackson 1T
D. Hewitt
K.J.F. Scotland
A.J.F. O'Reilly 1T
A.B.W. Risman 1T
A.A. Mulligan
H. R. Dawson
T.R. Prosser
R.H. Williams
W.A. Mulcahy
N.A.A. Murphy
J. Faull
H.J. Morgan

**16 July 1966 in Dunedin**
**British Isles 3  New Zealand 20**

S. Wilson 1PG
C.W. McFadyean
D.K. Jones
C.M.H. Gibson
D.I.E. Bebb
D. Watkins
R.M. Young
D. Williams
K.W. Kennedy
C.H. Norris
B. Price
M.J. Campbell-Lamerton
J. W. Telfer
A.E.I. Pask
R.A. Lamont

**6 August 1966 in Wellington**
**British Isles 12  New Zealand 16**

S. Wilson 3PG
A.J.W. Hinshelwood
C.W. McFadyean
C.M.H. Gibson
D.I.E. Bebb
D. Watkins 1DG
A.R. Lewis
D. Williams
F.A.L. Laidlaw
C.H. Norris
W.D. Thomas
W.J. McBride
N.A.A. Murphy
J.W. Telfer
R.A. Lamont

**27 August 1966 in Christchurch
British Isles 6  New Zealand 19**

S. Wilson
S.J. Watkins
C.W. McFadyean
C.M.H. Gibson
D.I.E. Bebb
D. Watkins 1T
R.M. Young
A.R. Lewis
W.D. Thomas
F. A. L. Laidlaw
C.H. Norris
M.J. Campbell-Lamerton
W.J. McBride
N.A. A. Murphy
A.E.I. Pask
R.A. Lamont 1T

**10 September 1966 in Auckland
British Isles 11  New Zealand 24**

S. Wilson 1PG, 1C
A.J.W. Hinshelwood 1T
C.W. McFadyean 1T
C.M.H. Gibson
D.I.E. Bebb
D. Watkins
R.M. Young
A.R. Lewis
D. Williams
K.W. Kennedy
R.J. McLoughlin
W.J. McBride
B. Price
A.E.I. Pask
J.W. Telfer
R.A. Lamont

**26 June 1971 in Dunedin
British Isles 9  New Zealand 3**

J.P.R. Williams
T.G.R. Davies
S.J.Dawes
C.M.H. Gibson
J.C. Bevan
B. John 2PG
G.O. Edwards*
J. McLauchlan 1T
J.V. Pullin
J.F. Lynch
W.D. Thomas
W.J. McBride
P.J. Dixon
T.M. Davies
J. Taylor

**10 July 1971 in Christchurch
British Isles 12  New Zealand 22**

J.P.R. Williams
T.G.R. Davies 2T
S.J. Dawes
C.M.H. Gibson
D.J. Duckham
B. John 1PG, 1DG
G.O. Edwards
J. McLauchlan
J.V. Pullin
J.F. Lynch
W.D. Thomas
W.J. McBride
P.J. Dixon
T.M. Davies
J. Taylor

* Replaced by R. Hopkins

## 31 July 1971 in Wellington
## British Isles 13  New Zealand 3

J.P.R. Williams
T.G.R. Davies 1T
S.J. Dawes
C.M.H. Gibson
D.J. Duckham
B. John 1T, 2C, 1DG
G.O. Edwards
J. McLauchlan
J.V. Pullin
J.F. Lynch
G.L. Brown
W.J. McBride
D.L. Quinnell
T.M. Davies
J. Taylor

## 14 August 1971 in Auckland
## British Isles 14  New Zealand 14

J.P.R. Williams 1DG
T.G.R. Davies
S.J. Dawes
C.M.H. Gibson
D. J. Duckham
B. John 2PG, 1C
G.O. Edwards
J. McLauchlan
J.V. Pullin
J.F. Lynch
G.L. Brown*
W.J. McBride
P.J. Dixon 1T
T.M. Davies
J. Taylor

* Replaced by W.D. Thomas

## 18 June 1977 in Wellington
## British Isles 12  New Zealand 16

A.R. Irvine 1PG
P.J. Squires
S.P. Fenwick
I.R. McGeechan
J.J. Williams
P. Bennett 3PG
D.B. Williams
P.A. Orr
R.W. Windsor
G. Price
A.J. Martin
M.I. Keane
T.J. Cobner
W.P. Duggan
T.P. Evans

## 9 July 1977 in Christchurch
## British Isles 13  New Zealand 9

A.R. Irvine
J.J. Williams 1T
S.P. Fenwick
I.R. McGeechan
G.L. Evans
P.Bennett 3PG
D.B. Williams
F.E. Cotton
P.J. Wheeler
G. Price
W.B. Beaumont
G.L. Brown
T.J. Cobner
W.P. Duggan
D.L. Quinnell

**30 July 1977 in Dunedin**
**British Isles 7  New Zealand 19**

A.R. Irvine 1PG
J.J. Williams*
S.P. Fenwick
D.H.Burcher
G.L. Evans
P.Bennett
D.B. Williams**
F.E. Cotton
P.J. Wheeler
G. Price
W.B. Beaumont
G.L. Brown
T.J. Cobner
W.P. Duggan 1T
D.L. Quinnell

* Replaed by I.R. McGeechan
** Replaced by D.W. Morgan

**13 August 1977 in Auckland**
**British Isles 9  New Zealand 10**

A.R. Irvine
H.E. Rees
S.P. Fenwick
I.R. McGeechan
G.L. Evans
P. Bennett
D. W. Morgan 1T, 1C, 1PG
F.E. Cotton
P.J. Wheeler
G. Price
W.B. Beaumont
G.L. Brown
J. Squire
W.P. Duggan
A. Neary

**4 June 1983 in Christchurch**
**British Isles 12  New Zealand 16**

H.P. MacNeill
T.M. Ringland
D.G. Irwin
R.A. Ackerman
G.R.T. Baird
S.O. Campbell 1DG, 3PG
T.D. Holmes*
I. Stephens
C.F. Fitzgerald
G. Price
M.J. Colclough
R.L. Norster
J. Squire
I.A.M. Paxton
P.J. Winterbottom

* Replaced by R.J. Laidlaw

**18 June 1983 in Wellington**
**British Isles 0  New Zealand 9**

H.P. MacNeill
J. Carleton
D.G. Irwin
M.J. Kiernan
G.R.T. Baird
S.O. Campbell
R.J. Laidlaw
S.T. Jones
C.F. Fitzgerald
G. Price
M.J. Colclough
R.L. Norster
J.B. O'Driscoll
I.A.M. Paxton*
P.J. Winterbottom

* Replaced by J.R. Beattie

**2 July 1983 in Dunedin**
**British Isles 8  New Zealand 15**

G. Evans
J. Carleton
J.Y. Rutherford 1T
M.J. Kiernan
G.R.T. Baird 1T
S.O. Campbell
R.J. Laidlaw
I. Stephens
C.F. Fitzgerald
G. Price
M.J. Colclough
S.J. Bainbridge
J.H. Calder
I.A.M. Paxton
P.J. Winterbottom

**16 July 1983 in Auckland**
**British Isles 6  New Zealand 38**

G. Evans 1PG
J. Carleton
D.G. Irwin
M.J. Kiernan
G.R.T. Baird
S.O. Campbell** 1PG
R.J. Laidlaw
S.T. Jones
C.F. Fitzgerald
G. Price
M.J. Colclough
S.J. Bainbridge
J.B. O'Driscoll
I.A.M. Paxton
P.J. Winterbottom

* Replaced by R.A.Ackerman
** Replaced by H.P. MacNeill

**17 June 1993 in Christchurch**
**British Isles 18  New Zealand 20**

A.G. Hastings 6PG
I.C. Evans
J.C. Guscott
W.D.C. Carling
R. Underwood
C.R. Andrew
C.D. Morris
N.J. Popplewell
K.S. Milne
A.P. Burnell
A.I. Reed
M.C. Bayfield
B.B. Clarke
D. Richards
P.J. Winterbottom

**26 June 1993 in Wellington**
**British Isles 20  New Zealand 7**

A.G. Hastings 4PG
I.C. Evans
J.C. Guscott
I.S. Gibbs
R. Underwood 1T
C.R. Andrew 1DG
C.D. Morris
N.J. Popplewell
B.C. Moore
J. Leonard
M.O. Johnson
M.C. Bayfield
B.B. Clarke
D. Richards
P.J. Winterbottom

**3 July 1993 in Auckland**
**British Isles 13  New Zealand 30**

A.G. Hastings 1C, 2PG
I.C. Evans
J.C. Guscott
I.S. Gibbs 1T
R. Underwood
C.R. Andrew
C.D. Morris
N. J. Poppewell
B.C. Moore
J. Leonard
M.O. Johnson
M.C. Bayfield
B.B. Clarke
D. Richards
P.J. Winterbottom

# Appendix IV

**24 June 1899 in Sydney**
**British Isles 3  Australia 13**

E. Martelli
A.M. Bucher
E.G. Nicholls 1T
C.Y. Adamson
G.P. Doran
M.M. Mullineux
G. Cookson
F.M. Stout
J.W. Jarman
T.M. W. McGown
J.S. Francombe
H.G. S. Gray
F.C. Belson
A. Ayre-Smith
G.R. Gibson

**22 July 1899 in Brisbane**
**British Isles 11  Australia 0**

C.E.K. Thompson
H.G.S. Gray
A.B. Timms
E.G. Nicholls 1T
G.P. Doran
C.Y. Adamson 1T, 1C
G. Cookson
F.M. Stout
J.W. Jarman
T.M. W. McGown
G.V. Evers
B.I. Swannell
W. Judkins
A. Ayre-Smith 1T
G.R. Gibson

**4 August 1899 in Sydney**
**British Isles 11  Australia 10**

C.E.K. Thompson
A.M. Bucher 2T
A.B. Timms 1T
E.G. Nicholls
E.T. Nicholson
C.Y. Adamson 1C
G. Cookson
F.M. Stout
J.W. Jarman
T.M. W. McGown
G.V. Evers
B.I. Swannell
W. Judkins
A. Ayre-Smith
G. R. Gibson

**12 August 1899 in Sydney**
**British Isles 13  Australia 0**

C.E.K. Thompson
A.M. Butcher 1T
A.B. Timms
E.G. Nicholls
E.T. Nicholson
C.Y. Adamson 1T, 1PG, 2C
G. Cookson
F.M. Stout
J.W. Jarman
T.M.W. McGown
G.V. Evers
B.I. Swannell
W. Judkins
A. Ayre-Smith
G. R. Gibson

**2 July 1904 in Sydney**
**British Isles 17  Australia 0**

C.F. Stanger-Leathes
W.M. Llewellyn 2T
A.B. O'Brien 1C
R.T. Gabe
E.T. Morgan
P.F. Bush 1T, 1DG
F.C. Hulme
D.R. Bedell-Sivright
D.H. Trail
D.D. Dobson
T.S. Bevan
S.M. Saunders
S.N. Crowther
B.I. Swannell
A.F. Harding 1C

**23 July 1904 in Brisbane**
**British Isles 17  Australia 3**

A.B. O'Brien 1T
W.M. Llewellyn 1T
R.T. Gabe
P.F. McEvedy
E.T. Morgan
P.F. Bush 1DG, 1GM, 1T
T.H. Vile
R.W. Edwards
D.H. Trail
D.D. Dobson
T.S. Bevan
S.M. Saunders
S.N. Crowther
B.I. Swannell
A.F. Harding

**30 July 1904 in Sydney**
**British Isles 16  Australia 0**

A.B. O'Brien 1C
W.M. Llewellyn 1T
R.T. Gabe 1T
P.F. McEvedy
E.T. Morgan 1T
P.F. Bush 1C
T.H. Vile
R.W. Edwards
D.H. Trail
D.D. Dobson
T.S. Bevan
B.F. Massey
S.N. Crowther
B.I. Swannell 1T
A.F. Harding

**30 August 1930 in Sydney**
**British Isles 5  Australia 6**

J.A. Bassett
C.D. Aarvold
H.M. Bowcott
A.L. Novis 1T
J.S.R. Reeve
R.S. Spong
P.F. Murray
H.O'H. O'Neill
S.A. Martindale
J.L. Farrell
D. Parker
F.D. Prentice 1C
B.H. Black
G.R. Beamish
I.E. Jones

**19 August 1950 in Brisbane**
**British Isles 19  Australia 6**

B.L.Jones 2C, 2PG, 1DG, 1T
D.W.C. Smith
J. Matthews
B.L.Williams 1T
M.C. Thomas
J.W. Kyle
W.R.Willis
J.D. Robins
D.M. Davies
T. Clifford
J.E. Nelson
J.R.G. Stephens
R.T. Evans
E.R. John
J.W. McKay

**26 August 1950 in Sydney**
**British Isles 24   Australia 3**

B.L.Jones 1PG, 1C
R. Macdonald 1T
J. Matthews
B.L. Williams
M.F. Lane
J.W. Kyle 1T
W.R. Willis
J.D Robins 2C
K.D. Mullen
T. Clifford
J.E. Nelson 2T
J.R.G. Stephens
R.T. Evans
E.R. John 1T
J.W. McKay

**6 June 1959 in Brisbane**
**British Isles 17  Australia 6**

K.J.F. Scotland 1DG
P.B. Jackson
D. Hewitt 2PG
M.J. Price
A.J.F. O'Reilly 1T
A.B.W. Risman 1C
R.E.G. Jeeps
H.F. McLeod
A.R. Dawson
S. Millar
W.A. Mulcahy
R.H. Williams
A. Ashcroft
J. Faull
G.K. Smith 1T

**13 June 1959 in Sydney**
**British Isles 24  Australia 3**

K.J.F. Scotland 1PG, 1C
P.B. Jackson
D. Hewitt 2C
M.J. Price 2T
A.J.F. O'Reilly 1T
A.B.W. Risman 1T
R.E.G. Jeeps
H.F. McLeod
A.R. Dawson 1T
S. Millar
W.R. Evans
R.H. Williams
N.A.A. Murphy
R.W.D. Marques
G.K. Smith

**28 May 1966 in Sydney**
**British Isles 11  Australia 8**

D. Rutherford 1PG, 1C
S.J. Watkins
D.K. Jones
M.P. Weston
D.I.E. Bebb
D. Watkins
R.M. Young
D. Williams
K.W. Kennedy 1T
R.J. McLoughlin 1T
M.J. Campbell-Lamerton
B. Price
J.W. Telfer
A.E.I. Pask
N.A.A. Murphy

**4 June 1966 in Brisbane**
**British Isles 31  Australia 0**

S. Wilson 1PG, 5C
S.J. Watkins
D.K. Jones 2T
M.P. Weston
D.I.E. Bebb 1T
D. Watkins 1DG, 1T
R.M. Young
D. Williams
K.W. Kennedy
R.J. McLoughlin
M.J. Campbell-Lamerton
B. Price
J.W. Telfer
A.E.I. Pask
N.A.A. Murphy 1T

**1 July 1989 in Sydney**
**British Isles 12  Australia 30**

A.G. Hastings 2PG
I.C. Evans
M.R. Hall
B.J. Mullin
R. Underwood
C.M. Chalmers 1PG, 1DG
R.N. Jones
D.M.B. Sole
B.C. Moore
D. Young
P.J. Ackford
R.L. Norster
D. B. White
D. Richards
F. Calder

**8 July 1989 in Brisbane**
**British Isles 19  Australia 12**

A.G. Hastings 1PG, 1T
I.C. Evans
S. Hastinys
J.C. Guscott 1T
R. Underwood
C.R. Andrew 1C, 1PG, 1DG
R.N. Jones
D.M. B. Sole
B.C. Moore
D. Young
P.J. Ackford
W.A. Dooley
M.C. Teague
D. Richards
F. Calder

**15 July 1989 in Sydney**
**British Isles 19  Australia 18**

A.G. Hastings 5PG
I.C. Evans 1T
S. Hastings
J.C. Guscott
R. Underwood
C.R. Andrew
R.N. Jones
D.M. B. Sole
B.C. Moore
D. Young
P.J. Ackford
W.A. Dooley
M.C. Teague
D. Richards
F. Calder

**30 June 2001 in Brisbane**
**British Isles 29 Australia 13**

M. Perry*
D. James 1T
B. O'Driscoll 1T
R. Henderson
J. Robinson 1T
J. Wilkinson 3C, 1P
R. Howley
T. Smith**
K. Wood***
P. Vickery
M. Johnson
D. Grewcock
M. Corry
S. Quinnell 1T
R. Hill

\* Replaced by I. Balshaw
** Replaced by J. Leonard
*** Replaced by G. Bulloch
**** Replaced by C. Charvis

**7 July 2001 in Melbourne**
**British Isles 14 Australia 35**

M. Perry*
D. James
B. O'Driscoll
R. Henderson
J. Robinson
J. Wilkinson** 3P
R. Howley***
T. Smith
K. Wood
P. Vickery****
M. Johnson
D. Grewcock
N. Back 1T
S. Quinnell
R. Hill*****

\* Replaced by I. Balshaw
** Replaced by N. Jenkins
*** Replaced by M. Dawson
**** Replaced by J. Leonard
***** Replaced by M. Corry

**14 July 2001 in Sydney**
**British Isles 23 Australia 29**

M. Perry
D. James*
B. O'Driscoll
R. Henderson
J. Robinson 1T
J. Wilkinson 1T, 2C, 3P
M. Dawson
T. Smith**
K. Wood
P. Vickery
M. Johnson
D. Grewcock
N. Back
S. Quinnell***
M. Corry

* Replaced by I. Balshaw
** Replaced D. Morris
*** Replaced C. Charvis

# Appendix V

(Mostly from 1910 onwards, as that was the year when the British Isles teams became fully representative)

## Most points by the Lions in a Test series

| POINTS | OPPONENTS | MATCHES | YEAR |
| --- | --- | --- | --- |
| 79 | South Africa | 4 | 1974 |
| 68 | South Africa | 4 | 1980 |
| 66 | Australia | 3 | 2001 |
| 59 | South Africa | 3 | 1997 |
| 51 | New Zealand | 3 | 1993 |
| 50 | Australia | 3 | 1904 |
| 50 | Australia | 3 | 1989 |
| 49 | South Africa | 4 | 1955 |
| 48 | New Zealand | 4 | 1971 |
| 43 | Australia | 2 | 1950 |
| 42 | New Zealand | 4 | 1959 |
| 42 | Australia | 2 | 1966 |
| 41 | Australia | 2 | 1959 |
| 41 | New Zealand | 4 | 1977 |

## Most points by a Lions player in a Test series

| POINTS | PLAYER | OPPONENTS | MATCHES | YEAR |
| --- | --- | --- | --- | --- |
| 41 | N. Jenkins | South Africa | 3 | 1997 |
| 38 | A.G. Hastings | New Zealand | 3 | 1993 |
| 36 | J. Wilkinson | Australia | 3 | 2001 |
| 35 | T.J. Kiernan | South Africa | 4 | 1968 |
| 30 | B. John | New Zealand | 4 | 1971 |
| 28 | A.G. Hastings | Australia | 3 | 1989 |
| 26 | P. Bennett | South Africa | 4 | 1974 |
| 21 | B.L. Jones | Australia | 2 | 1950 |
| 20 | P.F. Bush | Australia | 3 | 1904 |

## Most tries by the Lions in a Test series

| TRIES | OPPONENTS | MATCHES | YEAR |
|---|---|---|---|
| 10 | Australia | 3 | 1904 |
| 10 | South Africa | 4 | 1955 |
| 10 | South Africa | 4 | 1974 |
| 9 | Australia | 4 | 1899 |
| 9 | New Zealand | 4 | 1959 |

## Most tries by a Lions player in a Test series

| TRIES | PLAYER | OPPONENTS | MATCHES | YEAR |
|---|---|---|---|---|
| 4 | W.J. Llewellyn | Australia | 3 | 1904 |
| 4 | J.J. Williams | South Africa | 4 | 1974 |

## Most penalty goals in a Test series

| PENALTIES | OPPONENTS | MATCHES | YEAR |
|---|---|---|---|
| 13 | South Africa | 3 | 1997 |
| 12 | New Zealand | 3 | 1993 |
| 11 | South Africa | 4 | 1968 |
| 11 | South Africa | 4 | 1980 |
| 10 | Australia | 3 | 1989 |
| 9 | New Zealand | 4 | 1977 |
| 7 | South Africa | 4 | 1974 |

## Most penalty goals by a Lions player in a Test series

| PENALTIES | PLAYER | OPPONENTS | MATCHES | YEAR |
|---|---|---|---|---|
| 13 | N.Jenkins | South Africa | 3 | 1997 |
| 12 | A.G. Hastings | New Zealand | 3 | 1993 |
| 11 | T.J. Kiernan | South Africa | 4 | 1968 |
| 8 | A.G. Hastings | Australia | 3 | 1989 |
| 7 | J. Wilkinson | Australia | 3 | 2001 |
| 6 | P. Bennett | New Zealand | 4 | 1977 |

## Most dropped goals by a Lions player

| GOALS | PLAYER | OPPONENTS | MATCHES | YEAR |
|---|---|---|---|---|
| 2 | P.F. Bush | Australia | 3 | 1904 |
| 2 | B. John | New Zealand | 4 | 1971 |
| 2 | P. Bennett | South Africa | 4 | 1974 |

## Most conversions by a Lions player

| CONVERSIONS | PLAYER | OPPONENTS | MATCHES | YEAR |
|---|---|---|---|---|
| 5 | S. Wilson | Australia | 1 | 1966 |

## Most points by the Lions in a Test match

| POINTS | OPPONENTS | VENUE | YEAR |
|---|---|---|---|
| 31 | Australia | Brisbane | 1966 |
| 29 | Australia | Brisbane | 2001 |
| 28 | South Africa | Pretoria | 1974 |
| 26 | South Africa | Port Elizabeth | 1974 |
| 25 | South Africa | Cape Town | 1997 |
| 24 | Australia | Sydney | 1950 |
| 24 | Australia | Sydney | 1959 |
| 23 | South Africa | Johannesburg | 1955 |
| 22 | South Africa | Cape Town | 1980 |
| 21 | South Africa | Cape Town | 1938 |
| 20 | South Africa | Pretoria | 1968 |
| 20 | New Zealand | Wellington | 1993 |

## Most points by a Lions player in a Test match

| POINTS | PLAYER | OPPONENTS | VEUNE | YEAR |
|---|---|---|---|---|
| 18 | J. Wilkinson | Australia | Sydney | 2001 |
| 18 | A.P. Ward | South Africa | Cape Town | 1980 |
| 18 | A.G. Hastings | New Zealand | Christchurch | 1993 |
| 17 | T.J. Kiernan | South Africa | Pretoria | 1968 |
| 16 | B.L. Jones | Australia | Brisbane | 1950 |
| 15 | A.G. Hastings | Australia | Sydney | 1989 |
| 15 | N. Jenkins | South Africa | Cape Town | 1997 |
| 15 | N. Jenkins | South Africa | Durban | 1997 |
| 13 | S. Wilson | Australia | Brisbane | 1904 |
| 12 | S.O. Campbell | New Zealand | Christchurch | 1983 |
| 11 | P.F. Bush | Australia | Brisbane | 1904 |
| 10 | C.Y. Adamson | Australia | Sydney | 1899 |
| 10 | B. John | New Zealand | Wellington | 1971 |

## Most tries by the Lions in a Test match

| TRIES | OPPONENTS | VENUE | YEAR |
|---|---|---|---|
| 5 | Australia | Sydney | 1950 |
| 5 | South Africa | Johannesburg | 1955 |
| 5 | Australia | Sydney | 1959 |
| 5 | Australia | Brisbane | 1966 |
| 5 | South Africa | Pretoria | 1974 |

| 4 | Australia | Brisbane | 2001 |
| 4 | Australia | Sydney | 1904 |
| 4 | South Africa | Cape town | 1938 |
| 4 | New Zealand | Dunedin | 1959 |

## Most tries by a Lions player in a Test match

| TRIES | PLAYER | OPPONENTS | VENUE | YEAR |
|---|---|---|---|---|
| 2 | A.M. Bucher | Australia | Sydney | 1899 |
| 2 | W.M. Llewellyn | Australia | Sydney | 1904 |
| 2 | C.D. Aarvold | New Zealand | Christchurch | 1930 |
| 2 | J.E. Nelson | Australia | Sydney | 1950 |
| 2 | M.J. Price | Australia | Sydney | 1959 |
| 2 | M.J. Price | New Zealand | Dunedin | 1959 |
| 2 | D.K. Jones | Australia | Brisbane | 1966 |
| 2 | T.G.R. Davies | New Zealand | Christchurch | 1971 |
| 2 | J.J. Williams | South Africa | Pretoria | 1974 |
| 2 | J.J. Williams | South Africa | Port Elizabeth | 1974 |

## Most dropped goals by a Lions player in a Test match

| GOALS | PLAYER | OPPONENTS | VENUE | YEAR |
|---|---|---|---|---|
| 2 | P. Bennett | South Africa | Port Elizabeth | 1974 |

## Most penalty goals by the Lions in a Test match

| PENALTIES | OPPONENTS | MATCHES | CAREER |
|---|---|---|---|
| 6 | New Zealand | Christchurch | 1993 |
| 5 | South Africa | Pretoria | 1968 |
| 5 | South Africa | Cape Town | 1980 |
| 5 | Australia | Sydney | 1989 |
| 5 | South Africa | Cape Town | 1997 |
| 5 | South Africa | Durban | 1997 |
| 4 | South Africa | Johannesburg | 1938 |
| 4 | New Zealand | Wellington | 1977 |
| 4 | New Zealand | Wellington | 1993 |
| 3 | New Zealand | Christchurch | 1966 |
| 3 | South Africa | Cape Town | 1974 |
| 3 | New Zealand | Christchurch | 1977 |
| 3 | South Africa | Bloemfontein | 1980 |
| 3 | New Zealand | Christchurch | 1983 |
| 3 | Australia | Melbourne | 2001 |
| 3 | Australia | Sydney | 2001 |

## Most penalty goals by a Lions player in a Test match

| PENALTIES | PLAYER | OPPONENTS | VENUE | YEAR |
|---|---|---|---|---|
| 6 | A. G. Hastings | New Zealand | Christchurch | 1993 |
| 5 | T. J. Kiernan | South Africa | Pretoria | 1968 |
| 5 | A. P. Ward | South Africa | Cape Town | 1980 |
| 5 | A. G. Hastings | Australia | Sydney | 1989 |
| 5 | N. Jenkins | South Africa | Cape Town | 1997 |
| 5 | N. Jenkins | South Africa | Durban | 1997 |
| 4 | A. G. Hastings | New Zealand | Wellington | 1993 |
| 3 | V. G. J. Jenkins | South Africa | Johannesburg | 1938 |
| 3 | J. Wilkinson | Australia | Melbourne | 2001 |
| 3 | J. Wilkinson | Australia | Sydney | 2001 |
| 3 | S. Wilson | New Zealand | Wellington | 1966 |
| 3 | P. Bennett | South Africa | Cape Town | 1974 |
| 3 | P. Bennett | New Zealand | Wellington | 1977 |
| 3 | P. Bennett | New Zealand | Christchurch | 1977 |
| 3 | S. O. Campbell | New Zealand | Christchurch | 1983 |

## Most points by a Lions player in Test matches

| POINTS | PLAYER | MATCHES | CAREER |
|---|---|---|---|
| 66 | A.G. Hastings | 6 | 1989–1993 |
| 44 | P. Bennett | 8 | 1974–1977 |
| 41 | N.Jenkins | 3 | 1997 |
| 35 | T.J. Kiernan | 5 | 1962–1968 |
| 30 | S. Wilson | 5 | 1966 |
| 30 | B. John | 5 | 1968–71 |
| 28 | A.R. Irvine | 9 | 1974–1980 |
| 26 | B.L. Jones | 3 | 1950 |
| 26 | S.O. Campbell | 7 | 1980–1983 |
| 20 | P.F. Bush | 4 | 1904 |
| 20 | J.J. Williams | 7 | 1974–1977 |

## Most tries by a Lions player in Test matches

| TRIES | PLAYER | MATCHES | CAREER |
|---|---|---|---|
| 6 | A.J.F. O'Reilly | 10 | 1955–1959 |
| 5 | J.J. Williams | 7 | 1974–1977 |
| 4 | W.M. Llewellyn | 4 | 1904 |
| 4 | M.J. Price | 5 | 1959 |

## Most conversions by a Lions players in Test matches

| CONVERSIONS | PLAYER | MATCHES | CAREER |
|---|---|---|---|
| 6 | S. Wilson | 5 | 1966 |
| 4 | J.F. Byrne | 4 | 1896 |
| 4 | C.Y. Adamson | 4 | 1899 |
| 4 | B.L. Jones | 3 | 1950 |
| 4 | A. Cameron | 2 | 1955 |

## Most dropped goals by a Lions player in test matches

| GOALS | PLAYER | MATCHES | CAREER |
|---|---|---|---|
| 2 | P.F. Bush | 4 | 1904 |
| 2 | D. Watkins | 6 | 1966 |
| 2 | B. John | 5 | 1968–1971 |
| 2 | P. Bennett | 8 | 1974–1977 |

## Most penalty goals by a Lions player in Test matches

| PENALTIES | PLAYER | MATCHES | CAREER |
|---|---|---|---|
| 20 | A.G. Hastings | 6 | 1989–1993 |
| 13 | N. Jenkins | 3 | 1997 |
| 11 | T.J. Kiernan | 5 | 1962–1968 |
| 10 | P. Bennett | 8 | 1974–1977 |
| 7 | S.O. Campbell | 7 | 1980–1983 |
| 6 | S. Wilson | 5 | 1966 |
| 6 | A.R. Irvine | 9 | 1974–1980 |
| 5 | B. John | 5 | 1968–1971 |
| 5 | A.J.P. Ward | 1 | 1980 |
| 4 | B.L. Jones | 3 | 1950 |

## Scorers of all Lions points in a Test match

| POINTS | PLAYER | OPPONENTS | VENUE | YEAR |
|---|---|---|---|---|
| 18 | A.G. Hastings | New Zealand | Christchurch | 1993 |
| 12 | S.O. Campbell | New Zealand | Christchurch | 1983 |
| 9 | D.W. Morgan | New Zealand | Auckland | 1977 |
| 6 | T.J. Tiernan | South Africa | Port Elizabeth | 1968 |
| 6 | T.J. Tiernan | South Africa | Cape Town | 1968 |
| 6 | T.J. Tiernan | South Africa | Johannesburg | 1968 |

## Longest Lions career

| SEASONS | PLAYER | CAPS | CAREER |
|---|---|---|---|
| 13 | W.J. McBride | 17 | 1962–1974 |

## Most consecutive Lions caps

| CAPS | PLAYER | OPPONENTS | |
|---|---|---|---|
| 15 | W.J. McBride | 1966 NZ 2,3,4 | 1968 SA 1,2,3,4 |
| | | 1971 NZ 1,2,3,4 | 1974 SA 1,2,3,4 |
| 12 | C.M.H. Gibson | 1966 NZ 1,2,3,4 | 1968 SA 1(R), 2,3,4 |
| | | 1971 NZ 1,2,3,4 | |
| 12 | G. Price | 1977 NZ 1,2,3,4 | 1980 SA 1,2,3,4 |
| | | 1983 NZ 1,2,3,4 | |

## Most capped Lions player

| CAPS | PLAYER | CAREER |
|---|---|---|
| 17 | W.J. McBride | 1962–1974 |
| 13 | R.E.G. Jeeps | 1955–1962 |
| 12 | C.M.H. Gibson | 1966–1971 |
| 12 | G. Price | 1977–1983 |
| 10 | A.J.F. O'Reilly | 1955–1959 |
| 10 | R.H. Williams | 1955–1959 |
| 10 | G.O. Edwards | 1968–1974 |

## Most capped Lions in individual positions

| POSITION | PLAYER | CAPS | CAREER |
|---|---|---|---|
| Full-back | J.P.R. Williams | 8 | 1971–1974 |
| Wing | A.J.F. O'Reilly | 9 | 1955–1959 |
| Centre | C.M.H. Gibson | 8 | 1966–1971 |
| | J. Guscott | 8 | 1989–1997 |
| Fly-half | P. Bennett | 8 | 1974–1977 |
| Scrum-half | R.E.G. Jeeps | 13 | 1955–1962 |
| Prop | G. Price | 12 | 1977–1983 |
| Hooker | B.V. Meredith | 8 | 1955–1962 |
| Lock | W.J. McBride | 17 | 1962–1974 |
| Flanker | N.A.A. Murphy | 8 | 1959–1966 |
| Number eight | T.M. Davies | 8 | 1971–1974 |

## Most matches as captain

| MATCHES | PLAYER | CAREER |
|---|---|---|
| 6 | M. Johnson (3 victories) | 1997, 2001 |
| 6 | A.R. Dawson (3 victories) | 1959 |

## Results of British Isles Matches
*v South Africa*
Played 33    Won 10    Lost 19    Drawn 4

*v New Zealand*
Played31    Won 6    Lost 23    Drawn 2
*v Australia*
Played 20 Won 15 Lost 5 Drawn 0

## Most points scored by the Lions
*v South Africa*
28 pts (28–9) in Pretoria 1974
*v New Zealand*
20 pts (20–7) in Wellington 1993
*v Australia*
31 pts (31–0) in Brisbane 1966

## Most points scored against the Lions
*v South Africa*
35 pts (16–35) in Johannesburg 1997
*v NewZealand*
38 pts (6–38) in Auckland 1983
*v Australia*
35 pts (14–35) in Melbourne 2001

## Most tries scored against the Lions
7 by South Africa in Cape Town 1955